Attachment and Loss in the Works of James Joyce

Attachment and Loss in the Works of James Joyce

Linda Horsnell

LEXINGTON BOOKS
Lanham • Boulder • New York • London

Published by Lexington Books
An imprint of The Rowman & Littlefield Publishing Group, Inc.
4501 Forbes Boulevard, Suite 200, Lanham, Maryland 20706
www.rowman.com

86-90 Paul Street, London EC2A 4NE

Copyright © 2022 by The Rowman & Littlefield Publishing Group, Inc.

All rights reserved. No part of this book may be reproduced in any form or by any electronic or mechanical means, including information storage and retrieval systems, without written permission from the publisher, except by a reviewer who may quote passages in a review.

British Library Cataloguing in Publication Information Available

Library of Congress Cataloging-in-Publication Data

Names: Horsnell, Linda, 1961- author.
Title: Attachment and loss in the works of James Joyce / Linda Horsnell.
Description: Lanham : Lexington Books, [2021] | Includes bibliographical references and index. | Summary: "Using attachment theory as a frame of reference to critically analyse grief in the works of James Joyce, Attachment and Loss in the Works of James Joyce allows for new and innovative readings to emerge, opening another avenue in the debate regarding cognition and literature"— Provided by publisher.
Identifiers: LCCN 2021026304 (print) | LCCN 2021026305 (ebook) | ISBN 9781793635617 (cloth) | ISBN 9781793635624 (epub) | ISBN 9781793635631 (paperback)
Subjects: LCSH: Joyce, James, 1882-1941—Criticism and interpretation. | Joyce, James, 1882-1941—Characters. | Attachment behavior in literature. | Loss (Psychology) in literature. | Grief in literature. | Irish literature—20th century—History and criticism.
Classification: LCC PR6019.O9 Z5885 2021 (print) | LCC PR6019.O9 (ebook) | DDC 823/.912—dc23
LC record available at https://lccn.loc.gov/2021026304
LC ebook record available at https://lccn.loc.gov/2021026305

∞™ The paper used in this publication meets the minimum requirements of American National Standard for Information Sciences—Permanence of Paper for Printed Library Materials, ANSI/NISO Z39.48-1992.

For Terry
In gratitude of your unwavering love and support

Contents

Preface	ix
Acknowledgments	xi
Abbreviations	xiii
Introduction	1
PART I: THEORY	**9**
Chapter One: The Development of Attachment Theory	11
Chapter Two: Attachment Theory: A Universal Theory	19
Chapter Three: The Representation of Character and Reader Response	27
Chapter Four: Attachment Theory and Literary Interpretation	33
PART II: THE PORTRAYAL OF THE EMOTIONAL IMPACT OF BEREAVEMENT AND ENSUING GRIEF	**39**
Part II: Introduction	41
Chapter Five: "The Sisters": Anticipatory Grief in a Securely Attached Individual	45
Chapter Six: Master Dignam: Sudden Bereavement and Anxious/Ambivalent Attachment	59
Chapter Seven: "Eveline": Unresolved Grief and the Pull of the Dead	69

Chapter Eight: "The Dead": Disenfranchised Grief, Idealisation of the Deceased, and the Effect on the Living — 81

PART III: CHARACTER TRAITS AND INDIVIDUAL EXPRESSIONS OF GRIEF: STEPHEN DEDALUS, LEOPOLD BLOOM, AND MOLLY BLOOM — 91

Part III: Introduction — 93

Chapter Nine: Stephen Dedalus — 101

Chapter Ten: Leopold and Molly Bloom — 123

PART IV: JOYCE, RELIGION, AND THE PORTRAYAL OF THE GRIEF OF STEPHEN DEDALUS AND LEOPOLD BLOOM — 145

Part IV: Introduction — 147

Chapter Eleven: Joyce, Catholicism, and Family — 157

Chapter Twelve: Stephen Dedalus: Grief, Guilt, and Remorse of Conscience — 169

Chapter Thirteen: Leopold Bloom: Grieving in Isolation — 185

Summary and Conclusion — 205

Bibliography — 211

Index — 225

About the Author — 229

Preface

My interest in Joyce's work, as well as how individuals deal with their grief psychologically, led me to explore how Joyce portrayed grief with different characters in different scenarios. As I started researching it became apparent how central the psychological experience of bereavement and ensuing grief were in Joyce's work. Unlike many literary critics, I did not wish to rely on Freudian analysis, which looks at grief though the lens of repressed sexual desire. Placing emphasis on libidinal drives did not seem an adequate explanation to reflect the complexity of grief process. I therefore turned to the work of John Bowlby and his theory of attachment to use as a frame of reference when writing this book. Using this theory allowed for innovative readings of Joyce's representation of the grief process and exposition of the part played by childhood experiences. It also enabled detailed discussion of areas of the texts that previously had only be mentioned briefly.

Reading Joyce's work with a knowledge of Attachment Theory, his deep understanding of human behaviour became immediately apparent. This, along with the narrative techniques used and the sociological, domestic, and cognitive detail contained within his work leave it particularly open to the utilisation of a theory such as Bowlby's for critical analysis.

In this book I have chosen to concentrate on some of Joyce's short stories in *Dubliners* as well as on *Ulysses,* the main emphasis being on the principal protagonists of the latter. Bowlby argues that how one expresses grief is ultimately linked to the types of attachment formed in early life, hence reference is also made to *A Portrait of the Artist as a Young Man* when discussing Stephen Dedalus, particularly the representation of his time at Clongowes Wood College.

The work of psychologist Alexander F. Shand highlights the relationship between creative writing and the theory of grief put forward by Bowlby. He utilised the fact that creative writers had a long history of describing many of the features of grief in his study of human emotions and sentiments. It can be said that Joyce provides superior examples of such description in his work. What Bowlby later explicated in his theories of attachment, including grief and how this relates to the support available, can be seen as clearly portrayed within Joyce's work.

Acknowledgments

There are many people that have been instrumental in enabling me to write this book. I must thank Mark Sutton for introducing me to the joy of reading Joyce, sharing his knowledge with me, and providing feedback; Jeremy Noel-Tod and Matthew Taunton for the many readings of the drafts and the invaluable advice given; Enda Duffy for the sensitive and perceptive reading of the manuscript and recommendations; and my friends and family, who, although shall remain nameless here, have provided me with the support and encouragement that enabled me to succeed.

Short papers based on some of the content of Chapters 7 and 13 have been published in *Brief Encounters* and *Exclamation*, respectively, and I thank the reviewers for their thoughtful comments.

Abbreviations

In citing works in the notes, short titles have generally been used. Works frequently cited have been identified by the following abbreviations in the text:

AL followed by Volume number	John Bowlby. *Attachment and Loss.* 3 vols. London: Hogarth Press, 1969–1980, repr. London: Penguin, 1991. All references are to the 1991 editions.
D	James Joyce. *Dubliners.* London: Grant Richards, 1914; Hertfordshire: Wordsworth, 1993. All references are to the 1993 edition.
FW	James Joyce. *Finnegans Wake.* copyright edn. London: Faber and Faber, 1939, copyright ed., 1975. All references are to the copyright edition are given following usual academic practice with the page number and the line number preceded by the letters *FW.*
JB	Holmes, Jeremy. *John Bowlby and Attachment Theory.* The Makers of Modern Psychotherapy Series ed. by Laurence Spurling. London: Routledge, 1993, repr. East Sussex: Bruner-Routledge, 2004.
MB	John Bowlby. *The Making and Breaking of Affectional Bonds.* Tavistock, 1979; London: Routledge, 2005, repr. 2007. All references are to the 2007 edition.
P	James Joyce. *A Portrait of the Artist as a Young Man.* ed. by Seamus Deane. New York: B.W. Huebsch, 1916; edited edition, London: Penguin, 1992 repr. 2003. All references are to the 2003 edition.

SH	James Joyce. *Stephen Hero,* edited by Theodore Spencer, 2nd ed. Revised by John J. Slocum and Herbert Cahoon. Jonathan Cape, 1944; edited edition, London: Paladin, 1991. All references are to the 1991 edition.
U	James Joyce. *Ulysses,* edited by Hans Walter Gabler with Wolfhard Steppe and Claus Melchior. Paris: Shakespeare and Co., 1922; edited edition London: Bodley Head, 1986 repr. 2002. All references are to the Gabler edition and are given following usual academic practice in the form of episode and line number, preceded by the letter *U.*

Introduction

This book will explore how Attachment Theory, first formulated by John Bowlby, can elucidate Joyce's representation of the expression of grief caused by bereavement. It is a theory which recognises the integrated function of cognition, emotion, and behaviour and therefore this critical literary analysis can be placed within the field of "literature and the mind."[1]

Grief itself has been described as "one of the most compelling of literary subjects in the landscape of human experience."[2] Perhaps what makes this multifaceted response to loss so compelling is the fact that it is something that is not often discussed, despite it being a universal experience. Grief can be contained in front of others, with the bereaved "putting on a brave face." Reading literature can help the reader to compare and understand their own experiences of loss, the complex details of which, due to the relative silence in which they are often suffered, can remain elusive despite their commonality. Philosopher Jennifer Robinson states that: "If we really want to understand emotions in all their uniqueness and individuality" we would do well to turn "to the detailed studies of emotion that we find in great literature."[3]

Cognitive scientists use the term "theory of mind" or "mind reading" for "the evolved cognitive adaptation" that enables humans to attribute mental states to themselves, to other people, and to literary characters.[4] Discussing theory of mind, psychologist and anthropologist Robin Dunbar writes that we can "imagine how someone who does not actually exist might respond to particular situations" and hence produce literature that goes beyond "a simple description of events as they occurred, to delve more and more deeply into why the hero should behave in the way he does . . . ."[5] Joyce's use of interior monologue and stream of consciousness techniques allows such exploration of the psyche to occur.[6]

Lisa Zunshine makes that point that as a social species our "ability to communicate with others underlies every aspect of our existence" and therefore "our environment can also be defined as other minds."[7] In other words the minds of those with whom we commune and empathise and who ultimately can affect how we behave. Attachment Theory recognises and places emphasis on the environment in which individuals are raised in terms of the emotional support received, which is in turn inextricably linked to exhibited behavioural traits and grief reactions. From his oeuvre it is obvious that Joyce had a keen interest in, and was aware of, the effect of the environment, both physical and "other minds" on the individual. Indeed, Arthur Power, Joyce's friend whom he met in Paris, claims that "his [Joyce's] mind appeared to be occupied to the exclusion of everything else with two main problems—that of human behaviour and that of human environment—and then only as related to Dublin."[8] With Dublin life dominating his writing, his brother Stanislaus states that Joyce became "one of the most ruthless realists in literature" in his attempt to show "the life that passed before his steel-blue eyes and unblinking gaze at home and in the streets of Dublin."[9]

In his exploration of such lives and of the human mind, it is evident that grief became one of his main considerations, with death pervading his short stories and novels. From the opening story of *Dubliners* to Stephen's sickbed recollections in *Portrait*, to the multiple bereavements permeating *Ulysses*, the minds of the living are suffused with memories of the departed. At the time Joyce was residing in Dublin, the social conditions of many of the inhabitants in the city were such that a ubiquitous and hence prevalent emotional experience would have been that of losing a relative, friend, or neighbour. At the end of the nineteenth century, the slum tenements of Dublin, which had neither water nor sanitation, resulted in the city having "the worst urban adult mortality rates in the British Isles" and an infant mortality rate "higher than in Calcutta."[10] Joyce himself had witnessed the death of two siblings and the stillbirth of another before his mother died of cancer.[11] His grandfather had also died of a stroke whilst living in the Joyce household when James was just 12 years old, which Peter Costello claims was the "impetus" for "The Sisters" written 10 years later.[12] In his adult life, Joyce's future wife, Nora, had a miscarriage when he was actually writing *Ulysses,* which Richard Ellmann argues helped him portray Bloom's grief at the loss of his infant son Rudy.[13]

The originality of the work of both Joyce and Bowlby challenged the conventions and ideas within their own areas of work, with their innovative thinking dividing the critics and experts of their day. Joyce's unflinching and "ruthless" realism, as Stanislaus referred to it, resulted in *Ulysses* being banned. Similarly, Bowlby received a negative reception when he presented his ideas to the British Psychoanalytic Society in the late 1950s, which has since been ascribed to the fact that he disagreed with Freud.[14] However,

Joyce's *Ulysses* has since been described as "a book that attracts readers, holds them, moves them, and brings them back to re-experience it."[15] Likewise, Bowlby also received due recognition, being credited with having "laid the foundation for what has become one of the most heavily researched conceptual frameworks in modern psychology."[16] By the time Bowlby wrote the third volume of *Attachment and Loss* in 1980, other psychoanalysts were following his lead. He made clear that what he was offering was a new paradigm for "understanding personality development and psychopathology" and as such would be "alien to clinicians long used to thinking in other ways" (*AL*3: 1–2). Psychologists Mario Mikulincer and Phillip R. Shaver note that Bowlby "significantly altered and updated psychoanalytic theory by combining insights from then-current object relations psychoanalytic theories, post-Darwinian ethology, modern cognitive-developmental psychology, cybernetics (control systems theories), and community psychiatry to create Attachment Theory."[17] In other words he had effectively enabled psychoanalysis to move on from Sigmund Freud, Carl Jung and Jacques Lacan. I aim to show that his theories can also help literary criticism to do the same.

I have divided this book into four main parts. These focus on the theories which underpin my arguments, the emotional impact of bereavement and ensuing grief, character traits and individual expressions of grief, and the role of religion in the grief process, respectively.

Part 1, explicates the theoretical assumptions made, setting out how Bowlby developed his theories, whilst also recognising the work of the psychologist Alexander Shand who, writing as early as 1914, had delineated many of the main features of grief recognised by Bowlby. It discusses how Bowlby's theories differed from those postulated by Freud and Melanie Klein and how the core principles of Attachment Theory can be viewed as universal, traversing historical periods. With recent literary criticism looking toward literature and the mind and cognitive studies, the work of critics such as Jonathan Culpeper, who combine both textual and cognitive factors have been instrumental in my reading of Joyce's characters. The narrative techniques employed by Joyce encourage the readers to take a humanising approach and to ascribe mental states to them.

Part 2 discusses Joyce's portrayal of the emotional response to bereavement in four protagonists at different stages of maturity, from children through to adults, each of which are at different stage in the grief process. Michael Proeve and Steven Tudor have acknowledged how modernist texts in particular, with their portrayal of the inner lives of characters, have proved "a very effective narrative form of representing complex and nuanced human emotions."[18] Reading the inner lives of Joyce's characters with knowledge of Attachment Theory provides a particular understanding of their respective attachments and these, along with the differing circumstances of the bereavement suffered, is shown to play a part in the represented grief process.

As grief arouses so many emotions and with the theory of emotion being a separate subject in itself, the work of Keith Oatley, a cognitive theorist whose work dovetails with that of Bowlby and later attachment theorists, has been focused on in my consideration of the emotional aspect of loss. Oatley argues that emotions arise out of the meeting of the "two worlds" in which we live: "a finite world of embodiment in time, place, and biological nature and an infinite world of imagination, language, and culture."[19] Emotions are therefore often promoted by social situations since the infinite world which contains narratives of oneself, as well as one's plans and goals, have to interact with the external world of which only partial knowledge may be available and contains people with their own plans and quite often differing goals. Joyce himself stated to Arthur Power: "What makes most people's lives unhappy is some disappointed romanticism, some unrealisable or misconceived ideal" and he makes this view plain throughout his ouvre.[20]

Considering Oatley's argument from an attachment perspective, one's goals are toward perceived security and protection; toward a secure base. Yet the feeling of stability one gains from an attachment figure can be shattered at any moment as death can occur without warning. Attachment theorists argue that it is the cognitive rearrangement of one's own narrative and goals that evoke the myriad of emotions such as anger, sadness, and fear that accompany loss. C. S. Lewis, following the death of his wife, wrote: "No one ever told me that grief felt so like fear. I am not afraid, but the sensation is like being afraid."[21] Whilst arguing that Attachment Theory can provide a particular reading as to the emotional responses portrayed by Joyce, Part 2 also shows how he represents such emotion through his use of language and writing techniques, enabling empathy with the protagonists and identification with the psychological and social complexities of dealing with loss.

Part 3 discusses how knowledge of Attachment Theory provides a particular reading of the main protagonists of *Ulysses*, which in turn enables an understanding of Joyce's portrayal of their grief and simultaneously how central the making and breaking of emotional bonds was to his writing. Throughout *Ulysses* the protagonists recall memories from their childhood and adolescence, which are crucial to understanding Joyce's representation of their developed sense of self as adults. Stephen frequently thinks of his school days, creating an intertextual link to *Portrait*. For example, in "Telemachus" on top of the Martello Tower, at one point he recalls "carrying the boat of incense [. . .] at Clongowes" (*U,* 1.311). "It is known that Joyce originally planned to have the action of *Portrait* extend up to June 16, 1904, and manuscript fragments of *Portrait* (then *Stephen Hero*) material exist which represent the scene in the Martello tower that begins *Ulysses*."[22] Furthermore,

Joyce wrote to H. L. Mencken on 7 July 1915, "I [. . .] am engaged on a novel which is a continuation of *A Portrait of the Artist* and also of *Dubliners*."[23] This information makes plain that one is invited to read the character of Stephen across these different texts. Hence there is a considerable amount of knowledge available regarding Stephen's childhood.

Joyce presents the details regarding the lives of Molly and Leopold Bloom in a more fragmented manner, yet there is nevertheless a wealth of information within the novel. Luca Crispi summarises the way in which this information is imparted to the reader as follows:

> In general, everything that readers discover about the Blooms in *Ulysses* is represented as 1) being directly experienced by them on 16 June 1904, 2) by means of the characters' memories of their experiences, 3) by means of the other characters' stories about the Blooms' lives, or else 4) as information about the characters that is mediated through the varied, eclectic, and idiosyncratic narrative styles of the book's different episodes.[24]

John Henry Raleigh's *The Chronicle of Leopold and Molly Bloom* is invaluable to any Joyce scholar, as he has painstakingly chronicled each date and piece of information regarding the couple and their respective families from the information proffered by the narrator and represented recollections of the characters themselves in the text.[25] However, Crispi's genetic approach also takes into account how Joyce "wrote and re-wrote what purport to be the same stories, often in different episodes, over several years, and on different manuscripts," in order understand how the characters evolved and were perceived by Joyce.[26] The import of Joyce's decision to relay Stephen's separation from his family at a young age, Bloom's status as an only child with a relatively elderly Jewish father and Molly's lack of a mother figure will all be explored.

Part 4 focuses on Stephen Dedalus and Leopold Bloom and considers how Joyce portrays the role played by religion in the negotiation of their grief. Lee Kirkpatrick argues that "Attachment Theory focuses on human concerns about comfort and protection, and God is psychologically represented as a kind of parent figure."[27] Attachment Theory's strong link with social psychology not only aids understanding of individual actions but also those of collective groups, such as religious organisations. Since religion can be viewed as a belief system that allows for a continuing relationship with the deceased, it serves to keep a sense of identity and a continuing family system, with the deceased being present spiritually and symbolically, whilst the bereaved come to terms with the changes in their world. Studies have found that those who believe in the afterlife more readily resolve their grief, thus proving that religion can play a positive role in negotiating loss.[28] However, religion can also be a source of tension and both Bloom and Stephen are presented as having a very complicated relationship with the Church.

Stephen has had an intensely religious upbringing but has decided to walk away from its practices. Yet through Joyce's representation of the religious elements embedded in Stephen's psyche, the reader comes to understand that the teachings are so deeply engrained that total abandonment of them will prove all but impossible for him, in particular the need for introspection and psychological self-examination. Here the work of Proeve and Tudor on remorse provides a useful reference point. Their identification of the different concepts of remorse and guilt, (terms which they acknowledge are often used interchangeably in "everyday discourse"), facilitate my discussion of Stephen's grief reaction to his mother's death, most notably how such feelings intertwine with his internal working models of himself.[29]

Bloom is depicted as being of Jewish descent, and although he has been baptised both in the Catholic and the Protestant Church, he shows no conviction to any faith. However, it is his perceived Jewishness that makes him an outsider and consequently someone to be treated with suspicion. One only has to read Richard Wagner's *Judaism in Music,* known to be in Joyce's library, to understand the anti-Semitic feeling at the time when he was writing.[30] Joyce's portrayal of religion is therefore one of conflict, of opposing views and experiences: for Bloom the prejudice he experiences and his practical, secular view of life versus his acknowledgment of the comfort the rituals afford; for Stephen the comfort it gave his mother versus the nightmares caused by his refusal to pray; for the narrator the cold materialism of the church representatives and hence their hypocrisy versus the genuine attempts of the community to help the Dignam family.

Joyce said of *Ulysses*: "from it you may date a new orientation in literature—a new realism" when conversing with Arthur Power. He went on to add "the one thing you must admit that I have done is to liberate literature from its age-old shackles."[31] Together the following chapters will show that psychoanalytical literary criticism can be liberated from the "shackles" of Freud, Jung, and Lacan. As a theory which takes into account certain events and the meaning that an individual reads into them, Attachment Theory resonates with modernist literature, which Vargish and Mook have defined as being about "neither the objective world nor the subjective perceiver but their interaction."[32]

NOTES

1. Grief is defined as 'the primarily emotional (affective) reaction to the loss of a loved one through death.' Stroebe et al. "Bereavement Research: Contemporary

Perspectives" in *Handbook of Bereavement and Research Practice: Advances in Theory and Intervention,* eds. Margaret S. Strobe, Robert O. Hansson, Henk Schut, and Wolfgang Stroebe (Washington: American Psychological Association, 2008), 5. Bowlby acknowledges that he uses the word "mourning" where others may use "grief" and this will be evident when quoting from his work. However, when referring to the public display of grief he uses the term "mourning customs" (*AL*3: 16–18).

2. M. Freedman, "Notes on Grief in Literature' in *Loss and Grief: Psychological Management and Medical Practice*, ed. B. Schoenberg et al. (New York: Columbia University Press, 1970), 340.

3. Jennifer Robinson, *Deeper Than Reason: Emotion and Its Role in Literature, Music and Art* (Oxford: Oxford University Press, 2005), 99.

4. Lisa Zunshine, *Getting Inside Your Head: What Cognitive Science Can Tell Us About Popular Culture* (Baltimore: The Johns Hopkins University Press, 2012), ix.

5. Robin Dunbar, *Grooming, Gossip and the Evolution of Language* (Cambridge, MA: Harvard University Press, 1996), 101–2.

6. When referring to "Interior Monologue" and "Stream of Consciousness" throughout this book, I am using Robert Humphrey's definitions: Interior Monologue is defined as "the technique used in fiction for representing the psychic content and processes of character, partly or entirely unuttered, just as these processes exist at various levels of conscious control before they are formulated for deliberate speech. [. . .] It is concerned with the contents *and* processes of consciousness, not with just one of these." Using the analogy of an iceberg he explains that stream of consciousness fiction is "greatly concerned with what lies below the surface [. . .] a type of fiction in which the basic emphasis is placed on exploration of the prespeech levels of consciousness for the purpose, primarily, or revealing the psychic being of characters." Robert Humphrey, *Stream of Consciousness in the Modern Novel* (California: University of California Press, 1954), 4–25.

7. Zunshine, *Getting Inside Your Head,* 2.

8. Arthur Power, *Conversations with James Joyce* (London: Millington, 1974; repr. with corrections, Dublin: Lilliput Press, 1999), 60.

9. Stanislaus Joyce, *My Brother's Keeper: James Joyce's Early Years* (Cambridge: Da Capo, 2003), 93.

10. R. F. Foster, *Modern Ireland 1600–1972* (Allen Lane, 1988; London: Penguin, 1989), 437; Richard Fallis, *The Irish Renaissance: An Introduction to Anglo-Irish Literature* (Dublin: Gill and Macmillan, 1978), 183. For a wider historical context of the social, economic, and political conditions at the time Joyce was writing, I would refer the reader to the first chapter of Marguerite Harkness, *A Portrait of the Artist as a Young Man: Voices of the Text,* Twaynes Masterwork Studies No. 38 (Boston: Twayne, 1990), 1–6.

11. See Joyce, *My Brother's Keeper,* 133.

12. Peter Costello, *James Joyce: The Years of Growth 1882–1915* (West Cork: Roberts Rinehart, 1992), 125–28.

13. See Richard Ellmann, *James Joyce* (London: Oxford University Press, 1959; repr. 1966), 278. All references to the 1966 edition unless otherwise stated.

14. See Mario Marrone and Maricio Cortina, "Introduction: Reclaiming Bowlby's Contribution to Psychoanalysis" in *Attachment Theory and the Psychoanalytic Process* ed. Mauricio Cortina and Mario Marrone (London: Whurr Publishers, 2003), 12–13.

15. S. L. Goldberg, *The Classical Temper: A Study of James Joyce's Ulysses* (London: Chatto and Windus, 1961), 209.

16. Mario Mikulincer and Phillip R. Shaver, *Attachment in Adulthood: Structure, Dynamics and Change* (New York: Guilford Press, 2010), 4.

17. Mikulincer and Shaver, *Attachment in Adulthood*, 4.

18. Michael Proeve and Steven Tudor, *Remorse: Psychological and Jurisprudential Perspectives* (Surrey: Ashgate, 2010), 23.

19. Keith Oatley, *Best Laid Schemes: The Psychology of Emotions* (Cambridge: Cambridge University Press, 1992; repr. 1999), 14.

20. Power, *Conversations*, 113–14.

21. C. S. Lewis, *A Grief Observed* (London: Faber and Faber, 1961; repr. 1978), 7.

22. Sheldon Brivic, "James Joyce: From Stephen to Bloom" in *Psychoanalysis & Literary Process* ed. Frederick Crews (Cambridge: Winthrop, 1970), 142.

23. *The Letters of James Joyce*, ed. by Stuart Gilbert (London: Faber and Faber, 1957), 33.

24. Luca Crispi, *Joyce's Creative Process and the Construction of Character in Ulysses: Becoming the Blooms* (Oxford: Oxford University Press, 2015), 13.

25. John Henry Raleigh, *The Chronicle of Leopold and Molly Bloom: Ulysses as Narrative* (Berkley: University of California Press, 1977).

26. Crispi, *Joyce's Creative Process*, 12–14.

27. Lee A. Kirkpatrick, *Attachment, Evolution and the Psychology of Religion* (New York: Guildford Press, 2005), 19.

28. See Judith C. Hays and Cristina C. Hendrix "The Role of Religion in Bereavement" in *Handbook of Bereavement and Research Practice*, 340–41.

29. Proeve and Tudor, *Remorse*, 33.

30. See Richard Wagner, *Judaism in Music and Other Essays*, trans. W. Ashton Ellis (Lincoln: University of Nebraska Press, 1995)

31. Power, *Conversations*, 64.

32. Thomas Vargish and Delo E. Mook, *Inside Modernism: Relativity Theory, Cubism, Narrative* (New Haven: Yale University Press, 1999), 90.

PART I
Theory

Chapter One

The Development of Attachment Theory

Bowlby describes his conception of attachment behaviour as "any form of behaviour that results in a person attaining or retaining proximity to some other differentiated and preferred individual, who is usually conceived as stronger and/or wiser" (*MB*, 154). His early work on separation from attachment figures stemmed from his time working at the Child Guidance Clinic in the late 1930s and then post-war at the Tavistock Clinic's Department for Children. Jeremy Holmes, who writes comprehensively about Bowlby's work and ideas, explains that Bowlby's initial research showed that children who had been separated from their loved ones or bereaved, experienced "intense feelings of mental pain and anguish" (*JB*, 62). Significantly he found that in the long term such separations, which broke a fundamental bond between two people, could lead to "neurosis or delinquency in children and adolescents, and mental illness in adults" (*JB*, 62).

Bowlby continued his research by examining the nature and development of this bond. Although Attachment Theory owed much to psychoanalysis, Bowlby disagreed with Freud's drive theory and Klein's Object-Relations Theory because neither interpreted the attachment between a mother and her infant as a unique "psychological bond in its own right" (*JB*, 63). Even though, as Bowlby himself points out, Freud made the argument in his later work that anxiety in children "can be reduced to a single condition—namely, that of missing someone who is loved and longed for," he linked it to the child's requirement for libidinal gratification, rather than the need for a secure base (*AL*2: 48).[1] At odds with both Freudian and Kleinian theory, Attachment Theory therefore became "a discipline in its own right," contributing "as much to family and cognitive therapies as to psychoanalysis" (*JB*, 5).[2] Thus, although Attachment Theory can be viewed "as a variant of Object-Relations Theory," importantly for Bowlby a person "is not an isolated drive-driven creature in search of an object on whom to discharge the accumulated tension, but a person relating to other persons." He sees a person as relating to the world, "not just by unconscious phantasy but also by internal working models which include affective, cognitive and behavioural elements" (*JB*, 132).

Bowlby explains the link between maternal behaviour and patterns of attachment through his theory of internal working models as follows:

> What in a traditional theory is termed a "good object" can be reformulated within this framework as a working model of an attachment figure who is conceived as accessible, trustworthy, and ready to help when called upon. Similarly, what in traditional theory is termed a "bad object" can be reformulated as a working model of an attachment figure to whom are attributed such characteristics as uncertain accessibility, unwillingness to respond helpfully, or perhaps the likelihood of responding hostilely. In an analogous way an individual is thought to construct a working model of himself towards whom others will respond in certain predictable ways. (*MB*, 140)

Internal working models can be described in cognitive terms as schemas, which influence the individual's propensity to form affectional bonds. The type of attachments formed and the resultant behavioural traits are reliant on the environment to which the child is exposed, particularly the support offered by parents. Bowlby found that perceived security, especially at a young age, provides "a belief in the helpfulness of others and a favourable model on which to build future relationships," whereas perceived insecurity can lead to a less resilient personality, unable to deal with adverse events "among which rejections, separations, and losses are some of the most important" (*AL*1: 378). It can be seen, therefore, that Bowlby placed great importance on cognition and experience, which contrasts with Freud and Klein, who developed their theories by placing emphasis on internal fantasies.

Using the concept of faulty internal working models, Bowlby describes three main types of insecure attachment, based on the work of his colleague Mary Ainsworth. These insecure attachments were termed avoidant, ambivalent (sometimes also called anxious) and disorganised.[3] In this book I will be concentrating on anxious/ambivalent and avoidant attachments, as Joyce appears to have endowed his characters with such traits, which in turn allows for a certain interpretation of their grief. In both avoidant and anxious/ambivalent insecure attachments the internal working model is based on an inaccurate representation of the self and others and is seen as an adaptive response to the behaviour of the caregiver. Studies have shown that "mothers of insecure avoidants are *unresponsive*, and mothers of insecure ambivalents are *inconsistently responsive*" (*JB*, 107). Avoidant individuals "have an internal working model in which the *self* is represented as unloved and unlovable" and shun intimacy in order to be in control as their "self-esteem is short circuited within the self."⁴ The internal working model of the anxious/ambivalent child "represents the *self* as of low worth, ineffective and dependent" and tends to overemphasise their needs and distress in order to try and ensure a response.⁵ Thus, when I use the terms "avoidant" or "anxious/ambivalent" throughout this book I will be using them in a specific way to reflect a certain type of insecure attachment which is associated with certain behaviours. Both types of insecurely attached individuals contrast with those who have responsive parents and tend to be securely attached, who are able to reflect on their own story, to "find a middle path between being overwhelmed with emotion in ambivalent attachment and the switched-offness of the avoidant position."⁶

Bowlby's approach was to collect primary data by observing the behaviour of very young children in certain defined situations. He then endeavoured "to describe certain early phases of personality functioning and, from them, to extrapolate forwards"; a differing approach from that of Freud (*AL*1: 4). Whereas Bowlby's starting point was "an event or experience deemed to be potentially pathogenic to the developing personality," Freud looked to the "more or less developed personality" with a particular symptom and worked "from the end product backwards"(*AL*1: 4).

Maturing from infancy into adolescence and then adulthood, there is an opportunity for an individual to develop a wider range of attachment figures. Mikulincer and Shaver explain that adolescents and young adults spend a lot of time and energy "exploring the trustworthiness of potential attachment figures (e.g., friendly peers; one or more romantic partners; a devoted coach, teacher, or professional mentor)."⁷ Although Bowlby reports that data has suggested that the form a working model takes is "strongly determined" by childhood experiences, they can nevertheless be revised, but the facility to do so lessens as one gets older (*MB*, 140). Revisions may occur due to differences between responses to earlier caregivers/parents and new attachment figures. Most importantly changes that affect the "availability sensitivity and responsiveness of key attachment figures (e.g., death of a parent, parental stress, parental divorce, difficulties in parents' work life) can affect the quality of attachment interactions, thereby inducing revision and updating of working models."⁸ Equally, positive life events, such as finding a loving and supporting partner may also cause working models to be updated.

However, Bowlby also proposed that an individual may simultaneously operate two or more working models of both himself and his attachment figures and that his awareness of each of them may differ:

> In a person suffering from emotional disturbance it is common to find that the model that has greatest influence on his perceptions and forecasts, and therefore on his feelings and behaviour, is one that developed during his early years and is constructed on fairly primitive lines, but that the person himself may be

relatively, or completely, unaware of; while, simultaneously, there is operating in him a second, and perhaps radically incompatible, model, that developed later, that is much more sophisticated, that the person is more nearly aware of and that he may mistakenly suppose to be dominant. (*AL*2: 238–39)

This concept of multiple models implies "contradictory models of the *same* aspect of reality" where one should have only one model.[9]

Bowlby proposed that defensively excluding an emotionally significant event, such as bereavement, can lead to emotional disturbance where the personality will be prone to cognition, affect, and behaviour maladapted to the current situation.[10] He states that: "When the yearning for love and care is shut away, it will continue to be inaccessible. When there is anger, it will continue to be directed at inappropriate targets. Similarly, anxiety will continue to be aroused by inappropriate situations and hostile behaviour be expected from inappropriate sources."[11]

Following on from Bowlby's work the Adult Attachment Interview (AAI) was established. The questions contained therein focus largely on early attachment experiences in order to determine the internal working models of parents. Holmes points out that various retrospective studies have been shown to support the view "that attachment status is a function of the infant-parent relationship" by revealing a "70–80 percent correspondence between infant security and parent attachment status on the AAI" (*JB*, 113–14).

Since the schemata are derived from childhood experiences and attachments, they also influence how a person grieves, as grief itself is an expression of attachment. Bowlby and Parkes proposed a four-stage model of grief (discussed below). Yet acknowledgment must also be given to a founding member of the British Psychological Association and contemporary of Joyce, Alexander F. Shand, who had initiated the formulation of some of the "laws" that Bowlby and Parkes later refined. Shand's laws of sorrow, set out in *The Foundations of Character* (first published 1914, followed by a second edition in 1920) may not have provided a theory of grief that was fully comprehensive. However, as John Archer argues, they nevertheless covered more of its features than Freud's "Mourning and Melancholia" and consequently "would have provided a more sound basis for empirical research."[12] Unfortunately Shand's work was eclipsed by that of Freud, although Bowlby later acknowledged his contribution, noting how, using the texts of "English poets and French prose-writers," he not only set out "most of the main features of grief as we now know them" but also discussed systematically the relationship between fear, anger, and grief (*AL*3: 24–25).

Shand's ability to postulate his theories by reference to English and French literature suggests the presence of a relationship between literary representation and theories of grief put forward by psychologists. Although Freud also used literature to postulate and expand certain of his concepts, for example the Greek Oedipus myth and Shakespeare's *Hamlet*, this was not the case when he wrote "Mourning and Melancholia." It is therefore important to acknowledge Shand's work, who through his derivation of psychological theories from the data of literature, offered an alternative contemporary example to Freud and made a significant contribution to the understanding of the grief process.

Shand, like Bowlby after him, recognised the value of studying childhood behaviour and he acknowledged the astuteness of creative authors to discern such behavioural features, stating that:

> If there is no quality of character more important than "stability" or "steadfastness," and none that produces more disastrous consequences to individuals and nations than 'instability," we might suppose that the first manifestations in children of these qualities would have been carefully observed and recorded, and that they would have been traced to the natural tempers that either favour or thwart them. But the facts have not been systematically observed and if some of them have been recorded in literature, as is certainly the case, they have not been extracted from it.[13]

Children turn to those with whom they have affectional bonds for protection. How frequently and how intensively attachment systems are activated (or in Shand's terms how steadfast or stable a child is) will depend to a certain extent on the child's natural temperament; an assumption Bowlby himself made (see *AL2*: 219). However, Bowlby also argued that one of the "principal processes" involved in decreasing susceptibility to fear was "confidence in the availability of his attachment figure(s)" (*AL2*: 223). Currently, most researchers accept the likelihood of "a complex relationship between temperament and attachment, particularly insecure attachments."[14]

Bereavement can severely affect the perceived security of any person, whether child or adult. Bowlby developed the four-stage model of grief along with Colin Parkes, who initially called Bowlby's attention Darwin's ideas of the role of "the mourner's urge to recover the lost person" (*AL3*: xiii). They recognised that each person differs in regard to the duration and form of each stage and this can be related to the type of attachments formed. The four stages of the proposed are as follows:

1. Phase of numbing that usually lasts from a few hours to a week and may be interrupted by outbursts of extremely intense distress and/or anger.
2. Phase of yearning and searching for the lost figure lasting some months and sometimes years.
3. Phase of disorganisation and despair.

4. Phase of greater or less degree of reorganisation (*AL*3: 85).[15]

Several writers on Attachment Theory have pointed out that Bowlby did not view these stages of grief as prescriptive or fixed, although many have misinterpreted his postulations this way.[16] It was recognised that "people can move back and forth through phases so that years after bereavement, the discovery of a photograph in a drawer or a visit from an old friend can evoke another episode of pining."[17] The final phase, termed reorganisation, allows for continuing bonds by virtue of "redefinition of the self and situation," a "reshaping" of "internal representational models so as to align them with the changes that have occurred in the bereaved's life situation" (*AL*3: 94).

Again, Shand's insight and contribution to Attachment Theory can be seen as he had already recognised the validity of continuing bonds with the deceased. He described how following bereavement, love "through its sorrow, establishes a new union of thought in place of the sensuous union, and that which is lacking now it hopes to recover hereafter."[18] Continuing bonds allow for the fact that whilst the bereaved have to acknowledge that physical proximity to the deceased is no longer possible, they do not need to relinquish their attachment to that person, rather a cognitive rearrangement of internal representations allows the deceased to remain a symbolic source of comfort and of love.

The suggestion that the grief process can be successfully negotiated whilst having a continuous bond with the deceased is an area where Attachment Theory differs greatly to Freud's "Mourning and Melancholia." Freud's theory gives primacy to the libido and instinctual gratification over attachment bonds. He therefore argued that the bereaved person repeatedly attempts to invest the libido in the deceased, even though he knows this is not possible. Yet as he gradually accepts the reality of the situation, the libido is withdrawn from the loved object and once mourning is completed "the ego becomes free and uninhibited again."[19] Conversely, attachment theorists view grief as an extension of the separation reaction, which actually functions to keep the attachment figure close. Hence, search-related behaviour is quite common in the initial stages of grief; behaviour such as restlessness, going to places where the person is likely to be.[20]

Bowlby realised that the bereavement process can be seen to be reliant on several factors such as: the bereaved's own attachment history; the relationship with the deceased (parent, child, spouse, etc.); the circumstances of the death (sudden, suicide, long illness, etc.); the quality of the social network available (supportive friends and family); religious beliefs and practices.[21] These factors form an important part of my discussion in Parts 2–4 of this book.

NOTES

1. See Sigmund Freud, *Inhibitions, Symptoms and Anxiety*, trans. Alix Strachey, ed. and rev. James Strachey (London: Hogarth, 1936; rev. ed., 1961), 50–51.

2. Family Systems Theory looks at the individual as part of a family group rather than an isolated individual. Cognitive Theory looks at how the thoughts of an individual determine their emotions and behaviour.

3. It should be noted that at one time the "three category model of adult attachment style was developed into a four-category model" as two types of avoidance were distinguished, but this has since shown to be high and low levels of avoidance and anxiety. See John Archer, "Theories of Grief: Past, Present and Future Perspectives," in *Handbook of Bereavement and Research Practice*, 59. Some authors use the term "avoidant," "insecure-avoidant" or "anxious-avoidant" to describe what I have called avoidant individuals. Similarly, some authors use the terms and "insecure-ambivalent," "anxious-ambivalent" or just "anxious" or "ambivalent" to refer to what I have termed anxious/ambivalent.

4. David Howe, *Attachment Across the Lifecourse: A Brief Introduction* (Basingstoke: Palgrave Macmillan, 2011), 44; Holmes, *The Search for a Secure Base: Attachment Theory and Psychotherapy* (East Sussex: Brunner-Routledge, 2001; repr. 2002), 10.

5. Howe, *Attachment Across the Lifecourse*, 45.

6. Holmes, *The Search for a Secure Base*, 3.

7. Mikulincer and Shaver, *Attachment in Adulthood*, 34.

8. Mikulincer and Shaver, *Attachment in Adulthood*, 135.

9. Mary Main, "Metacognitive Knowledge, Metacognitive Monitoring, and Singular (Coherent) vs. Multiple (Incoherent) Model of Attachment: Findings and Directions for Future Research," in *Attachment Across the Lifecyle*, ed. Colin Murray Parkes, Joan Stevenson-Hinde and Peter Marris (London: Routledge, 1991), 132.

10. John Bowlby, "The Role of Childhood Experience in Cognitive Disturbance," in *Cognition and Psychotherapy*, ed. Michael J. Mahoney and Arthur Freeman (New York: Plenum Publishing, 1985), 197.

11. Bowlby, "The Role of Childhood Experience," 197.

12. John Archer, "Theories of Grief," 46.

13. Alexander F. Shand, *The Foundations of Character: Being a Study of the Tendencies of the Emotions and Sentiments*, 2nd ed. (London: MacMillan, 1920), 163.

14. Howe, *Attachment Across the Lifecourse*, 204.

15. Note that in his work Bowlby uses the term "mourning" but acknowledges in Chapter 1 the term "grieving" may be used instead, 16–17.

16. For example, see Margaret S. Strobe et al., "Bereavement Research: Contemporary Perspectives," in *Handbook of Bereavement and Research Practice*, 10.

17. Colin Murray, Parkes *Bereavement: Studies of Grief in Adult Life*, 3rd ed. (London: Penguin, 1988), 7.

18. Shand, *The Foundations of Character*, 365–66.

19. Sigmund Freud, *Collected Papers*, Vol. 4 trans. supervised by Joan Riviere (London: Hogarth, 1925; 10th repr., 1957), 154.

20. For a fuller description and explanation of searching behaviours see Colin Murray Parkes and Holly G. Prigerson, *Bereavement: Studies of Grief in Adult Life*, 4th ed. (London: Routledge, 2010), 55–57.

21. Luis J. Juri and Mario Marrone, "Attachment and Bereavement," in *Attachment Theory and the Psychoanalytic Process*, 248–50.

Chapter Two

Attachment Theory
A Universal Theory

Attachment Theory views itself as describing universal elements of human experience and phenomena that are not culturally specific. Thus, when considering the disruption of attachment bonds due to loss, the resultant grief has been described by John Archer as "a natural human reaction, [. . .] a universal feature of human existence irrespective of culture."[1] Mary Ainsworth, who classified the different types of insecure attachments, carried out her initial studies in Uganda and then Baltimore, with largely black participants, before carrying out further work in Europe.[2] It is therefore unsurprising that Attachment Theory has been persuasively characterised as "a cross-cultural theory."[3] A recent review of research papers carried out by Germán Posada and Jill M. Trumbell in order to establish "what is universal and what is culturally specific in attachment relationships" revealed that "there are several key factors of attachment that seem to be common across cultures and contexts."[4]

Bowlby grounded his theory in evolutionary and ethological science, viewing attachment behaviour as adaptive, helping to keep the individual safe; something also seen in other mammals and birds. He argues that:

> In defining attachment behaviour as the output of a safety regulating system emphasis is placed on the biological function attributed to it, namely that of protecting the mobile infant and growing child from a number of dangers, amongst which in man's environment of evolutionary adaptedness the danger of predation is likely to have been paramount. To an ethologist a proposal of this kind is obvious enough. (*AL*1: 375)

Although humans are generally no longer in danger from predators, other potential dangers do exist and, as Bowlby states, "genetic biases built in over millions of years cannot be eradicated overnight" (*AL*2: 172). Therefore, as it is statistically safer to be with a companion, it is unsurprising that we seek and find comfort with others (see *AL2*: 172–73).

The propensity of a person who has suffered a loss to exhibit protest and anger, anxiety and despair as well as searching for the lost person, can all be seen as natural response to locate and thus recover the lost person. In other words, seeking for the lost person is a nonadaptive response to the goal directed mechanism of finding comfort and safety with that person that has been dislocated. However, when looking at grief in humans, one must also consider the psychological reorganisation that needs to occur. The internal working models regarding our loved ones also form part of our identity, our sense of self, and adapting to those changes, whatever one's cultural background, is an emotionally painful and timely process.

Attachment Theory, a theory that espouses an underlying universal experience of grief, can be seen to oppose arguments put forward by historicist critics. Such critics hold that grief (like all other human experiences) is manifested and translated in different languages and cultures and hence experiences of death are highly specific to their historical period. Of course, one needs to acknowledge that Joyce's work was written at a particular time in history, and there are certain factors evident within the texts which reflect that period. For example, the views and consequent reactions to death by suicide and the prejudicial behaviour toward the Jews are particularly relevant to Leopold Bloom. Nevertheless, critics such as Frederic Jameson, who starts the Preface to *The Political Unconscious* with the phrase "Always historicise!" and goes on to "denounce" the use of psychological theories for interpretation, would find Attachment Theory as a critical tool difficult to subscribe to, viewing such a theory as creating "a system of allegorical interpretation." He argues that "the data of one narrative line are radically impoverished by their rewriting according to the paradigm of another narrative, which is taken as the form's master code or ur-narrative and proposed as the ultimate hidden or unconscious *meaning* of the first one."[5] He takes an "Anti-Oedipus" stance in order to "reassert the specificity of the political content of everyday life and of the individual fantasy experience."[6] Although he is referring to the work of Freud and Lacan, such a stance would be equally incompatible with Attachment Theory and also, I would argue, with the way in which Joyce's *Ulysses* uses its Homeric parallel. As the events of Homer's *Odyssey* are superimposed on modern Dublin, Joyce's novel implies that fundamental elements of the human experience, such as the emotional response to death and love, are experienced in similar ways by modern Dubliners and Ancient Greeks.

It is possible to find passages in the literature of earlier eras that, although using language alien to twentieth-century psychology, nevertheless describe some of the behaviours that Bowlby and Parkes have since discerned in their proposed stages of the grief process. For example, Robert Burton, writing in the seventeenth century, describes grief as a "domineering passion" that makes "all other passions vanish." It is something that "perverts the good estate of body and minde, and makes them weary of their lives, cry out, howle and roare for very anguish of their soules." He refers to examples of such behaviour described in the Bible: "*David confessed as much, Psalm. 38.8 I have roared for the very disquietnesse of my heart.*"[7] These descriptions of grief and the outbursts of distress can be understood in attachment terms as manifestations of the first stage that Bowlby and Parkes describe. Burton also goes on to note how: "*I.S.D. in Hildesheim,* fully cured a patient of his, that was much troubled with melancholy, and for many years, *but afterwards by a little occasion of sorrow: he fell into his former fits and was tormented as before.*"[8] Putting this in attachment terms, Burton is describing how the patient started to work through the stages of grief, but moved back through the stages due to another sorrow that seemingly acted as a trigger; something which Parkes acknowledges can happen even years later.

Advancing from the seventeenth century to the nineteenth, both Charles Darwin (biologist and naturalist) and Carl Lange (a physician and psychologist) discuss certain aspects of grief which again correlate with the first stage of grief proposed by Bowlby and Parkes termed "numbing," where the bereaved may feel "ill" or "solid."[9] Darwin describes how the bereaved may initially be "frantic with grief," but once "fully conscious nothing can be done" then "deep sorrow" ensues. "The sufferer sits motionless, or gently rocks to and fro; the circulation becomes languid; respiration is almost forgotten, and deep sighs are drawn. All this reacts on the brain, and prostration soon follows with collapsed muscles and dulled eyes." He terms this a "silent, motionless, grief."[10] Lange comments on the "motor weakening" caused by sorrow, resulting in "a feeling of lassitude" and, like Darwin, describes the person as preferring to "sit silent and lost in thought."[11] Both Lange and Darwin do of course reference the tears of the bereaved and, following his detailed description of how the facial expressions change, Darwin concludes they are "rudiment vestiges of the screaming-fits, which are so frequent and prolong during infancy."[12] Commenting on Darwin's description, Bowlby states that this is the way children attract or recover a missing mother and in grief, consciously or unconsciously, the bereaved has the same objective in mind; that is, trying to recover the lost person (*AL3*: 90).

Early in the twentieth century, Shand also used the term "sorrow" rather than "grief." Shand claimed there were four types of sorrow and what I believe he is describing in the first two types, if considered in attachment terms, are the differences in grief shown by those with different attachment traits. He notes that how a man expresses his sorrow "seems to rest on innate differences of temper or character, or on different stages of mental development.

The child approximates to the first type; the man with his self-control to the second. But there are men also with the expansive, emotional character of the child. [. . .] There are others as innately disposed to reserve, and to repress emotional expression."[13] It is possible to equate the final two sentences of this quotation with the overemphasis of distress shown by those with anxious/ ambivalent traits and the repression shown by those with avoidant traits. He goes on to describe "a third type of sorrow," which is "conditioned by loss of energy and physical depression" and "a fourth type" which is the opposite of the third type and "illustrates the frequent union of sorrow with anger in energetic natures."[14] This clearly relates to the different aspects of the first stages of grief, that is to say, numbness and outburst of anger and despair.

There are, then, some grounds for considering grief as not purely historically contingent but rather as an immutable emotional response to loss through time. Although the terms "passion," "melancholy," or "sorrow" may be used, an attachment theorist would see them as manifestations of the same underlying emotional response. With Shand turning to the fiction of authors such as Shakespeare and Racine in order to construct his theory of grief, it is clear that fictional descriptions of this emotional response have been a powerful resource for refining psychological models of grief. That the human experience and expression of grief is analogous across time and space can be seen whether consulting the study by Parkes of London widows, who when recalling the lost person or speaking about him, sometimes experienced "uncontrollable sobbing"(see *AL2*: 89); or reading in Joyce's *Ulysses* how Stephen Dedalus "wept alone" (*U*, 9.224); or in Homer's *Odyssey* how Telemachus, who wanted to "lament in peace" his "private loss" finds his eyes growing "bright with tears"; the described responses are analogous (II, 67–78).[15]

A comparable argument can also be made regarding the terminology used by Bowlby and Ainsworth to discuss insecure attachment traits and that used by Shand in his study of certain elements of behaviour. Although different language may be used, what is being discussed is evidently the same phenomenon. For example, Shand refers to the "stability" and "steadfastness" of children, which can be seen to equate to how often their attachment behaviours are invoked. Shand also argued that to understand character it is necessary to "investigate the forces [by which he meant emotions] at the base of character, and the part they play in the general economy of the mind." He adds that from observation of "a man's expression and gestures, from his speech and conduct, we may be able to refer results to motives, the ends accomplished to their determining emotions and sentiments."[16] This argument relates to Bowlby's theory regarding the different conduct (in other words behaviour patterns), exhibited by individuals depending on whether they are insecurely or securely attached and how they are motivated by the desire to keep the attachment figure close (see Chapter 1).

THE UNIVERSAL ELEMENTS OF JOYCE'S WRITING

Joyce, like Shand, had a keen interest in observing expressions and gestures and also like Shand used different language to that adopted by attachment theorists when discussing behaviours and emotions. Joyce's friend Philippe Soupault recounts how Joyce "chose Dubliners as his example, but he was aiming at mankind" and expresses his belief that "[n]o one has illustrated better than he that road leading from the particular to the general. He relates how "[o]bserving gestures and what might be called their harmonics, reading facial expressions, provoking reactions" were part of "Joyce's daily work."[17] Richard Ellmann elaborates further on how Joyce gathered information, stating that: "Since the material of *Ulysses* was all human life, every man he met was an authority, and Joyce carried dozens of small slips of paper in his wallet and loose in his pockets to make small notes."[18] Joyce's writing called on the minutiae of his own emotional experiences as well as those noted and observed, with the result that certain attachment behaviours are accurately presented, although of course they are not referred to as such. An example of this, discussed further in Chapter 10, is Bloom's need to be petted after his disagreement with Molly, an action designed to keep his wife, his main attachment figure, close (see *U*, 18.1245–48). Similarly, Stephen's inability to get close to or trust anyone can be read as behavioural traits seen in those who form insecure avoidant attachments.

Critics have also acknowledged the existence of such traits within Joyce's work, although again without using Bowlby's terminology. For instance John Paul Riquelme, using as an example Stephen's conversation with Mulligan at the beginning of in the "Telemachus" episode of *Ulysses,* comments on how Stephen "uses language as a shield for coldly keeping others at a distance while the teller (i.e., the narrator) uses language to represent thoughts" and notes how Stephen's "physical act of drawing back indicates his habit of psychological withdrawal."[19] In other words Riquelme reads within the character of Stephen the emotional repression or "switch-offness" of avoidant individuals to which Holmes refers.

Attachment Theory is often expressed in terms of affect regulation, so how Joyce represents emotion through subjective thoughts and feelings, physical responses and body language are of central importance to this book.[20] The represented thoughts of the characters are just as significant as their respective actions. Indeed, referring to Rodin, Frank Budgen notes that: "What a man does is only a part, and that the smaller part, of his character. What he thinks and dreams is the greater part."[21] Throughout Joyce's oeuvre, primacy is given to the thoughts of the characters, in which recall plays a prominent role, although the representational techniques develop with each piece of work.

Joyce relates the thoughts and memories of the main protagonists of *Dubliners* through the narrator, be it in first or third person, so the reader is provided with information only from a particular viewpoint. Nevertheless, Ezra Pound wrote of the stories therein that Joyce "deals with common emotions which run through all races" and the "universal element" beneath the things about him.[22] In *Portrait*, the memories are articulated with a different narrative style in each section as Stephen grows and the reader witnesses his psychological development along with his changing views of the world. Stephen comments in the latter part of *Portrait:* "The artist, like the God of the creation remains within or behind or beyond or above his handiwork, invisible, refined out of existence, indifferent, paring his fingernails" (*P*, 233). Joyce has this ambition come into its own in *Ulysses*. Utilising interior monologue and stream of consciousness techniques to grant access to the interior world of the protagonists, the third person narrator of *Ulysses* is far less prominent than in his previous work.[23]

The stream of consciousness technique, which, it has been argued is "based on a realisation of the force of the drama that takes place in the minds of human beings" is key in evoking the depth of emotional experience of the characters. It provides a particular representation of emotion; one in which language is often duplicitous, symbolism prolific, views subjective and thought associations complex. The reader is therefore privy to the very individual emotional response to bereavement Joyce has created within each of the main characters, along with their manifold associated memories, which in turn are shown to be triggered by sensual inputs.

Since Attachment Theory views attachment behaviours associated with grief as universal qualities, immutable across cultures and throughout history, the sociohistorical contexts of Joyce's fiction will only be referred to where of significant relevance in what follows. Whilst Bowlby's theory came into being several decades after Joyce was writing, this does not negate the possibility of using Attachment Theory as a frame of reference when reading of his work. I agree with the argument put forward by Luke Thurston when discussing the extent of Joyce's familiarity with the writings of Freud. He concludes that it did not really matter as "the case for using psychoanalytic ideas to understand his work would be essentially the same since the argument is based not on contingent historical circumstances, but on general claims about the nature of the human subject."[24] This view is echoed by Robert Jones who, acknowledging Joyce's "remarkably fresh insights in to the human experience of emotion" in *Portrait*, goes on to state that: "Although Joyce's writings predate much of contemporary psychological investigation, his individual insights into the human condition in general, and the unconscious mind in particular, has led to significant interest from psychology."[25]

In representing the human subject, the thoughts, behaviours, and motivations behind certain actions, although Joyce was writing before Bowlby and therefore using different terminology, attachment traits can be clearly discerned in his portrayal of the main protagonists within his work.

NOTES

1. John Archer, *The Nature of Grief: The Evolution and Psychology of Reactions to Loss* (London: Routledge, 1999), 1.

2. See L. Alan Sroufe, "Attachment Theory: A Humanistic Approach for Research and Practice Across Cultures," in *Attachment Across Clinical and Cultural Perspectives: A Relational Psychoanalytic Approach*, ed. Sonia Gojman-de-Millan, Christian Herreman and L. Alan Sroufe, Psychoanalytic Inquiry Book Series (London: Routledge, 2017), 6.

3. L. Alan Sroufe, "Attachment Theory," 1.

4. Germán Paosada and Jill M. Trumbell, "Universality and Cultural Specificity in Child-Mother Attachment Relationships: In Search for Answers," in *Attachment Across Clinical and Cultural Perspectives: A Relational Psychoanalytic Approach*, ed. by Sonia Gojman-de-Millan, Christian Herreman, and L. Alan Sroufe, Psychoanalytic Inquiry Book Series (London: Routledge, 2017), 30 and 46.

5. Fredric Jameson, *The Political Unconscious: Narrative as a Socially Symbolic Act* (Ithaca: Cornell University Press, 1981), 9–22.

6. Fredric Jameson, *The Political Unconscious*, 22.

7. Robert Burton, *The Anatomy of Melancholy*, ed. Thomas C. Faulkner, Nicolas K. Kiessling, and Rhonda L. Blair, 6 vols. (Oxford: Henry Cripps, 1621, ed. copy, Oxford: Clarendon Press, 1989), 1:257–58.

8. Colin Murray Parkes, *Bereavement*, 7; Robert Burton, *The Anatomy of Melancholy*, I:258.

9. Colin Murray, Parkes *Bereavement*, 66.

10. Charles Darwin, *The Expression of the Emotions in Man and Animals*, 3rd ed. (Great Britain: John Murray, 1872; London: Harper Collins, 1889, repr. 1998), 84–85.

11. Carl Georg Lange, "The Emotions: A Psychophysiological Study," in Carl Georg Lange and William James, *The Emotions* (New York: Hafner, 1922 repr. 1967), 40–41. Lange's monograph was published in Danish in 1885 and translated in German by Dr. Kurella in 1887. The version quoted is a translation into English by Istar A. Haupt from Kurella's German version.

12. Darwin, *The Expression of the Emotions in Man and Animals*, 194.

13. Shand, *The Foundations of Character*, 302.

14. Shand, *The Foundations of Character*, 303–4.

15. Homer, *The Odyssey*, trans. by Robert Fitzgerald New York: Doubleday, 1962), 33.

16. Shand, *The Foundations of Character*, 3–4.

17. Philippe Soupault, "James Joyce," in *Portraits of the Artist in Exile: Recollections of James Joyce by Europeans*, ed. Willard Potts (Seattle: University of Washington Press, 1979), 112–13.

18. Ellmann, *James Joyce*, 453.

19. John Paul Riquelme, *Teller and Tale in Joyce's Fiction: Oscillating Perspectives* (Maryland: Johns Hopkins University Press, 1983), 163.

20. See Howe, *Attachment Across the Lifecourse*, 24.

21. Frank Budgen, *James Joyce and the Making of Ulysses*, 2nd ed. (London: Grayson & Grayson, 1937), 92.

22. Ezra Pound, "'Dubliners' and Mr James Joyce," *Egoist*, I, 14, (1914), 267 in *James Joyce: The Critical Heritage*, ed. by Robert H. Deming, 2 vols., (London: Routledge, 1970), I:67.

23. When referring to "Interior Monologue" and "Stream of Consciousness" throughout this book, I am using Robert Humphrey's definitions: Interior Monologue is defined as "the technique used in fiction for representing the psychic content and processes of character, partly or entirely unuttered, just as these processes exist at various levels of conscious control before they are formulated for deliberate speech. [. . .] It is concerned with the contents *and* processes of consciousness, not with just one of these." Using the analogy of an iceberg he explains that stream of consciousness fiction is "greatly concerned with what lies below the surface [. . .] a type of fiction in which the basic emphasis is placed on exploration of the prespeech levels of consciousness for the purpose, primarily, or revealing the psychic being of characters." Robert Humphrey, *Stream of Consciousness in the Modern Novel* (California: University of California Press, 1954), 4–25.

24. Luke Thurston, "Scotographica: Joyce and Psychoanalysis," in *A Companion to James Joyce*, ed. by Richard Brown (Oxford: Blackwell Publishing Ltd, 2008), 410.

25. Robert S. P. Jones, "Language, Form and Emotion in James Joyce's Portrait of an Artist as a Young Man: A Literary Analysis," *Advances in Language and Literary Studies*, no. 8 (2017): 158–60.

Chapter Three

The Representation of Character and Reader Response

Esliabetta Cecconi, who discusses Joyce's secondary characters, opens her preface with the statement: "Character has always been a problematic category in narrative theory."[1] Although an uncomplicated sentence, it implies the many complex debates around fictional characters. For example, the way in which the reader interprets and relates to them and the philosophical questions that also arise around the question of reader response, such as the "paradox of fiction."[2] To consider these questions in any great detail is beyond the scope of this book. However, there are certain theories that have influenced my reading, such as the work of Jonathan Culpeper, Murray Smith, and Suzanne Keen.

Culpeper notes that, "broadly speaking" there are two opposing stances that can be taken by critics when considering "the ontological status of character." The first consists of those who "humanise" characters, arguing that to a certain extent characters can be considered and discussed "independently of the text." They "make the assumption either that the characters are imitations or representation of real people, or—the more extreme view—that they are actually real people."[3] The latter chimes with Frank Budgen's comment that, in his view, "the characters are, in the first place, living breathing human beings. The life of the book comes first and the philosophy afterwards."[4] Budgen is firmly in the humanising camp. The opposing dehumanising view is that characters are purely functional and what matters is the effect of the actions of the character, rather than the cause. To use Jonathan Culler's phrase, they are "actants rather than personages."[5] However, Culpeper has put forward the case for an integrated approach, where both textual factors and the cognitive factors (the reader's prior knowledge) together can give a certain view of a character to the reader.[6] A simple example of using prior knowledge is when, in *Ulysses,* Bloom refers to "the wife's admirers" instead of the wife's advisors (*U*, 12.767). If one has knowledge of Freud and the unconscious, and this being what is termed in popular culture as a "Freudian slip," one becomes aware that Joyce is presenting Bloom as a character preoccupied with his wife's liaison with Boylan. Similarly reading Joyce's work with knowledge of Attachment Theory will provide a revealing reading of the main characters.

The fact that critical debate has moved toward an integrated approach has led to the more humanising stance often taken by readers being discussed at some length in the last decade, notably in a special edition of *New Literary History*, edited by Rita Felski in 2011. She suggests that "the impact of cognitive science on the humanities has triggered a new wave of interdisciplinary scholarship devoted to the puzzle of elucidating our intellectual curiosity about, and emotional attachment to, people who do not exist."[7] Murray Smith's paper "On the Twofoldness of Character," in that special edition, takes a similar approach to that of Culpeper. Turning to the long running radio drama *The Archers* as an example, Murray Smith notes how listeners "respond to and talk in sustained fashion about characters as if they were real." For example, when the character Nigel Pargetter "died" fans spoke "of their "grief" for [him and] at least one eulogy [. . .] was written in his memory."[8] However, referring to the work of Greg Currie he goes on to make the point that despite this humanising approach, readers are aware that characters are not real people but that they are "disposed to finding meaningful connections" within the narrative work.[9] In other words our cognition that the narrative is designed in a particular and functional manner means that connections are made over and above those that would normally be made in real life.

Other essays in Felski's special issue take an interest in the ways readers who are not professional literary critics read character, often in a humanising way. In "Readers' Temperaments and Fictional Character," Suzanne Keen argues that, rather than separating theories about fiction and the experience of actual readers, the "shaping influences of readers on character should be acknowledged." She "calls for a revival of reader-response studies, informed by evidence of the high degree of variability in reactions to fictional characters." Keen's argument is that when considering character, the reader's own character has an important part to play, it is not purely a notion controlled by the text and its author; but that "critics and theorists generalise from their own experiences without acknowledging the roles played by their own personalities."[10]

Taking into account the above arguments, any critical response to character will involve not only the critic's knowledge and tendency to make meaningful inferences but also his or her "personality, disposition and experience."[11] Such a critical stance allows for a wide variety of readings; readings that destabilise arguments put forward by, for example, genetic critics of Joyce such as Luca Crispi, who argues against a humanising approach. Whilst I do not wish to negate the importance of genetic studies and the invaluable information they provide to scholars, this book does not dismiss as "indefensible" what Crispi refers to as "common-sensical notions" regarding "narrative and human character and character traits."[12] Rather, taking an integrated approach, I acknowledge how Joyce's realism, which focuses on the internal lives of his characters and consequent actions, encourages a more humanising approach to the text and hence promotes emotional engagement with them.

Crispi argues that understanding when in the writing process certain biographical information was added regarding the respective characters of *Ulysses* can lead to "more grounded and nuanced debates" in terms of how the character can be understood to function in a particular text.[13] Nevertheless, he does concede that:

> It will remain impossible to conceive a coherent and convincing methodological approach to the concept of character in narratives as long as the concept remains ontologically ambivalent.
> [. . .]
> The most engaging literary works of art encourage us to believe that the narrative stories that unfold in a book imitate the world we live in [. . .]. Throughout history narratives have helped readers explore and define the understanding of the world and their fellow human beings. Narratives will continue to do so regardless of the philosophical and critical debates about the status of characters in art and what we variously understand as human character that have and will continue to resurface and then recede temporarily.[14]

Here Crispi is making a clear demarcation between literary criticism and reader response—a separation that Keen argues against. Taking an integrated approach to character gives credit to the reader's prior knowledge, whether gained through scholarly experience or actual life events, and thus allows for fictional texts to be read with knowledge of Bowlby's theories. This in turn provides an understanding of the grief and also the empathic emotional response that may be experienced by the reader. For example, I am aware that the experience of having witnessed the sudden death of my own father at the time of writing this book has contributed to my critical interpretation, particularly that of Master Dignam and the initial shock felt. As Keen has argued, this is a legitimate response to the text and narrative empathy ("feeling with the text") needs to be acknowledged, even though it means relinquishing "the relative tidiness of models based on description of textual strategies."[15] But critical forays into such theoretical realms can give way to novel readings. Indeed Jonathan Culler argues for what he terms "overinterpretation" of the text:

> [I]f critics are going to spend their time working out and proposing interpretations, then they should apply as much interpretive pressure as they can, should

carry their thinking as far as it can go. [. . .] They have a better chance, it seems to me, of bringing to light connections or implications not previously noticed or reflected on than if they strive to remain "sound" or moderate.[16]

Joyce, it appears, would not object to Culler's argument, if one takes into account his conversation with Arthur Power, where he reportedly stated: "people may read more into *Ulysses* than I ever intended, who is to say that they are wrong"; for, as he added, "do any of us know what we are creating?"[17] This book provides a reading that utilises knowledge of Bowlby's work in order to apply "interpretive pressure" to Joyce's texts, whilst also being cognisant of the connections the reader may make due to narrative empathy or awareness of the "purposeful design" of the text.[18]

FORM AND CHARACTER

In 1998, Cupchik et al. carried out a study using extracts from stories in *Dubliners* to monitor participants' emotional response. They found that "emotional" excerpts that allowed for easy identification "prompted fresh emotions and emotional memories almost equally, whereas descriptively dense passages evoked more fresh emotions than memories." They go on to state that "it is generally thought [. . .] that first-person narration promotes identification, as compared with third-person narration which promotes a spectator set" and that "if such variations, chosen by the writers, are as effective as the variation of set in our study, the writer has this means, too, of varying aesthetic distance, and hence the mix of fresh emotions and emotional memories."[19] In *Ulysses*, Joyce provides a masterclass at how the aesthetic distance can be manipulated partly through the various styles implemented in the different episodes. However, the point I want to make here is that whatever blend of form and language Joyce elects to transfer and convey emotion in *Ulysses*, the character traits of Bloom and Stephen are always identifiable. Therefore, whether it be in "Oxen of the Sun" episode at the lying in hospital, where different literary styles show the development of language; or in the "Circe" episode where waking dreams and hallucinations predominate; or in the "Ithaca" episode at Bloom's house where a catechistic form which negates empathic intimacy with the characters; the reader can clearly identify the "scientific" bent of Bloom in contrast with the "artistic" leaning of Stephen (*U*, 17.560).

Gotfried describes the differences in the way that Stephen and Bloom use language particularly well:

Both characters are indeed similar to the sentences they speak. [. . .] Stephen's sentences read like the bon mots of the artist (those indeed of Joyce himself): rhetorically balanced, polished, and finished like the marble surfaces of great statues. He is able to mould language, to fashion it into something. [. . .] Bloom, on the other hand, [. . .] seems often at the mercy of language's twists and turns; and he is used by language as much as he uses it. His sentences are loose, open to whims of leaping association and capricious in the syntactical connections.[20]

Blooms "leaping associations" often refer to scientific theories and debate (whether or not remembered correctly). Thus in the "Oxen of the Sun" episode, in a section where Joyce uses Latinate Prose style (see *U*, 14.334–428) Stephen, after reference to the promised land and clearly bitter at the loss of his mother, nevertheless reflects poetically: "And thou hast quenched me forever. And thou has left me alone for ever in the dark ways of my bitterness: and with a kiss of ashes hast thou kissed my mouth" (*U*, 14.377–80). However Bloom, showing his scientific bent is found echoing "the eighteenth century assumption that electricity was fluid" when trying to calm Stephen during the thunder storm which ensues shortly after Stephen's speech: "it was no other thing but a hubbub noise that he heard, the discharge of fluid from the thunderhead, look you, having taken place, and all of the order of a natural phenomenon" (*U*, 14.424–28).[21] The poetic versus the factual.

Similarly, in the "Ithaca" episode, one finds the dramatic played off against the scientific as both conjure up a scene in a hotel. Stephen's scenario of a young man and a young woman is filled with emotional tension by virtue of his staccato prose. Conversely Bloom's prose, although referring to the emotionally devastating suicide of his father, is akin to a legal/scientific report, using one long sentence to describe times and locations and how his father used "2 parts of aconite liniment to 1 part chloroform liniment" in order to take his own life (Cf *U*, 17.611–32).[22] Despite their clearly identifiable character traits, what they both have in common is the continued grief for a lost parent and this will be discussed at length.

NOTES

1. Elisabetta Cecconi, *"Who Chose This Face for Me?" Joyce's Creation of Secondary Characters in Ulysses*, European University Studies Series XIV, Anglo Saxon Language in Literature (Bern: Peter Lang, 2007), 13.

2. "The Paradox of Fiction" looks at three propositions regarding reactions to literary characters which are "jointly inconsistent: (a) We often have emotion for fictional characters and situations known to be purely fictional; (b) Emotions for objects logically presuppose beliefs in the existence and features of those objects; (c) we do not harbour beliefs in the existence and features of objects known to be fictional." This

has been debated widely by philosophers and various theories proposed. See Jerrold Levinson, "Emotion in Response to Art," in *Emotion and the Arts*, ed. Mette Hjort, and Sue Laver (Oxford: Oxford University Press, 1977) 22–23.

3. Jonathan Culpeper, *Language and Characterisation: People in Plays and Other Texts* (Edinburgh: Pearson Education, 2001), 6.

4. Frank Budgen, *James Joyce*, 274.

5. Jonathan Culler, *Structuralist Poetics: Structuralism, Linguists and the Study of Literature* (London: Routledge & Kegan Paul, 1975), 230.

6. Culpeper, *Language and Characterisation*, 11. Culpeper defines the reader's prior knowledge as "the past knowledge and experience stored in the mind," particularly the "long-term memory," 28.

7. Rital Felski, "Introduction," *New Literary History* 42, no. 2 (2011): v–vi.

8. Murray Smith, "On the Twofoldness of Character," *New Literary History* 42, no. 2 (2011): 277–78.

9. Smith, "On the Twofoldness of Character," 289. Smith is making reference to the work of Gregory Currie, "The Capacities that Enable us to Produce and Consume Art," in *Imagination, Philosophy and the Arts*, ed. Matthew Kiernan and Dominic McIver Lopes (London: Routledge, 2003), 296–97.

10. Suzanne Keen, "Readers' Temperaments and Fictional Character," *New Literary History*, 42, no. 2 (2011): 295–302.

11. Keen, "Readers' Temperaments and Fictional Character," 307.

12. Crispi, *Joyce's Creative Process*, 21.

13. Crispi, *Joyce's Creative Process*, 2.

14. Crispi, *Joyce's Creative Process*, 18–21.

15. Keen, "Readers' Temperaments and Fictional Character," 296.

16. Jonathan Culler, "In Defence of Overinterpretation," in *Interpretation and Overinterpretation*, ed. Stefan Collini (Cambridge: Cambridge University Press, 1992, digital, 2004), 110.

17. Power, *Conversations*, 102–3.

18. Smith, "On the Twofoldness of Character," 289.

19. Gerald C. Cupchik, Keath Oatley, and Peter Vorderer, "Emotional Effects of Reading Excerpts from Short Stories by James Joyce," *Poetics* 25 (1998): 363 and 376. The "spectator set" felt sympathy for the protagonist whereas the "identification set" imagined what it was like to be the protagonist.

20. Roy K. Gottfried, *The Art of Joyce's Syntax in Ulysses* (London: Macmillan, 1980), 33–34.

21. Don Gifford with Robert J. Seidman, *Ulysses Annotated: Notes from James Joyce's Ulysses*, revised and expanded edition (California: University of California Press, 1989), 421.

22. Whilst the innovative form and style are important to any Joyce scholar, this has been written about extensively in the past and is not the focus of this book, although as with the historical context, it will be mentioned where relevant.

Chapter Four

Attachment Theory and Literary Interpretation

With a tendency to "avoid those subjects of which he had only passing or partial knowledge, one of which was English literature," Bowlby, unlike Freud, did not turn to the works of creative writers to elucidate his concepts (*JB*, 96).[1] However, he did acknowledge how Shand, (who I believe can be described as the forefather of Attachment Theory in terms of his work on grief), had put the work of such writers to good use in the construction of his own theories. It therefore seems reasonable to suggest that Attachment Theory could also be extended to provide a ready model for readings of literature.

RELATION BETWEEN THEORETICAL STANCE TAKEN AND THE TEXT

Much regarding the relation between the theoretical stance taken and Joyce's work has already been discussed in the previous chapters. Most importantly I have argued that although Joyce would not have been using the language of attachment theorists, his portrayal of grief and how it is experienced is still commensurate with that described by Bowlby. Aided by the self-reflexive elements of his writing, along with his interest and hence close scrutiny of human behaviour, Joyce has instilled within his characters behavioural elements that can be interpreted from an attachment perspective.

In discussing the role of the novelist L. A. G. Strong argues that "novelists have often been the best psychologists," defining their task as one that is "to feel, to understand, and to present: to concentrate on the particular instance with such power and honesty that the reader's imagination leaps, in terms of the truth presented, to the truth beyond it."[2] Reading Joyce with knowledge of Attachment Theory one could argue that, for example, the "power" with which he describes the distressing experiences of the young Stephen Dedalus at Clongowes Wood College after being removed from the family home at a young age, leads one to the truth beyond the text; that Joyce is creating a scenario where Stephen, if he were a real person, would be prone to avoidant behavioural traits. That the text then goes on describe his emotional insularity and in particular the later emotional distance from his mother, which despite his efforts he is unable to rekindle, leads the reader, to use Murray Smith's argument, to make the "meaningful connection" between his portrayed childhood history and consequent emotional detachment and therefore to read Stephen as indeed exhibiting avoidant traits.[3] (This will be discussed in detail in Chapter 9.)

In Stephen Joyce is portraying a certain type of character, one that is largely autobiographical. Armed with the knowledge that Joyce was sent away from his mother at the age of six and a half years; that he developed, according to Strong, into "a thinker who had suppressed his feeling side" again helps the reader to make such connections both with and within the text.[4] Of course it is accepted that Stephen is not Joyce but, as Morris Beja comments, "the more we have come to learn about the smallest details of Joyce's life, the more we have come to see correspondences between that life and his art."[5]

Brook Thomas acknowledges the many alternative readings that Joyce's work may produce but he also makes plain that, since reading is a temporal process, it is not possible to produce more than one reading, or as he refers to it "one pattern" of words, at any one time:

> We can no more perceive all the alternative readings in our mind at the same time than—to use a visual example that does seem applicable in this particular case—we can simultaneously see both rabbit and duck of the famous gestalt figure. To produce one pattern we have to go through an act of reading, and to produce another pattern we need to go through another act of reading, creating an endless number of structures.[6]

Critics are inevitably forced to choose a particular perspective, a particular way in which to interpret the text. Thus, using Attachment Theory as a frame of reference produces a reading that is restricted and only partial, but this will be true of any critical stance taken.

Whilst probing the possible advantages and disadvantages of using Attachment Theory as a frame of reference, I would like to return to the work of Jonathan Culler who encourages critics to "carry their thinking as far as it can go." His argument is that "like most intellectual activities, interpretation is interesting only when it is extreme. Moderate interpretation, which articulates a consensus, though it may have value in some circumstances is of little interest."[7] Critics who read characters merely as actants, or like Jameson take a more Marxist view, may find an interpretation of Stephen as exhibiting avoidant traits difficult to subscribe to. Focusing on the portrayal of a protagonist's experiences and environment in terms of whether he has a secure base and making connections between those and his portrayed thoughts and consequent actions may be seen by some as projecting a narrative or, as Jameson has argued, creating an ur-narrative.[8] Yet, to quote Richard Kain, "the amazing air of reality" that Joyce achieves "proceeds not from ordinary external description but from a reliance upon the psychological sensations presented to the mind."[9] An argument can be made that in concentrating upon the minds of his protagonists, Joyce encourages readers to make such connections, to ascribe to them a theory of mind, and to take a more humanising approach to his characters. Indeed this is attested to by the recent publication of the book *Cognitive Joyce*, which discusses his texts in light of recent developments of cognitive sciences, the "Introduction" of which comments on how "Joyce thoroughly explores the workings of the human mind across his work" from *Dubliners* through to *Finnegans Wake*.[10]

If one accepts the arguments put forward by Culpeper and Keen, that critics call on their own knowledge and experiences when making interpretations (see Chapter 3) such an approach can be viewed as a mechanism by which to apply interpretive pressure to the text, to help make connections that have hitherto been unexplored. Using one's knowledge of a theory such as Bowlby's, which takes into account insights from post-Darwinian ethology, modern cognitive-developmental psychology, and community psychiatry, amongst others, allows for a more comprehensive psychoanalytical interpretation than Freudian theory, which concentrates on libidinal drives.

ATTACHMENT THEORY AND THE PROVISION OF ALTERNATIVE INTERPRETATIONS

Jeremy Holmes discusses how the various emotional reactions to bereavement, which have been meaningfully relayed by creative writers, can be seen to correlate with Bowlby's defined stages of grief by virtue of his analysis of three poems: Tennyson's *In Memoriam,* Milton's *Lycidas,* and John Donne's "A Valediction: forbidding mourning," the latter of which is concerned with anticipatory grief (*JB*, 96–102). In discussing "A Valediction" Holmes notes both attachment and the "rhythm of sexuality," which is associated with birth and death, are "held together by the central image of the secure base," which, he argues, shows that attachment can be viewed as a "unifying principle that reaches from the biological depths of our being to its furthest spiritual reaches" (*JB*, 102).

Bowlby was adamant, however, that on a *conceptual* basis sexual behaviour and attachment behaviour should be seen as distinct. This is an important point when using Attachment Theory as a frame of reference to interpret literary texts since, unlike Freudian theory, it allows for interpretations that are not linked to libidinal drives and satisfaction. Previously, Jung had critcised what he termed "Freud's 'dogma' of infantile sexuality" and "his strict adherence to the Oedipus complex" as a key motivational force for behaviour.[11] Bowlby did admit that attachment behaviour, parental behaviour and sexual behaviour could sometimes overlap, giving the example of a person who treats his sexual partner as though they were a parent and the partner reciprocating by "adopting a parental attitude" (*AL*1: 233). Nevertheless, he argued for their conceptual discreteness for the following reasons: "the two systems vary independently of one another"; "the class of objects towards which each is directed" may differ and the "sensitive phase in the development of each are likely to occur at different ages" (*AL*1: 230–33).

Sheldon Brivic's critical reading of Joyce's work is a good example of a Freudian interpretation where the attachment and sexual motivations of the protagonists are conflated. He proposed that it is possible to describe the meaning of *Portrait* and *Ulysses* as "one central problem of relationship," arguing that Stephen from *Portrait* onwards shows "the standard Oedipus complex distinguished by particularly strong castration anxiety."[12] He also goes on to interpret Bloom in a similar way. From an attachment perspective, whilst one can certainly agree with Brivic that relationships have played an important part in the portrayed development of Stephen and Bloom, the reasoning behind this statement would be based on perceived security and the development of internal working models, not psychosexual perspectives. As I will show, this will lead to a very different interpretation and understanding of the represented thoughts and actions of the protagonists than those offered by Freudian critics.

Critics approaching Joyce from a Freudian perspective have acknowledged the importance of early memories within his writing. For example, John Rickard sees memory as being at the core of *Ulysses* and hence influencing its content and form. He looks at different forms of memory within the text, and argues that "Joyce's writing involves itself in [. . .] the effects the past has on the present and future."[13] Rickard defines mourning as a "ritualised, public form of memory" and when discussing why Stephen and Bloom have are still mourning the loss of their loved ones he turns to Freud's "Mourning and Melancholia," arguing that their lack of detachment of the libido from the lost object has been caused by repression, or as he terms it a "mnemic abscess [. . .] in the psyche."[14] Equally, reading Joyce from an attachment perspective, it is possible to see how the past memories affect the current portrayed actions of the protagonists and by tacit implication, their future. The representation of memories as organising principles in terms of a sense of self, relationship formation and ultimately how one reacts to loss, provide a strong impetus to the narrative structure. Whilst attachment theorists provide a different model of the grief process to that proposed by Freud, they do acknowledge that "attachment related feelings are subject to repression no less than those dominated by sexuality or aggression."[15]

Of course, psychoanalytical interpretations of Joyce's work have not just been based on Freudian theory. Lacanian and Jungian theories have also been used as a framework for critical readings of Joyce. It is worth noting that Joyce was familiar with Jung's work as Jung treated Joyce's daughter, Lucia, for her schizophrenia. Jung also wrote two articles on *Ulysses*. In the first, which was written in 1930 and never published, he stated, "Joyce's book was made an example of the schizophrenic mind."[16] In 1932 he wrote a further article, published in the Europaishce Revue, in which he wrote: "In the whole book no Ulysses appears, the book itself is Ulysses, a microcosm of James Joyce. The world of the self and self of the world in one."[17] Certainly the self-referential aspects of Joyce's work help to shape his characters and their behaviours. Elucidating the insecure attachment traits portrayed in the characters provides a basis for understanding their thoughts, behaviours and individual reactions to bereavement, providing alternative interpretations and new insight in Joyce's work.

NOTES

1. With reference to U. Bowlby, personal communication, 1991
2. L. A. G. Strong, *The Sacred River: An Approach to James Joyce* (London: Methuen, 1949), 99.
3. Smith, "On the Twofoldness of Character," 277–78.
4. Strong, *The Sacred River*, 88.
5. Morris Beja, *James Joyce: A Literary Life*, Literary Life Series (Basingstoke: Macmillan, 1992), ix.
6. Brook Thomas, *James Joyce's Ulysses: A Book of Many Happy Returns* (Louisiana State University Press, Baton Rouge, 1982), 162; See E. H. Gombrich, *Art and Illusion* (London: Paidon Press, 1972)
7. Jonathan Culler, "In Defence of Overinterpretation," 110.
8. Jameson, *The Political Unconscious*, 9–22.
9. Richard M.,Kain, *Fabulous Voyager: James Joyce's Ulysses* (Chicago: University of Chicago Press, 1947), 20.
10. Sylvain Belluc and Valérie Bénéjam, "Introduction," in *Cognitive Joyce*, ed. Sylvian Belluc and Valérie Bénéjam, Cognitive Studies in Literature and Performance Series (Basingstoke, Palgrave Macmillan, 2018), 1.
11. David Tacey, *How to Read Jung* (London: Granta, 2006), 3.
12. Sheldon Brivic, "James Joyce," 118.

13. John S. Rickard, *Joyce's Book of Memory: The Mnemotechnic of Ulysses* (Durham: Duke University Press, 1999), 2.

14. Rickard, *Joyce's Book of Memory*, 41–42.

15. Jeremy Holmes, "Superego: An Attachment Perspective," *International Journal of Psychoanalysis* 92 (2011): 1228.

16. Ellmann, *James Joyce*, 641.

17. Carl Jung, quoted in Stephen Parker, *Jung's Essay on Ulysses*, accessed 05 January 2012, http://jungcurrents.com/jungs-essay-on-ulysses.

PART II

The Portrayal of the Emotional Impact of Bereavement and Ensuing Grief

Part II

Introduction

Part 2 focuses on how Joyce represents and thus conveys to the reader, through his writing techniques and use of language, the emotional impact of bereavement and the ensuing stages of the grief process as defined by Bowlby. Joyce's detailed portrayal of the thoughts of the main protagonists of "The Sisters," "Eveline" and "The Dead" in *Dubliners* at formative moments in the texts and also Master Patrick Dignam's interior monologue in *Ulysses,* provide prime examples of how loss gives rise to various emotions. Each of these texts portray a different aspect of the emotional impact of bereavement by virtue of the differing circumstances of each death and the specific relationships the bereaved had with their attachment figure.

Joyce's "new form of realism" was one in which Joyce "want[ed] the reader to understand always through suggestion rather than direct statement."[1] However, from his early work, it was evident that Joyce was not a traditional realist, as Phillippe Soupult sums up succinctly: "That which is to be perfected in *Ulysses* is already foreshadowed in *Dubliners*."[2] Although Joyce's literary technique developed throughout his oeuvre, his ethos was that art, instead of insisting on its "religious, its moral, its beautiful, its idealising tendencies," should show "life as we see it before our eyes, men and women as we meet them in the real world" was ever present.[3] This particular aspect of his realism, his unapologetic representation of the often base business of life, required keen observation of people's behaviour and actions, speech and body language, which he is known to have practiced (see Chapter 2). Joyce's work and particularly his portrayal of the emotional response to grief, therefore, not only leaves it open to readers experiencing narrative empathy but also to interpretation using Attachment Theory by virtue of the fact it encourages a humanising approach.

Before going on to discuss the portrayal of emotion in Joyce's work, it is worth taking time to consider how the term "emotion" came to be applied in the way it is today. Historian Thomas Dixon writes:

> It is an immensely striking fact of the history of English-language psychological thought that during the period between *c.* 1800 and *c.* 1850 a wholesale change in established vocabulary occurred such that those engaged in theoretical discussions about phenomena including hope, fear, love, hate, joy, sorrow, anger and the like no longer primarily discussed the passions or affections of the soul, nor the sentiments but almost invariably referred to "the emotions."[4]

Dixon argues that this was due to the "secularisation of psychology" which no longer needed to negotiate questions of the will and Christian morality.[5] Although Joyce's work is saturated with religious references, themes, and tensions, he himself, "rejected its dogma [and] refused to pay allegiance to its spiritual power."[6] His writing, which invites the reader to immerse themselves in the "real world" of the inhabitants of Dublin, lays bare the duplicity that can sometimes be found in those who portray themselves as pious Christians.

Keith Oatley is one of many psychologists who espouse the notion that, depending on the ability of the artist he can not only "depict emotions," but additionally "allow readers to be moved by their own emotions as they read and also to reflect on them."[7] As is evident, this is in agreement with Joyce's statement as recalled by Arthur Power: "The object of any work of art is the transference of emotion; talent is the gift of conveying that emotion."[8] Oatley describes a typical emotion that is fully developed as: "A kind of readiness elicited by some event that impinges on a person's concerns. It will have a tone that is experienced consciously, and it will include accompaniments of conscious preoccupation, bodily disturbance, and expression. It will also issue in some course of action prompted by the emotion."[9] However, he does add that his own studies have shown that not all of these features may be present in every emotional episode.[10] When reading one will not take any action but, as Peter Goldie argues, this lack of action does not mean "that our external emotional responses to fictional stories are radically distinct from, or less genuine, than our real life emotional responses."[11]

Oatley and Mitra Gholamain have argued that there are five processes in reading a fictional narrative that enable the reader to connect to the text emotionally: the psychological processes of "identification" and "sympathy" with the protagonist(s) and one's own "autobiographical memory," plus aspects of "fictional presentation to the reader" which include "reaction to the aesthetic object" (the ability of the author to "achieve what Longinus called "the sublime," which involves profound thought, intensity of emotion, and material for reflection") and "response to the discourse level."[12]

In life, Oatley argues, emotions are derived from one's goals and plans, with happy or distressing emotions occurring depending on whether they are achieved or go badly, respectively.[13] He posits that part of the enjoyment of stories comes from the fact "they invoke planlike sequences and set problems, not just for the story characters but for the readers."[14] He goes on to argue that "[n]arrative form decouples the event or story sequence from the discourse sequence. In so doing an arena of creativity emerges—not just the writer's creativity but the reader's."[15] Joyce's shifts in narrative voice, his use of the stream of consciousness technique, interior monologue and the narrative gaps all facilitate the aforementioned "creative arena" and hence connection to the text via the use of one's own schemata and autobiographical memory. The judgements made as part of the creative process also enable consideration of the questions that are implicit within the text and so enable the reader's participation in the meaning of the text. This is exemplified particularly well by the various interpretations of the relationship between the boy and the priest in "The Sisters."

Both "The Sisters" and the interior monologue of Master Dignam present the emotional response to bereavement from a child's perspective but due to the differing circumstances of their losses and their support base, their portrayed experiences are, as I discuss, quite distinct.

NOTES

1. Budgen, *James Joyce*, 21.

2. Philippe Soupault, "James Joyce," 109.

3. James Joyce "Drama and Life," in *James Joyce: The Critical Writings*, ed. Ellsworth Mason and Richard Ellmann (New York: Cornell University Press, 1989), 44–45.

4. Thomas Dixon, "From Passions to Emotions," in *Emotions: A Social Science Reader*, ed. Monica Greco and Paul Setnner, Routledge Student Reader Series (London: Routledge, 2008), 30.

5. Thomas Dixon, "From Passions to Emotions," 30.

6. Hélène Cixous, *The Exile of James Joyce*, trans. Sally A. J. Purcell (New York: David Lewis, 1972), 418.

7. Oatley, *Best Laid Schemes*, 256.

8. Power, *Conversations*, 113.

9. Oatley, *Best Laid Schemes*, 21.

10. Oatley, *Best Laid Schemes*, 21. With reference to K. Oatley and E. Duncan, "Structured Diaries for Emotions in Daily Life."

11. Peter Goldie, "Narrative and Perspective; Values and Appropriate Emotions," in *Philosophy and the Emotions,* ed. Anthony Hatzimoysis (Cambridge: Cambridge University Press, 2003), 214.

12. Keith Oatley and Mitra Gholamain, "Emotions and Identification: Connections Between Readers and Fiction," in *Emotion and the Arts,* ed. by Mette Hjort and Sue Laver (Oxford: Oxford University Press, 1997), 268–73. For more detailed

explanations of these terms see Longinus, "On the Sublime," in *Classical Literary Criticism*, trans. Penelope Murray and T. S. Dorsch, 2nd ed. (London: Penguin, 2000), 113–66.

13. See Oatley, *Best Laid Schemes*, 44.

14. Oatley, *Best Laid Schemes*, 247.

15. Oatley, *Best Laid Schemes*, 246, defines "discourse structure" as "the sequence of events presented in a narrative, and this subject to all the transformations that writers use including figures of rhetoric, the tenses, aspects, and modes of the narrative."

Chapter Five

"The Sisters"

Anticipatory Grief in a Securely Attached Individual

"The Sisters" provides one of Joyce's least traumatic fictional representations of the effects of bereavement. By providing the main protagonist of the story, the unnamed boy and first person narrator, with a secure base in the form of his family life and non-abusive relationship with Father Flynn, Joyce has furnished him with the potential to be able to deal with loss more easily than many of his other protagonists I will be discussing throughout this book.[1] Furthermore, as the death of the priest was not unexpected, he has also been furnished with the potential to experience anticipatory grief; the emotional response to a potential loss.

Bowlby argues that perceived support provides "a belief in the helpfulness of others and a favourable model on which to build future relationships" and in "The Sisters" I believe Joyce portrays such support (*AL*1: 378). With no mention of the boy's parents it seems reasonable to assume that Joyce is presenting a child who is being raised by his uncle and aunt. This assumption is further supported by the disclosure that the boy had known Cotter long enough to become bored with his stories and also his visits to Father Flynn had evidently taken place over some period of time, having had occasion to learn the responses of the mass "by heart" (*D*, 4). The apparent lack of any siblings also points to his aunt and uncle being his main attachment figures. That the boy has a secure base and support within the domestic setting is evidenced by virtue of his uncle's conversation with Old Cotter. Much like the young Stephen Dedalus, whom Joyce was later to portray in *Portrait,* the boy is shown to have an interest in intellectual activities rather than physical pursuits. His uncle's expressed belief in the importance of taking physical exercise and learning "to box his corner" makes plain the significance he places on active experience rather than purely focusing on intellectual endeavours (*D*, 2). Yet with no indication that his uncle has enforced his views, Joyce appears to be suggesting that the boy is free to pursue what interests him, allowing him to develop his sense of self within the world. There is no hint within the text of any emotional insecurity on the part of the boy within the domestic setting. Although his uncle jokingly refers to the boy as a "Rosicrucian" it appears to be a term of endearment and he seems proud that Father Flynn had "had a great wish for him" (*D*, 1–2).[2] Thus, reading with knowledge of Attachment Theory and making the connection between Bowlby's comments regarding the helpfulness of others and the building of future relationships, one could envisage that the boy would have found it easy to form a trusting friendship with Father Flynn and as a teacher and mentor form an attachment with him.

Bowlby notes that whilst there may be some differences, children from their fourth year onwards "tend to mourn in ways very similar to adults" (*AL3*: 290). How one reads the boy's reaction to the priest's death depends on whether or not one interprets the priest as having abused that trust. Father Flynn can be seen as a father figure, both as representative of God the father within the Christian faith, but also through the interest he has taken in the boy. From attachment studies it has been found that when a parent dies who has been sexually and/or physically abusive, rather than being "cause for celebration," it can cause feelings of anger to resurface or "even give rise to feelings of guilt if the child was repeatedly told that the abuse was a punishment for his or her faults."[3] The boy is not represented as showing any such feelings toward the priest. However, critics who question the priest's integrity have focused on Cotter's "unfinished sentences" regarding the priest, the boy's dream and also his reported "sensation of freedom" following the priest's death (*D*, 2–3). It is therefore worth considering each of these occurrences in turn.

With the continued use of ellipses in Cotter's sentences Joyce creates the impression of a man who is choosing his words carefully; who has something which is socially delicate or perhaps shocking to say but does not want to speak of the matter directly: "No, I wouldn't say he was exactly . . . but there was something queer . . . there was something uncanny about him" (*D*, 1). Some form of impropriety is further implied by his comment that he would not like his children "to have too much to say to a man like that" (*D*, 2). However, Joyce also exposes Cotter's duplicity when he has the boy comment: "When we knew him first he used to be rather interesting, talking of faints and worms; but I soon grew tired of him and his endless stories about the distillery" (*D*, 1). Whereas Cotter apparently had no qualms in engaging the boy's time with his stories, he criticises him for spending time with the priest instead of running about and playing with boys of a similar age. This in turn stimulates questions as to how one is to read the purpose and validity of his comments regarding the priest. One could easily imagine a tinge of jealousy mixed with old Cotter's view of Father Flynn, partly because of the priest's superior knowledge, but also induced by the disappointment of being deprived of the chance to tell his own stories and relive his own memories through his conversations with the boy. I am not suggesting that Cotter is to be seen as behaving maliciously. Rather that implicit within the narrative are various subjective influences colouring his expressed views and concerns.

Cotter's remarks, along with Eliza Flynn's later statement that "something had gone wrong" with her brother have led to various interpretations regarding the behaviour and morality of the priest (*D*, 6). David Pierce, for example, has no hesitation in labelling him syphilitic.[4] However, Margot Norris takes a more circumspect approach and looks to differing explanations. Whilst she recognises the possibility of "guilty" readings, of perhaps a syphilitic priest or of a priest who has molested or sodomised the boy, she also acknowledges there could equally be "innocent" readings of the priest's illness and his relationship with the boy.[5] That such different yet plausible interpretations can be made highlights Joyce's artistry. Joyce not only obliges each individual reader to participate in the act of creation, but the resultant ambiguity enables him to realistically represent how a few vague sentences and gossip can lead to unsubstantiated conclusions. In other words, he portrays how in real life we use our imagination to create "another's perspective" when communicating with them.[6] However, whilst Joyce has tantalisingly hinted at some form of misdemeanour and indirectly raised the issue of the sexual desires of priests and their enforced celibacy, it is the boy's puzzlement that I believe ultimately leads to a more "innocent" reading of his relationship with Father Flynn.

The only information available to the reader that can elicit an understanding of the boy's relationship with the priest and hence his emotional response to his death, is purely from the boy's perspective. With the provision of this limited subjective view, one needs to analyse carefully the portrayal of his memories, feelings and reactions toward both Cotter and Father Flynn: the language used, any hint of hyperbole or inconsistencies that could imply any unreliability within the narrative. From the language and sentence structure with which Joyce furnishes the first person narrator, he is clearly to be viewed as older than when the events took place and as looking back on what was probably his first memorable experience of the death of someone with whom he was 'great friends' (*D*, 1). However, the narrator appears to immerse himself in that memory and present it from the perspective of a young boy.

That he was interested in language from a young age is registered at the beginning of the story by his curiosity of the sound of what Norris refers to as "bookish words."[7] Of import from an attachment perspective is the supportive environment under which the boy is able to pursue his quest for knowledge. Joyce's depiction of how the boy is treated by Father Flynn contrasts strongly with his portrayal of how the priests act toward the young and equally inquisitive Stephen Dedalus of *Portrait* whilst at Clongowes Wood. At Father Flynn's house, "difficult questions" are put to the boy and in the event of a "foolish reply" the priest's response is to merely "smile and nod his head twice or thrice" (*D*, 3–4). There is no one there to ridicule him or give him the pandybat should he not know how to respond. Most importantly for gaining an understanding of the boy's relationship with the priest, there is an obvious lack of any indication within the narrative of a lasting disquiet on the boy's part when in the presence of Father Flynn. Reporting that initially he felt "uneasy" when the priest "let his tongue lie on his lower lip" when he smiled, he also describes this feeling as dissipating once he "knew him well" (*D*, 4). With the language used to recount their meetings being factual, to the point and devoid of any negativity or anxiety and his behaviour toward the priest sympathetic (emptying the snuff into his box for him as he had trembling hands), Joyce gives no substantiation to Cotter's veiled insinuations. Indeed, by having the narrator list the subjects they discussed and also explain the priest's lack of annoyance should he give a wrong response, Joyce creates a sense that the boy was both proud of the knowledge he had acquired from Father Flynn and appreciative of his understanding attitude.

Garry Leonard, reading from a Lacanian viewpoint, interprets the boy's visits to the priest and fascination with words as forming part of the process of self-authentication, "allow[ing] him to narrate silently his own story (his[s]tory) in deliberate contrast to the narration of the various adults who frequently surround him."[8] However, one could alternatively read the importance of the visits to the boy as relating to the opportunity of learning from someone whom he valued as a friend as well as being tutor of greater wisdom than himself, and had therefore formed an attachment to him. It is of note that when the story first appeared in the *Irish Homestead* in 1904 the visits were circumstantial. The boy was depicted as going to the shop with his aunt, who would occasionally bring some snuff for the priest and it was in the aunt's presence that he would converse with the boy.[9] In *Dubliners*, by portraying the visits as unaccompanied and taking place on a voluntary basis to quench the boy's thirst for knowledge, Joyce presents a less formal and friendlier aspect to their meetings.

The narrator's expressed view of the priest contrasts strongly with his assessment of Cotter. Whereas at one time the boy appeared to enjoy his visits he is shown to now find them annoying: "Tiresome old fool" (*D*, 1). However, on the day of Father Flynn's death, disdain and irritation are overridden by astonishment and puzzlement as Cotter describes the priest as "uncanny," "queer," and his situation as "peculiar" (*D*, 1). The boy describes "staring" at Cotter, reflecting his inability to identify with the description of the Father Flynn that alludes to a type of strangeness or abnormality in his make-up (*D*, 1). His incomprehension as to why old Cotter is speaking in this way, or indeed what exactly he is implying, allows the reader to identify with him as, at this point (and as it transpires for the rest of the story), it is impossible to discern the precise meaning of Cotter's words. With the sexual nuances being evident to the reader, but no further information forthcoming, this exemplifies an aspect of Joyce's writing technique that Norris refers to as the "silent discourses" that "create interpretive dilemmas."[10]

In this story the "interpretive dilemma" is at least as challenging for the boy as for the reader. Being young, one can read him as probably not understanding the sexual nuances. Nevertheless, he is portrayed as being astute enough to know that whatever Cotter's words are implying, they are not complimentary. Initially, when Cotter is speaking, although the boy finds himself staring, there is no indication of any other involuntary physical response from him, be it a blush, increased heart rate, or any other form of anxiety. It could therefore be argued that he is to be read as not equating whatever Cotter is insinuating as pertaining to any involvement on his own part. The only discomfort mentioned comes from the boy's recognition that he was being examined by Cotter's "beady black eyes," not because he viewed his words as exposing some hidden truth regarding his relationship with Father Flynn (*D*, 1–2).

As Cotter continues to gossip about the priest, it is clear that the boy can only feel anger toward the old distillery worker. Taking Oatley's point that emotions are derived from one's goals or plans, it is possible to reason that what Joyce is depicting here is the result of the boy's self-enforced silence. His determination not to show any reaction in front of Cotter means abandoning his preferred course of action (i.e., his goal) to speak out in support of the priest, in turn fueling his emotional response, which in this case translates into anger. In his state of incomprehension and irritation, Cotter's words are viewed by the boy as displaying his befuddled thinking, as made patent by his further embellished description of him: "Tiresome old red-nosed imbecile" (*D*, 2).

The narrator recounts how Cotter's allusions played on his young mind and affected his dreams that night: "It was late when I fell asleep [. . .] I puzzled my head to extract meaning form his unfinished sentences. [. . .] I imagined that I saw again the heavy grey face of the paralytic" (*D*. 2). Both Bowlby and Parkes, commenting on studies carried out on widows and widowers, note how the bereaved often sense the presence of, or dream of, the deceased (*AL*3: 96–11).[11] Bowlby also notes how this can occur in the case of bereaved children (*AL*3: 287). Dreaming can be viewed "as a type of problem-solving behavior" and what Joyce is portraying here appears to be analogous with such behaviour.[12]

It is of note that the smiling face of the dream is not referred to as Father Flynn or the priest, but rather as "the paralytic" and then even more remotely as "it" (*D*, 2). The use of the term "it" could simply be the boy acknowledging that the priest is no longer mortal. Yet, that being said, his imagined presence negates the boundaries of life and death, and it is not until the next day when he reads the card that he is shown to be truly persuaded that Father Flynn is indeed dead. The otherness evoked by the term "it" could also, therefore, be an indication of his inability to reconcile Father Flynn with the suggestion that he was someone to be kept away from. Hence the ethereal priest that needs to "confess" cannot be fully equated with the priest he knew or his "murmuring voice" entirely understood (*D*, 2). Just as, during the boy's waking hours, Cotter's words were at once about and yet did not equate to the priest he knew, so in his dream the vision is and is not "the paralytic" (*D*, 2).

Although "The Sisters" is littered with fragmentary allusions, what is evident is that Father Flynn saw the boy as a potential priest: "they say he had a great wish for him" (*D*, 1).[13] Yet with the boy's cognitive abilities still developing and his understanding of priesthood coming from a man that found its duties "too much for him" (*D*, 6) he appears to view such a vocation with reverence and awe:

> His questions showed me how complex and mysterious were certain institutions of the Church which I had always regarded as the simplest acts. The duties of the priest towards the Eucharist and towards the secrecy of the confessional seemed so grave to me that I wondered how anybody had ever found in himself the courage to undertake them. (*D*, 3)

Although this description exemplifies the boy's timorous feelings toward the grave duties of the priest, the boy's dream also depicts how his imagination has been stimulated by the mystery of the church. The conflation of the confessional and "Persia"—the "long velvet curtains," antique lamp, and strange customs—create an image that is both exotic and other (*D*, 4).

As the boy continues to negotiate his dream state, occupying the indeterminate space between subject and object, he feels that the priest wants to confess and describes his soul as receding into a place which is both agreeable yet at the same time brutal: "into some pleasant and vicious region" (*D*, 2). Reading from a Freudian viewpoint, Edward Brandabur interprets this description, as a "clue" toward what he concludes is a sadomasochistic relationship between the priest and the boy.[14] Arguing against a reading of them "engaging in overt sexuality," he sees Father Flynn gaining pleasure by inflicting his "revolting presence" on the boy and also by setting him difficult questions, whilst the boy in turn gains pleasure from "being seduced into a state of paralyzed passivity."[15] This explanation seems to fall short since, as already noted, the boy overcame any discomfort initially presented by the priest's appearance. Arguably, on a symbolic level, if one interprets the priesthood as a state of "paralysed passivity" then one could see the boy being persuaded into such a role, but, as discussed above, his feelings toward this vocation foster nervousness rather than passivity. Furthermore, taking his reaction to Cotter's "endless stories" as an indication, he is not represented as a boy who would allow himself to be "seduced" into such a state.

Brandabur also interprets the smile exchanged by the priest and the boy in his dream as "a smile of mutual understanding, mutual acquiescence, and mutual pleasure in a sadomasochistic system."[16] Whilst there may be an implied mutual understanding here, I fail to read this as consequential to a sadomasochistic relationship. That priests tend to have a certain smile is referred to repeatedly by Joyce in his writing and is something that he would have experienced daily whilst at Clongowes Wood. In fact rules 6 and 7 of the Jesuit Rules of Modesty state that: "The lips must not be too much closed not too much open" and "[t]he whole face should display hilarity rather than sadness or any other less moderate affection," respectively.[17] Joyce has Bloom refer to this obligatory countenance in the "Lotuseaters" episode of *Ulysses* when he describes Father Farley as someone who "looked a fool but wasn't. They're taught that" (*U,* 5.333). Father Flynn is not portrayed as a Jesuit as the initials S. J. are not stated after his name on the notification of his death on the door. However, acknowledging Joyce's own enduring image of the priestly expression, which would have been with him throughout his Jesuit education, this aspect of the boy's dream where he believes the smiling face is confessing to him, can be read as representing a mutual understanding that he is taking the role of a priest, and hence he is portrayed as also adopting the "feeble smile'" (*D,* 2).

Thomas Connolly describes Father Flynn as having "drifted from the activity of the spiritual life" and hence become "a remainder after something else has been removed, a gnomon," which in can be seen as "a type of paralysis, an incompleteness."[18] This is quite a deft description of Joyce's portrayal of the priest's life, supported further in the text by the aunt's statement that the priest "was a disappointed man" (*D,* 6). Yet despite his own failure, with his "great wish" for the boy, he is also shown to trust in his ability to teach him to succeed where he had been left wanting. Therefore, Father Flynn's motivation and any attachment he has subsequently formed with boy can be viewed as a consequence of his attempt to overcome the family disappointment, albeit vicariously, rather than any sexual deviance. Moreover, knowing of Father Flynn's wish, the "pleasant and vicious region" of the dream could equally be read as an expression of the boy's ambivalent views toward entering the priesthood and the ensuing incumbent duties, including the confessional.

Reading this dream as the reaction to the loss of a clergyman who was an attachment figure for the boy frees it from an interpretation that necessarily involves any psychosexual element. I noted in Chapter 4 that Bowlby saw sexual behaviour and attachment behaviour as distinct, one of the reasons being "that the class of objects towards which each is directed may be quite different," which seems particularly pertinent in the scenario portrayed by Joyce (*AL*1: 230–33). The description of the boy's dream appears to relate to what Parkes has shown in his studies: that "bereaved dreamers continue to go over in their minds the vivid mental images that preoccupy their waking hours and, out of them, create the action, setting and cast of their dreams."[19] Combining his last image of the priest, his views of the priesthood and his puzzlement over Cotter's words, the boy creates an image of the priest who is at once familiar and yet, following Cotter's esoteric allusions unfamiliar, in a place with strange customs. The boy's mixed feelings toward the priesthood also provide, at least in part, an explanation as to the dislocation of his immediate sense of loss, which critics who produce less innocent readings of the text may interpret as being suggestive of former sexual abuse.

Rather than being in a "mourning mood" the boy reports "I felt even annoyed at discovering in myself a sensation of freedom as if I had been freed from something by his death" (*D*, 3). That "something" could be interpreted as a strong sense of obligation to consider the wishes of his friend and mentor when choosing his future vocational path. His reported annoyance and "wonder" at his feeling that way tends to negate any less innocent readings of the boy's relationship with the priest (*D*, 3). His wondrous state indicates that not only was such a feeling unexpected but also that he did not welcome it; the implication being that he felt this to be disrespectful toward the priest who "had taught [him] a great deal" (*D*, 3). Bernard Benstock explains the boy's lack of distress at the death of Father Flynn by arguing that his feigned indifference shown in front of Cotter and his family had "evolved into a sustained absence of emotional response" by the time he reads the card on the door of the shop.[20] However, it is possible to provide an alternative interpretation when taking into account the boy's understanding that there was "no hope" for the priest (*D*, 1). Whilst acknowledging that his sense of vocational release has played a part in his reaction, the boy can also be viewed as having experienced anticipatory grief. This is in fact something which Benstock himself touches upon when he makes the point that "'The Sisters' is less a story about the boy's *shock* at unexpected death than it is a story of the stages of reactions to expected death."[21]

Bowlby states that, when discussing the emotional reaction of parents to the news that their child is fatally ill, "the mourning process starts at the moment that the diagnosis is conveyed to them" (*AL*3: 115–16). What he is describing here is anticipatory grief (also referred to as anticipatory mourning), which is the anticipation of a future loss and can contain many of the elements of normal grief (post-death grief). There is a lot of debate over this concept and whether or not it aids normal grief.[22] However, Paul Rosenblatt, who has studied nineteenth-century diaries using Attachment Theory and Family Systems Theory, amongst others, found that "the data suggest that when survivor and decedent were not co-resident and, hence, the survivor had no involvement in care of the dying, the longer the period of anticipation of loss the less the grief, at least in the first year of bereavement."[23] He states that data suggested "that one can, during the anticipation period, disconnect from memories, ideas, and behaviour patterns if one is not living with the dying person."[24]

When "The Sisters" was originally printed in the *Irish Homstead*, the opening sentences state that the boy had gone and looked at the "lighted square of the window" of the priest's house for "three nights in succession."[25] However, when published in 1914, Joyce had obviously decided to give the boy's visits a different temporal frame. Changing the narrative to "night after night" alters how one reads the boy's behaviour (*D*, 1). With the implication that the boy had been expecting Father Flynn's death for some time, he can be viewed as having had time to start the cognitive rearrangement of his relationship with the priest, and hence the grief process, before the death actually occurred. This does not mean that he would not have been shocked to hear of his death, since "even when death is expected, its arrival comes as a shock, lasting from a few minutes to a few days."[26] In this short story the boy is portrayed as being able to overcome his shock quickly enough to feign disinterest in front of Cotter, rather than being overcome by emotion. He is also shown to be able to take note of the conversations going on about him rather than being stunned and distracted. This suggests that he may have already overcome the initial phase of grief, of "numbing," "distress and/or anger" that Bowlby describes (*AL3*: 85).

Supporting this reading are the boy's continual visits to check the window in Father Flynn's house. Bowlby describes the second phase of grief as "yearning and searching" (*AL3*: 85).[27] This involves an urge to "move towards possible locations of the lost object" and it appears that the boy is unable to keep away from the location of their meetings.[28] Hence through the actions of the boy, Joyce has portrayed certain behaviours indicative of normal grief before the actual death of the priest. At the beginning of the story the boy relates how Father Flynn had often told him "I am not long for this world" and he had "thought his words idle" (*D*, 1). This could be read as a form of denial. However, after hearing "there was no hope for him this time," he realised the priests words "were true" and much like the parents described by Bowlby, the boy can be viewed as having started the grief process (*D*, 1). Disbelief (denial) can also occur at this second phase of grieving (*AL3*: 87) and as already noted, the boy needed to visit the shop to be "persuaded" that

Father Flynn was dead, yet once persuaded he was "disturbed" to find himself "at check" (*D*, 3). In other words, he found himself not knowing what to do. As he then goes on to describe what normally happened at his visits, Joyce implies that he was almost expecting him not to be dead and to have "gone into the little dark room behind the shop" (*D*, 3).

Having read the card on the door the boy discloses that he "had not the courage to knock," although Joyce does not have him reveal the reason for his inhibition (*D*, 3). However, the use of the word "courage" indicates that, if he did knock, he would have to face something frightening. This in turn takes the reader to the beginning of the boy's narrative and his admission that the word "paralysis" had "filled [him] with fear" (*D,* 1). Total paralysis, with loss of muscle function and sensation, means one is alive and yet inert. It is a state of being and yet not-being: an existence. If one then considers how death is portrayed in the Christian world, which espouses belief in an afterlife, it can be said that the dead are viewed as in a state of not-being and yet still being: a continued existence. With his view of paralysis as "maleficent" plus its association with death being such that it could almost be viewed as a metaphor, one can interpret the boy's need for courage as a prerequisite to enable him to witness the effects of death (*D,* 1).

Fear stimulates the attachment system and it is only in the reassuring presence of one of his main attachment figures—his aunt—that the boy is shown to feel able to enter the house of mourning. Here, apprehension again overrides his inquisitiveness, as represented by his hesitation at the door of "the dead-room" (*D,* 4). This is an interesting choice of phraseology in itself, implying that he expected the whole room to have taken on the characteristics of death. Overcoming his anxiety enough to enter the room, he is portrayed as entering "on tiptoe" (*D,* 4). In relating this action, Joyce underscores the religious notion of the dead as resting or sleeping, as reinforced in the Catholic Requiem Mass with its repeated supplication to "give" or "grant eternal rest to him (her)."[29]

Once inside the "dead-room" the boy notes in detail the "mutterings" of Nannie Flynn, her clothing, her shoes, the light in the room, the odour of the flowers (*D,* 4–5). Garry Leonard interprets what he defines as the boys "obsessive concern for fully describing every detail of what he sees" as a "defence against the possibility that his reality might be fiction."[30] In other words Leonard is arguing that, as the signifier (words) represent the subject (in this case the boy), he is trying to avoid the Lacanian Real (what cannot be expressed) and hence his lack-in-being by carefully describing what he knows. He suggests this has been triggered by the death of the priest. However, reading the boy as having experienced anticipatory grief brings this interpretation into question. If visiting the priest had helped him to maintain a sense of self, then his inability to see him and his starting of the grief process would surely have caused the boy to question his precarious sense of self before this point in time. It seems that what Joyce is relaying with the rendering of the boy's heightened sensory awareness is a state of anxiety due to being in close proximity to the cadaver of Father Flynn. Although the boy has the reassuring presence of his aunt, when entering a "dead-room" in a state of fearful unease, it is unsurprising that he is portrayed as taking in every detail, analysing it, considering whether anything therein is strange or inexplicable. He would therefore note even the trivial, including Nanny Flynn's attire and the way her heels are "trodden down on one side" (*D*, 4).[31]

Joyce further maintains a sense of anxiety by virtue of the boy disclosing his "fancy" that the priest was smiling, as he kneels in prayer by the coffin; raising the possibility that the boy's dream was an actual spiritual visitation (*D*, 4). Since Father Flynn's facial expression is not revealed until after the prayers have been said, the reader is placed in the same position of uncertainty, not knowing if this is the result of an overactive imagination influenced by his anxiety, or an intuitive presentiment of some significance. Having generated a sense of anxious anticipation, Joyce ensures that this is negated just as quickly by the defining statement "But no" (*D*, 4). He therefore creates a sense of disappointment, both for the boy with his gothic imagination and also for the expectant reader, when it becomes evident that no physical manifestation or mystery had been revealed when the priest's face had seemingly appeared. It really was just a dream. However, as is often the case with Joyce, he also creates a certain sense of irony as the boy notices the cadaver's "truculent" expression whilst its hands are "*loosely* retaining a chalice" (*D*, 4–5, my emphasis).

"In the little room downstairs," as the boy's aunt converses with the sisters, Joyce shows that Cotter's words have infiltrated her psyche. Her response to the explanation provided by Eliza of the onset of the priest's breakdown: "And was that it? [. . .] I heard something" seems to finally dismiss any veiled insinuations (*D*, 7). In her own anticlimactic epiphanic moment, she realises that his dropping of the chalice and subsequent illness was really all there was to tell.[32] Yes, she had "heard something" but there had been no substance, hence the ellipsis, as she is unable to state precisely what Cotter had been insinuating. Joyce chooses to give no description of the boy's emotional response to Eliza's somewhat pathetic story of Father Flynn's life, signifying that he has remained composed and unruffled by her words. Whilst Eliza's narrative gives a greater understanding as to the onset of Father Flynn's initial illness, unlike that of Cotter, her report is not intended to be gossipy and potentially defamatory. The communal sense in the room therefore remains one of loss rather than one of speculation or unease, despite the aunt's momentary interjection.

The custom of viewing of the dead not only enabled neighbours to broach the subject of loss with the bereaved, but additionally "remembering the dead in a communal context also confirmed and legitimised grief."[33] Yet the boy's presence during his visit is marked by his silence, possibly due to his status as a minor (discussed further in Chapter 6) but also as a reflection of his own emotional needs. He relates how, in the room where he used to sit with Father Flynn, he sat in his usual chair as opposed to with his aunt. No longer fearful he does not need to stay close to his attachment figure. However, that Joyce has him mention his physical position within the room implies this was important to him and he can also be read as locating himself with the sisters as a symbolic gesture of his emotional alliance. It is as though he wants to accept the words of condolence from his aunt with them and therefore to listen rather than to speak. Reading the boy's silence and physical positioning in this light, it is possible to see that what is being highlighted here, despite the boy's previous sense of release, is that he too will "miss" the priest (*D*, 6). Hence, in his silent and understated manner, he is asking for some acknowledgment of his own pain of losing a friend, thereby enabling him to legitimise his own feelings of loss.

By presenting the boy as being secure in his domestic life and having had time to become accustomed to the fact that Father Flynn's life was ebbing away, Joyce has portrayed a child who was able to cope relatively well with the loss of his friend and mentor. In other words, reading with knowledge of Attachment Theory, one can discern that his work depicts what attachment theorists have referred to as the securely attached individual's ability to cope better with adverse events and also the role played by anticipatory grief in dealing with his loss.

NOTES

1. Mario Mikulincer and Phillip R. Shaver in "An Attachment Perspective on Bereavement" write that "secure individuals' positive models of others allow them to continue to think positively about the deceased, and their positive models of self allow them to cope with the loss." In *Handbook of Bereavement and Research Practice: Advances in Theory and Intervention*, eds. Margaret S. Stroebe et al. (Washington DC: American Psychological Association, 2008), 99.

2. A Rosicrucian is a "member of a worldwide brotherhood claiming to possess esoteric wisdom handed down from ancient times." J. Gordon Melton, "Rosicrusian Religion," in *Encyclopaedia Britannica Online*, www.Brtannica.com/topic/Rosicrusians

3. Parkes and Prigerson, *Bereavement*, 174.

4. David Pierce, *Reading Joyce* (Harlow: Pearson Longman, 2008), 69.

5. Margot Norris, *Suspicious Readings of Joyce's Dubliners* (Pennsylvania: University of Pennsylvania Press, 2003), 18–29.

6. Paula Leverage et al., "Introduction," in *Theory of Mind and Literature*, eds. Paula Leverage et al. (Williams, IN: Purdue University Press, 2011), 1–11.

7. Norris, *Suspicious Readings*, 16.

8. Garry M. Leonard, *Reading Dubliners Again: A Lacanian Perspective* (Syracuse: Syracuse University Press, 1993), 24–25.

9. See Forence L. Walzl, "Joyce's 'The Sisters': A Development," *James Joyce Quarterly* 50 (2013): 80.

10. Norris, *Suspicious Readings*, 10–11.

11. Parkes and Prigerson, *Bereavement*, 70–73.

12. Parkes and Prigerson, *Bereavement*, 73, are referring to J. A. Hadfiled, *Dreams and Nightmares* (Harmondsworth: Penguin, 1954).

13. Some critics may query this. For example, Richard Wall, *An Anglo-Irish Dialect Glossary for Joyce's Works* (Gerrards Cross: Smythe, 1986), 29 explains that "great wish" meant "great esteem" or "respect" and "does not connote desire." However, Bernard Benstock *Narrative Con/Texts in Dubliners* (Hampshire: Macmillan, 1994), 59 comments that for Joyce to "practice such rigid economy of style requires that [. . .] words serve multiple purposes." Therefore, with Joyce's knowledge of language, its different connotations and also double meanings, which particularly comes to the fore in *Finnegans Wake*, I would argue that it is possible to interpret this phrase as meaning at once both "esteem" and "desire."

14. Edward Brandabur, *A Scrupulous Meanness: A Study of Joyce's Early Work* (Urbana: University of Illinois Press, 1971), 38.

15. Brandabur, *A Scrupulous Meanness*, 38–43.

16. Brandabur, *A Scrupulous Meanness*, 44.

17. Edward Boyd Barrett, *The Jesuit Enigma* (London: Cape, 1928), 129.

18. Thomas E. Connolly, *James Joyce's Books, Portraits, Manuscripts, Notebooks, Typescripts, Page Proofs Together with Critical Essays About Some of His Works*, 5th ed. (New York: Mellen, 1997), 171–72.

19. Parkes and Higgerson, *Bereavement*, 73.

20. Benstock, *Narrative Con/Texts in Dubliners*, 33. Benstock does not refer to any specific theory of grief here.

21. Benstock, *Narrative Con/Texts in Dubliners*, 143.

22. See for example Robert Fulton, "Anticipatory Mourning: A Critique of the Concept," *Morality*, 8 (2003): 342–51.

23. Paul, C. Rosenblatt, *Bitter, Bitter Tears: Nineteenth Century Diarists and Twentieth Century Grief Theories* (Minneapolis: University of Minnesota Press, 1983), 51. Rosenblatt comments that he is "unable to detect [. . .] any difference that would invalidate the use of nineteenth-century diaries to understand grief in the twentieth century," 9.

24. Rosenblatt, *Bitter, Bitter Tears*, 50.

25. Colin MacCabe, *James Joyce and the Revolution of the Word* (London: MacMillan, 1979; repr. 1981), 33.

26. David Charles-Edwards, *Counselling Issues for Managers No. 1: Death and Bereavement and Work* (London: CEPEC, 1992), 33.

27. Bowlby acknowledges the work of Shand and his "suggestion that searching for the lost person is an integral part of mourning," *AL3*: 87.

28. Parkes and Higgerson, *Bereavement*, 55–56.

29. The Society of St. Pius X, accessed 1 November, 2013, http://www.sspx.co.uk/mass/requiem/index.htm

30. Leonard, *Reading Dubliners Again*, 25.

31. Leonard makes an alternative argument regarding the boot heel: "Increasingly he [the boy] is aware of some lack at the center of his own being that he would like to fill with the truth about himself. As a result of this impulse (which can be viewed as Desire in Lacan's sense of the term), he is drawn to those objects whose presence is undercut by an absence,' including Nannie's boot heel." *Reading Dubliners Again*, 26.

32. Charles Rossman, "The Reader's Role in '*A Portrait of the Artist as a Young Man*,'" in *James Joyce: Critical Assessments of Major Writers*, ed. Colin Milton, 4 Vols (Abingdon: Routledge, 2012), 264. Referring to *Dubliners, Portrait* and *Ulysses* Rossman explains that: "Joyce has arranged the facts in these books so that the reader is led toward complex, epiphanic, narrative moments which reveal a situation, a circumstance, or a character but leave their meaning . . . still unuttered."

33. Julie Marie Strange, *Grief and Poverty in Britain, 1870–1914* (Cambridge: Cambridge University Press, 2005), 81.

Chapter Six

Master Dignam

Sudden Bereavement and Anxious/ Ambivalent Attachment

In *Ulysses* Joyce takes a different approach in his portrayal of childhood bereavement in comparison to that taken in "The Sisters," in terms of narrative technique, circumstance, and brevity. Whilst in the short story the narrative related to an adult looking back on his childhood experience of a death that he did not actually witness, in *Ulysses* Joyce portrays the interior monologue of Master Dignam, a child who has recently witnessed the sudden death of his father and who is in the very early stages of coming to terms with his loss.

Attachment theorists have noted how the way in which a loved one dies, the support available to the bereaved, and the individual attachment traits of the bereaved (which in turn are linked to the parenting received) all have an effect on the grief process.[1] Joyce's narrative regarding Master Dignam enables consideration for each of these factors and their ensuing emotional impact, despite his relative absence within the text of *Ulysses*, which is set on the day of his father's funeral. In the "Hades" episode he is referred to simply as "the boy" who is given a wreath to carry (*U*, 6.634) and in the "Wandering Rocks" episode Joyce affords less than 60 lines of text to the "dawdling" boy who cuts a lonely figure as he traverses the Dublin streets with the "pork steaks he had been sent for" (*U*, 10.1122–23). Perhaps, at least in part, due to his relative absence critics appear to afford him little discussion or do not interpret him as unduly suffering from his loss. For example, Dettmar argues that Master Dignam "seems to have been almost completely unaffected by the death of his father. A few short hours after the funeral, he is both physically and mentally miles away from death, absorbed by the boxing advertisement."[2] However, with reference to the work of Bowlby and other attachment theorists, I will discuss how, within a short number of lines he is afforded, the trauma he has experienced as a result of the sudden death of his father is in fact made explicit.

Sudden deaths in themselves are far more traumatic to cope with than those that have been anticipated, giving loved ones no time to prepare for an event that will effectively alter their sense of identity.[3] Nigel Field has postulated that experiencing the death of a parent during childhood or directly witnessing a death (both of which Joyce portrays as happening to Master Dignam at once) can be "inherently frightening in alerting the bereaved to the fact that they are helpless to protect the self or loved ones from danger."[4] It is entirely apposite, therefore, that when Joyce presents the internal monologue of Master Dignam, he relates the shock and incomprehension which accompanies the recognition of his father's mortality as he tries to process the reality of death: "Never see him again. Death that is. Pa is dead. My father is dead" (*U,* 10.1169–70). The repetition can be construed as Master Dignam trying to assimilate all that has happened and convince himself that his father is indeed dead. However, his language is also shown to change from a more personal phrase, using the word "pa," to a more public utterance of "my father." With the jumbled thoughts that accompany a loss, particularly an unexpected and sudden death, there is also the knowledge that one will have to somehow communicate this to others and converse with them. Therefore, Master Dignam can also be viewed as trying to find the right phrase in preparation for talking to his school friends. The simplicity of the phrase "my father is dead" seems somewhat inadequate when considering the description of all he has witnessed. Yet the lack of additional exposition on the part of the boy can be read as paving the way for his friends to enquire further, thereby encouraging them to engage with him and ultimately to understand his experienced anxiety and sense of loss.

As has already been noted, Bowlby terms the first stage of grief "numbing," where the bereaved person feels "stunned" and unable to take in all that has happened, which "usually lasts for a few hours to a week" (*AL3*: 85). For a young mind such as Master Dignam's to apprehend that an intimidating father, who was standing there "boosed" and "bawling" one moment, could instantaneously transform into a state of helplessness would certainly be difficult to negotiate psychologically (*U,* 10.1167–68). Hence, just as Joyce had the young Stephen Dedalus of *Portrait* question what it means to kiss and why, when confused by Wells, so he has Master Dignam question "How was that?" as he tries to comprehend his father's death; his thoughts jumping from the removal of the coffin to the moments preceding his father's death (*U,* 10.1167). How was that, that someone can be looking "butty" one moment and be dying the next (*U,* 10.1169)? How was it possible to be surrounded by a complete family and within an instant to find oneself fatherless and the senior male of the household? How could this happen? These are the type of questions that one can imagine emanating from his brief enquiry, the answers to which would be beyond the comprehension of a young boy. He can be viewed as being incapable of rationalising all that he has seen as his young age would preclude an understanding as to the physiological causes of heart failure or how excessive drinking could have contributed to this. All he would know is that his family life has changed irreversibly without any warning. Hélène Cixous describes *Ulysses* as "a work balanced on the void, on chaos and the improbable, drawing its existence from the very incoherence of reality."[5] At this point in the novel Master Dignam seems to encapsulate that precarious equilibrium, balancing on the edge of a dense void of total inscrutability.

Joyce's portrayal has caused Clive Hart to comment that with Master Dignam "we are not really admitted into the inner reaches of a personality, as we are when Stephen and Bloom contemplate the effects of death on their lives. [. . .] Master Dignam is all periphery, responding to a succession of stimuli."[6] Hart's discerning comment emphasises Joyce's stance to present life as it really is; to present him any other way would have negated such artistic ambition.[7] Being young, Master Dignam's cognitive abilities would be less well developed and therefore inferior to those of both Stephen and Bloom. Thus, his comprehension and facility to articulate would also be less advanced. Moreover, he is represented as at a very different stage of the grief process to them. At this early stage, life can often take on a sense of "unreality" and normal functioning can be impaired, so one can be seen as merely existing and devoid of one's normal personality.[8]

Joyce, no doubt calling on his own experience of loss within his immediate family, would have been painfully aware of this and therefore chooses to present a mind briefly contemplating received visual inputs, but which cannot help continually returning to the image of his father's death and reliving that moment. He relates the replaying in Master Dignam's mind of how his father's "tongue and his teeth" were moving in an attempt to speak in his final moments; how the termination of his earthly life extinguished the colour of that life from the face of his "poor pa"; and how, in his permanent state of inertia, a fly could walk unheeded over his face (*U,* 10.1161–72). When reading one can, as Strong states, move from "the truth presented to truth beyond it" and therefore understand that at such an early stage in the grief process, it would be difficult for his thoughts to move beyond this traumatic vision to any form of introspection, however naïve.[9]

The emotional distress experienced by young Master Dignam is represented as having been further exacerbated by the witnessing of the undignified removal of the cadaver from the house. The bumping down the stairs of the coffin is seemingly uncaring and disrespectful: "Pa was inside" (*U,* 10.1165). Frank Budgen says of *Ulysses*: "There are moods of pity and grief in it, but the prevailing mood is humour."[10] Certainly the description of "ma crying in the parlour" whilst the men carrying the coffin appear to be stuck at a corner and his uncle is shouting instructions, appears to be one of comedic chaos (see *U,* 10.1165). However, the fact that some aspects of dealing with death and its consequences can result in such situations is probably not something a child would envision and as such would be difficult to negotiate psychologically. It therefore seems pertinent that Joyce does not allow Master Dignam's thoughts to dwell on the pandemonium for long but instead regains a sense of dignity by turning to the physical attributes of the coffin, of which he seems proud; taking time to think how "large" and "high and heavylooking" it was (*U,* 10.1166–67).

As Master Dignam walks alone in the street, Joyce is able to raise the question of the emotional support available to him by virtue of his thoughts regarding the passing schoolboys and his intention to delay his return to school. His question "Do they notice I'm in mourning?" can be explored in two different ways (*U,* 10.1158–59). Firstly, one could assume that unlike Bloom, whose dark clothing has been commented on throughout the day, he does not expect to be noticed and therefore his state of grief will remain invisible to them. At a time in Western social history where children were supposed to be "seen and not heard" and their psychological needs following bereavement had not been fully recognised, it is plausible to imagine that the mourners at his father's wake would have naturally conversed with his mother, but paid little attention to him as a minor, thereby predicating his thoughts of imperceptibility.

Bowlby has espoused that, just as for bereaved adults, it is the important for a child to have someone "on whom they can lean and who is willing to give [them] comfort and aid," arguing that "whereas most adults have learned that they can survive without the more or less continuous presence of an attachment figure, children have no such experience" (*AL3*: 290). Joyce seemed all too aware that the needs of bereaved children were going unrecognised, as he had originally highlighted the issue more directly in *Stephen Hero*, relating the funeral of Stephen's sister. The narrator comments how Stephen receives sympathies which are all focused on his mother: "Nearly all the men said "And how is the poor mother bearing it?" and nearly all the women said "It's a great trial for your poor mother" (*SH,* 173). Whilst noting the lack of empathy toward his own grief, Stephen is also depicted as finding these platitudes "unconvincing" (*SH,* 173). Similarly, Master Dignam's simple, but nevertheless telling comment, regarding the mourners "jawing" and "sighing," portrays an atmosphere of artificiality rather than sincerity (*U,* 10.1128–29).

Ostensibly, what Joyce is conveying in both *Stephen Hero* and *Ulysses*, along with the emotional needs of minors, are the limitations of language. It is something that he had previously referred to in his short story, "The Dead," where Gabriel Conroy envisions the death of his aunt and the prospect of only finding "lame and useless words" to console her sister (*D,* 160). Yet where words may fall short and appear insincere, actions may succeed and in *Ulysses* the efforts of Cunningham and Bloom are portrayed as arising out of true concern for the Dignam family. In addition to making "a whip for the youngsters," they also take steps to ensure that Mrs. Dignam receives her husband's insurance rather than the moneylender, Bridgeman (*U,* 6.564). Even though this latter action could be viewed as morally and legally suspect, since they are effectively attempting to defraud Bridgeman "on a technicality," they are represented as genuinely trying to find ways to help their late friend's widow (see *U,* 12.763–65).[11] In contrast to the mother, who is receiving the support of the community, Master Dignam is portrayed as somewhat alone and adrift with his emotions. His physical battle with his shirt collar can be seen as symbolically mirroring his emotional battle with the memories of his father's last moments, which will not be kept down.

Secondly, although not mutually exclusive from the above reading, Master Dignam's comment regarding whether he will be noticed could also be interpreted as signalling his own realisation that he needs support and therefore that he wants to be noticed. In addition to his choice of phraseology for talking to his friends in order to promote engagement with him, his proposal to "stay away [from school] till Monday" can be seen as equating to what attachment theorists describe as an ambivalent/anxious strategy in order to ensure a response, often employed by children whose parents/caregivers are unable to respond to them in a consistent manner (*U,* 10.1157–58).[12] His expressed conscious behavioural strategy, which gives time for his peers to read his father's obituary in the newspapers, can certainly be read as being calculated to increase the dramatic effect when he does return to school and hence promote support from his classmates.

In my discussion of "The Sisters" I noted how one could see a link between the child's grief reaction and the available support system in terms of his home life. This is also possible with Joyce's portrayal of Master Dignam, albeit requiring reference to other episodes within *Ulysses* other than "Wandering Rocks." Before going on to discuss this point, I would like to further elaborate on how attachment style and grief are linked. When studying the anxiety exhibited by children who were unwillingly separated from their mothers, Bowlby found that they showed a typical sequence of behaviour of "protest," "despair" and eventually "detachment" (*AL2*: 46). He explained that when he began to analyse these observations it became apparent to him that:

> Each of the three main phases of the response of a young child to separation is related to one or another of the central issues of psychoanalytic theory. Thus

the phase of *protest* is found to raise the problem of separation anxiety; *despair* that of grief and mourning; *detachment* that of defence. [. . .] [T]he three types of response—separation anxiety, grief and mourning, and defence—are phases of a single process and that only when they are treated as such is their true significance grasped. (*AL2*: 47)

Following on from Bowlby's observations and subsequent postulation, John Archer has argued that, with the reaction to separation being "a distinctive part of the attachment style" and grief being "an extension of this separation reaction," it should be possible "to predict different types of grief reactions from different attachment styles, which in turn reflect different reactions to parenting."[13]

Making such connections within the text and also using an integrated approach such as that espoused by Culpeper (see Chapter 3) it is possible for the reader to comprehend Master Dignam's exhibited ambivalent/anxious strategies. Joyce portrays Master Dignam's home life and hence parental support system predominantly through Bloom's stream of consciousness and the conversation of the mourners on the way to Dignam's funeral in the "Hades" episode. Here, comments made by Simon Dedalus and Martin Cunningham primarily focus on his decency and describe his sudden death being caused by a "breakdown" of the "heart" (*U*, 6.303–5) even though they are later shown to acknowledge Dignam had lost a job through drink (see *U*, 6.570–73). Freud noted the tendency of individuals to not criticise the dead and to ignore possible transgressions and this is precisely what Joyce depicts.[14] However, it is Bloom's thoughts, complete with a comic sense of irony, that convey the truth as to the major contributory factor to Paddy Dignam's demise: "Blazing face: redhot. Too much John Barleycorn. Cure for a red nose. Drink like the devil till it turns adelite. A lot of money he spent colouring it" (*U*, 6.307–9).

What becomes immediately evident, especially through the acknowledgment of his job loss, is that Paddy Dignam is to be viewed as having forsaken his due responsibility toward his family in favour of his alcohol consumption. Moreover, it would not have been an unusual occurrence for Master Dignam to see his father "boosed" (*U*, 10.1167). Joyce therefore appears to be creating a domestic scenario in which Paddy Dignam's response to the needs of his children would have been dependent on his state of inebriation (or which point of the recovery process he was at) at any particular time and therefore would have been inconsistent.

Public health reports at the beginning of the twentieth century showed that alcohol was responsible for the most prevalent diseases in Dublin and that its consumption often took preference over food. The reports suggested that this was due "in large measure from the urge to escape appalling living conditions for the relative warmth, comfort and spaciousness of the pub."[15] With Master

Dignam being one of five children, his father seems to have preferred the relative peace and sanctuary of the public house; spending what little money he had on alcohol. Hence, the financial situation of the family is depicted as, at the very least, precarious.

Although the mention of the loan is clearly an indicator of their financial position, Joyce's decision to use the word "paltry" to denote Bloom's perception of the funeral is most profound (*U,* 6.498). A remaining legacy of the Victorian era was that the amount of money spent on a funeral was "equated with respect and affection for the deceased."[16] Therefore the bereaved, whatever their financial circumstances, did whatever they could to provide a decent burial for their loved ones. At the funeral, although mutes have been hired to carry in the coffin, there are only three carriages. The carriage in which Bloom and his companions have travelled, with its "crumbs" and "mildewed leather," appears not to have been cleaned after its use by lovers, or so the mourners deduce ("After all [. . .] it's the most natural thing in the world" [*U,* 6.97–109]). For the refreshments following the funeral it is Master Dignam's uncle who is shown to provide the "superior tawny sherry" for the ladies to sup (*U,* 10.1127). The austerity of Mrs Dignam's public display of her grief can therefore be read as a clear indication of her limited financial resources.

Trying to raise her family with restricted financial means and with little support from a husband who was often drunk, Mrs. Dignam can be read as being under considerable strain and stress in her daily life. Additionally, with five children to care for, the amount of time to devote to each of them would be limited. Master Dignam's comment that he "could easy do a bunk on ma" represents his perception that his actions are not always noticed (*U,* 10.1137). Again, as in the case of his father, although for differing reasons, Joyce provides a portrait of a mother who would have been unable to respond consistently to her children's needs.

Bowlby has noted that those who make anxious/ambivalent attachments "are far more likely than those who grow up secure to have had parents who, for reasons stemming from their own childhoods and/or from difficulties in their marriage, found their children's desire for love and care a burden and responded to them irritably—by ignoring, scolding, or moralizing" (*AL3:* 218). From the glimpses that Joyce gives the reader of Master Dignam's home life, Bowlby's findings appear to have been illustrated within the text of *Ulysses.* Ambivalent/anxious attachment behaviour is "an adaptive response to parental inability to provide quality care giving" and results in behaviour that "reflects a strategy of fighting for more attention."[17] The portrayal of Master Dignam is one that indicates he is probably used to generally adopting such strategies since, although quite disorientated by his bereavement, his calculation to stay away from school to promote the maximum effect came to mind quite easily.

Reading Master Dignam as being an insecurely attached child who is finding it hard to come to terms with what has happened and is thus seeking attention and reassurance, one may expect him to be represented as finding solace in his religious belief. As Lee A. Kirkpatrick notes, psychologically God will often be thought of as a "father figure" and therefore someone to turn to for additional comfort and emotional support.[18] However, through his portrayal of a sudden death, Joyce actually highlights that there can sometimes be conflicting consequences of religious indoctrination. In relating Master Dignam's concerns over his father's spiritual state: "I hope he is in purgatory now because he went to confession to Father Conroy on Saturday night," Joyce shows that such beliefs can also be a source of angst (*U,* 10.1172–74).

Foregrounding Master Dignam's disquiet is the conversation that takes place in the carriage on the way to his father's funeral. A reference to Paddy Dignam's "sudden death" is followed by the comment "poor fellow" which can be viewed as reflecting not only sorrow for his passing, but an acknowledgment that he had been denied a chance to receive the last rites (*U,* 6.311). Conversely, having no religious conviction, Bloom sees a sudden death as "the best death" from the point of view that there is no suffering, much to the wide-eyed astonishment of his Christian companions (*U,* 6.312). Joyce is not ridiculing Master Dignam, or indeed his father's friends, for their beliefs. Rather he is in effect making a comparison between what he would refer to as myth (what the Christian faith professes to be true) and fact (that it is impossible to confirm this "truth") and hence emphasising, through the resulting tension, that all Master Dignam really has is something which is in the void between the two: his hopes.

Joyce has a created a definite sense of a character who is struggling emotionally: struggling to come to terms with all that he has witnessed and what death actually means; struggling to feel confident of his father's spiritual rest; most importantly, struggling in his isolation and the absence of anyone to share these anxieties with. In this episode, where Joyce focuses on the city as a whole and therefore the minor characters as well as the main protagonists, he portrays Master Dignam as consumed by his father's death, occasionally responding to various external stimuli. Like Stephen and Bloom, he is portrayed as experiencing an apparent lack of anyone with whom he can openly express his true inner feelings of loss. As if to symbolise this lack of support, Joyce turns his narrative attention away from Master Dignam to the cavalcade. Having been deserted not only by his father but also by the narrator, a certain moment of poignancy is created, as the grieving child is left alone and on the street to raise "his new black cap" as the cavalcade passes and his collar again symbolically springs up (*U,* 10.1267–68). By his switch of narrative focus, Joyce promotes a sense of concern for Master Dignam, in addition to the sympathy already elicited through his recollections.

Such unease regarding Master Dignam is further magnified by the earlier disclosure in the "Hades" episode that Martin Cunningham is attempting to try to secure a place for him in what Mr. Kernan refers to as "Artane" (*U*, 6.537). Artane is actually a small village outside Dublin where the O'Brien Institute for Destitute Children was situated at the time.[19] From a practical viewpoint, should Master Dignam board there one could see that this would relieve his mother of one mouth to feed. However, considering the emotional aspects of such an action, one could envisage the traumatic effect of a possible separation from his main attachment figure and his siblings at this time. For a child who is depicted as showing signs of what Bowlby refers to as anxious or ambivalent attachment, this would be perceived as total abandonment. Additionally, it is possible to imagine that his anxiety could be increased due to the fact his physical distance from his mother would also inhibit him from keeping his father's last wish "to be a good son to ma" (*U*, 10.1170–71). To a young mind, being good would mean helping with chores and with his younger siblings—an impossibility if physically removed from the household. Having portrayed the emotional turmoil following a sudden death, leaving Master Dignam's future and consequent psychological well-being open and thus uncertain, can create a sense of anxiety in the reader, so mirroring the emotion Master Dignam himself is portrayed as feeling.

Joyce has created two distinct experiences of childhood bereavement in the narratives discussed thus far which, reading with knowledge of Attachment Theory, allows the emotional impact of the loss to be viewed as reflecting the stage of the grief process the bereaved are at, as well as their support base and hence attachment traits. Although "The Sisters" depicts the recollection of the protagonist's experience reproduced in later life, his factual reporting and lack of hyperbole implies that he is able to reflect on his loss without emotional difficulty. I have argued that he can be read as a securely attached individual and attachment theorists have noted that "secure individuals' positive models of others allow them to continue to think positively about the deceased, and their positive models of self allow them to cope with the loss."[20]

The depiction of how the boy of "The Sisters" dealt with his loss contrasts considerably with the portrayal of Master Dignam. Relating to the fact that Master Dignam's loss has been both unexpected and very recent, his thoughts are transient, responding to stimuli and instantly returning to his father's death. However, the information that one is able to ascertain regarding Master Dignam's home life creates a picture of tension and little emotional support; an environment where it may be necessary to devise strategies in order to get some recognition of his trauma. It is interesting that Joyce chooses to focus on the internal monologue of Master Dignam rather than his mother. This suggests that, with the support she is represented as receiving support from the community, there is no undue cause for concern, whereas Master Dignam, alone yet seemingly crying out for attention, is worthy of consideration. He can therefore be viewed as a representative of the many children who were seen, but whose emotional cries were not heard.

NOTES

1. For example, see Parkes and Priggerson, *Bereavement.*
2. Kevin J. H. Dettmar, *The Illicit Joyce of Postmodernism: Reading Against the Grain* (Madison: University of Wisconsin Press, 1996), 196.
3. Parkes, *Bereavement*, 129 and 225.
4. See Nigel P. Field, "Unresolved Grief and Continuing Bonds: An Attachment Perspective," *Death Studies*, 30 (2006): 742–43.
5. Cixous, *The Exile of James Joyce*, 727.
6. Clive Hart, "Wandering Rocks," in *James Joyce's Ulysses: Critical Essays*, eds. Clive Hart and David Hayman (Berkeley: University of California Press, 1977), 192.
7. See James Joyce, "Drama and Life," 45.
8. Rudi Dallos and Arlene Vetere, *Systemic Therapy and Attachment Narratives: Applications in a Range of Clinical Settings* (London: Routledge, 2009), 140–41.
9. Strong, *The Sacred River*, 99. See "Relation Between Theoretical Stance Taken and the Text" section in Chapter 4 for full quote.
10. Budgen, *James Joyce*, 72.
11. Hugh Kenner, *Ulysses* (London: Allen and Unwin, 1980), 103.
12. For example, see Kirkpatrick, *Attachment*, 192.
13. Archer, *The Nature of Grief*, 177.
14. See Alan Warren Friedman, *Fictional Death and the Modernist Enterprise* (Cambridge: Cambridge University Press, 1995), 122. Friedman is referring to Freud's *War and Death.*
15. Andrew Gibson, "Macropolitics and Micropolitics in 'Wandering Rocks,'" in *Joyce's "Wandering Rocks,"* ed. Andrew Gibson and Steven Morrison, European Joyce Studies (Amsterdam: Rodopin, 2002), 38. Gibson is referring to Sir Charles A. Cameron, *Report upon the State of the Health in the City of Dublin for the Year 1902* (Dublin: Cahill, 1903)
16. Strange, *Grief and Poverty in Britain*, 98.
17. Kirkpatrick, *Attachment,* 192. With reference to J. S. Chisholm, "The Evolutionary Ecology of Attachment Organisation," *Human Nature*, 7 (1996), 1–138.
18. Kirkpatrick, *Attachment*, 19.
19. Don Gifford with Robert J. Seidman, *Ulysses Annotated*, 116.
20. Mario Mikulincer and Phillip R. Shaver, "An Attachment Perspective on Bereavement," in *Handbook of Bereavement and Research Practice*, 99.

Chapter Seven

"Eveline"

Unresolved Grief and the Pull of the Dead

Joyce's initial exploration of the death of a parent and the psychological effect of their last wishes can be found within the pages of *Dubliners*. In the short story "Eveline" Joyce considers the effects the loss of a mother can have on the living, something he went on to explore further in his portrayal of Stephen Dedalus in *Ulysses*. In his portrayal of the eponymous character, Eveline Hill, he illustrates how unresolved grief in relation to a key attachment figure can inhibit the search for a new secure base and the formation of new attachment figures.

Bowlby describes "healthy mourning" as "the successful effort of an individual to accept both that a change has occurred in his external world and that he is required to make corresponding changes in his internal, representational world and to reorganise, and perhaps to reorient, his attachment behaviour accordingly" (*AL3*: 18). "Reorganise" is the key word here. Bowlby does not advocate detaching from the lost person, but rather rearranging the psychological representation of the self and the deceased. This allows "proximity seeking" to be aimed at the living, rather than the deceased, who can in turn "become major providers of protection, security, and comfort."[1] In her relationship with Frank, a sailor who wants to take her away to Buenos Aires, Eveline has found the possibility of "protection, security and comfort" and at the moment Joyce introduces her to the reader, time is "running out" if she is to fulfill her intention of eloping with him (*D*, 25). However, she is shown as unable to motivate herself to move and instead remains seated by the window, deliberating on her domestic life and whether she should leave.

The time that Joyce spends detailing Eveline's home life is significant in that it creates an image of a young lady who lacks a secure base and, as already noted in previous chapters, perceived insecurity affects how one deals with one's loss. Like Master Dignam, Joyce portrays Eveline as living in a home that upholds the Christian faith but has retained little spiritual peace and harmony, particularly since the death of her mother. As she sits by the window, she reflects on how she has been left to contend with a father who is often drunk. Although she is able to recollect one recent act of kindness by her father when she was ill, the only other example that is forthcoming goes back to when her mother was alive. His current overriding behaviour is portrayed as being emotionally abusive, with a recent threat of this escalating to physical abuse: "she sometimes felt herself in danger of her father's violence" (*D*, 24). With Eveline's remembered acts of her father's kindness being so few, dealing with his persistent emotional abuse can be read as a longstanding issue. It has been noted by Suzanne Keen that, "empathetic responses to fictional characters and situations occur more readily for negative emotions, whether or not a match in details of experience exists."[2] The introduction by Joyce of a possible element of physical menace therefore only serves to heighten the reader's engagement with Eveline and her plight.

Eveline reports that lately her father "had begun to threaten her and say what he would do to her only for her dead mother's sake," although precisely what action he has threatened is not disclosed (*D*, 24). This is a good example of what Andrew Gibson terms "the latent content that fails to find expression or is only half expressed."[3] Looking to Peter Costello's account of Joyce's early life, one could read the prospect of sexual violence as being couched within the narrative in Joyce's effort to portray "life as we see it before our eyes." Costello notes how John Joyce, who was frequently drunk, could be both abusive and violent and that the young girls of the Joyce household needed to be shielded from him. He also finds it plausible that "a man of his excessive sexual drive may have tried to comfort himself with his own children, as was so often the case in rural Ireland and the poorer quarters of the city," especially as "his younger daughters later recoiled from him, as he himself admitted."[4] With the known existence of a popular, although anonymous, Victorian pornographic novel, *Eveline*, which involves an incestuous relationship with the father, Joyce's choice of title for his short story only further supports the possibility of such a reading.[5] It is entirely plausible that Joyce wanted to raise the issue of the threat of incest to young women, albeit by tacit implication, whilst simultaneously helping the reader to engage with Eveline's goal to leave for the sake of her well-being.

With Joyce's use of free indirect speech, the question "Was that wise?" is at once rhetorical whilst simultaneously also inviting the reader to make a judgement on her proposed elopement (*D*, 23). As a character Eveline is shown to be thoughtful and fair-minded rather than impulsive and resentful, as she mentally probes the wisdom of her decision to leave. However, the underlying question regarding the sagacity of her decision appears to be whether she has reached her limit both emotionally, and with her recent onset of palpitations, physically. Put succinctly: can she suffer her father's behaviour any longer?

In a real-life scenario, the lack of responsive care from her father would gesture toward the development of an insecure attachment to him. Within the pages of the text, Eveline's self-reliance, a behavioural trait typical of avoidant individuals, along with her unresolved grief, which I will discuss in detail, supports such a reading of her character. Her lack of security (both physical and emotional) and the "hard work" it takes "to keep the house together" creates a sense of a bleak and unfulfilling future for Eveline should she remain in the family home (*D*, 24). With apparently little reason to question the wisdom of her planned elopement, the indecisiveness she presents could be read as being out of concern for "the two young children who had been left to her charge" (*D*, 24). However, the namelessness and lack of detail regarding them suggests they may not be her primary concern. As the narrative unfolds, the cause of her wavering appears to be due to the burden of her mother's last coherent wish, a plea to "keep the home together as long as she could," which still looms large despite the many difficulties her continued adherence to it presents (*D*, 25).

The "coloured print of the promises of the Blessed Margaret Mary Alacoque," which Eveline has seen every day, although only briefly mentioned by the narrator, is an important reference point here. It could be viewed as constant subliminal reinforcement of her mother's wishes (*D*, 23). As Donald Torchiana explains:

> Although Joyce does not name the promises, they and the print are still easy to come by in Dublin. These promises made to the Blessed order, radiate clockwise from a figure of Christ standing with His arms outstretched; beneath Him is space for the signatures of father, mother, children, and presiding priest, all to be signed under the Caption "Consecration of the Family to the Sacred Heart."[6]

The signatures of her family continually before her can be read as a persistent reminder of the family unit as it once was and the onus her mother placed on her to stop it from disintegrating.

When an attachment figure dies, working through the grief process as proposed by Bowlby and Parkes, eventually one will cognitively rearrange how one sees oneself in relation to that person. Yet "[r]eorganisation toward full acknowledgment of the permanence of the loss is a gradual and emotionally painful process" and is therefore something that does not occur quickly.[7] However, as one acknowledges physical contact is no longer possible, continuing attachment bonds with the deceased can continue in a symbolic form. Much like when adolescents become young adults, and the hierarchy of attachment figures is adjusted, proximity seeking can be aimed toward new partners. Eveline, at the age of nineteen, even without the death of her mother would be at the stage in her life when she would seek new attachments and relationships. The loss of her mother would have taken her toward that process of cognitive editing perhaps earlier than it would otherwise occurred.

It is not known how long Eveline's mother has been dead, but nevertheless her agreement to go away with Frank suggests that when she made that commitment she considered herself to be in control of her own life, capable seeking a new attachment figure and not controlled by her departed mother. But grief is not a linear process and, as Colin Parkes argues, people can "move back and forth" between the different stages of grief with, for example, the finding of an old photograph even years later, causing a new episode of pining.[8] In this story, the street organ music is shown to take Eveline back to her mother's final night and create a new phase of yearning. The formal arrangement of the narrative here can be said to mimic the nonlinear emotional experience of grief, moving as it does through intricate temporal and emotional spheres.

Infiltrating Eveline's senses as she leans against the dusty curtains, the music directs the trajectory of her thoughts toward "the last night of her mother's illness" (D, 25). As she listens to the familiar air, the past combines with the present and she again hears her mother's final words, "Derevaun Seraun! Derevaun Seraun!" (D, 25). William Tindall comments that Patrick Henchy interpreted these words as corrupt Gaelic for "the end of pleasure is pain."[9] As such they could be seen to foreshadow Stephen's more lucid conversation with his mother in *Ulysses,* in which she cries over the words "love's bitter mystery" (U, 1.253). Both Eveline's mother and Stephen's mother are portrayed as having sacrificed their lives for the love of a man who has turned to drink; a recurrent theme in Joyce's work and a reflection of his own family life.

Garry Leonard views the dilemma Eveline is facing as relating to which of her mother's utterances to adhere to: a choice between whether to heed her coherent request, or whether to heed her final words, which urge her to "flee from the house at her first opportunity."[10] Yet, in the light of her initial coherent request, one could question whether her mother was actually urging Eveline to leave. Could she instead be warning her against marriage in general? Although this is not implausible, the translation offered by Wim Tigges, provides an alternative perspective. Tigges relates how, when he quoted out of context the phrase "Derevaun Seraun!" to a friend who originated from Tralee, County Kerry, she immediately translated is "as "I have been there; you should go there!" taking it to be the Irish "do raibh ann, siar ann." This is pronounced in English roughly, "derivaun sheraun."[11] He notes that with the lack of personal pronoun, the sentence could read "one has gone there, go there."[12] Although the spectre of incest is present, I am not suggesting that with this interpretation of her words Eveline's mother is to be seen as directing her into her father's arms. Rather, contrary to the question posed above, it seems that she could in fact be directing Eveline to marry. In this scenario, Eveline's trembling as she recalls those words can be seen as representing her inner conflict since, to enter into marriage with Frank, she needs to abandon her mother's original wish as it would require her not only have to leave the family home but Ireland itself.

Whether one interprets the words as a warning to leave or a plea to marry the implication for Eveline will be the same. If the end of pleasure is pain, or if she is to go where her mother has gone, her elopement with Frank means that she is setting herself up to follow in her mother's footsteps, to repeat her mistakes, albeit in a different country. Perhaps this is why Joyce represents her view of her mother's insistence as "foolish" (*D*, 25). However, her decision to leave now becomes dubious. By introducing this element of doubt as to the consequences of eloping, Joyce ensures that the reader remains engaged with the choice with which Eveline is faced: to stay at home despite her father's behaviour, or to trust that Frank will indeed provide her with a new and fulfilling life in a strange land.

It is of note that, having written this story sometime between July and September 1904, it was published in *The Irish Homestead* in September 1904, only weeks before Joyce and Nora Barnacle left Ireland together on 8 October. It is possible Joyce's own awareness of the trust he was asking Nora to place in him was being explored within this story. Nora had already escaped the violence of her uncle's house in Galway and run away to Dublin.[13] Now Joyce was asking her to leave Ireland altogether and what little security she had, a scenario he recreates with Eveline and Frank. However, Nora "was her own woman" unlike the character of Eveline that Joyce presents.[14] With the loss of her mother Eveline has also lost part of her identity. Although a teenager, she has been forced to take on both a maternal role toward her charges and the general role of housekeeper and cook to the family unit as a whole whilst also maintaining her job as junior shop assistant. She is always answering to someone else and has no one on whom to rely. This portrayal of Eveline makes it clear that for some time she has been many things to many people, whilst at the same time no one. The names that she is called in the story, "Miss Hill," "Eveline," "Poppens," and "Evvy," are employed depending on the situation, "as if names could not warrant a fixed identity anymore but only different roles of the individual in society."[15]

Eveline can therefore be read as a young woman who has not only physically "elbowed her way through the crowds" but emotionally has had to continually elbow her way through life since her mother's death, trusting and depending on no one but herself (*D*, 24). She psychologically represents

Frank as the person who has the ability to provide the secure base she so desperately needs; the attachment figure on whom perhaps she could depend. With the deaths of her brother and her best friend, plus her remaining brother away, at present she is shown to be devoid of any constant support mechanism. Although she acknowledges that her home provided her with "shelter and food" and that "she had those whom she had known all her life about her," the reported additional threat of violence from her father means that there is certainly no safe and secure base available to her (*D*, 23). In Eveline's eyes Frank could provide all that is missing and as such her decision to elope is not unrealistic. Not only would he give her an identity as his wife but moreover she believes: "He would take her in his arms, fold her in his arms. He would save her" (*D*, 26). The language used here, very much in the mode of a romantic novel, provides a strong image of protection. Love and care are something that attachment theorists have shown those with avoidant traits actually crave, despite their self-sufficiency (see *MB*, 165).[16]

I have already referred to the fact that as a person matures and attachments to parent figures become less significant a person will seek in a sexual bond (which in a strict Catholic community in the early nineteenth century would generally also equate to a marital bond) and a similar kind of security that he or she previously sought from parents.[17] Although Joyce creates the impression that Frank will indeed provide Eveline with a secure base by continually providing any information regarding Frank from her perspective, conversely he also deftly manages to infuse some ambiguity as to the reliability of such an impression. With her admission that her colleagues at the store may "say she was a fool" he raises the question as to why she imagines them thinking in this way (*D*, 23). Although admittedly she would be going to a foreign land where she does not know anyone else, her escape from the drudge of Dublin life, along with the romance of her story, could equally be seen as promoting envy rather than scorn. Another, more disquieting, rationale for this thought therefore offers itself to the reader: an indirect acknowledgment that what she knows of this seemingly "kind" and "open hearted" man is not very detailed (*D*, 24). Under her rhetoric of safety one can also read a certain amount of doubt.

Although her character in some ways appears unassuming, when practical necessities dictate, she is shown to stand up for what she needs. Her preparedness to squabble with her father every Saturday is based on a need for money for sustenance. Similarly, that she is prepared to consider eloping is based on her need for escape and security rather than the complexities of love. At no point does Joyce create the illusion that this is a passionate relationship. Whilst Eveline recalls how she came to "like" Frank, she also confesses to feeling "pleasantly confused" when "he sang about the lass that loves a sailor" (*D*, 25). Again, there is more than one way this comment could be construed. Firstly, as Eveline's emotional feelings toward him are portrayed as somewhat vague, the mention of love could be seen to cause her some consternation. Secondly, although not quoted in "Eveline," the actual words of the song, which was written by Charles Dibdin (1745–1815), denote men who loved their wives, but loved the sea even more and with it the girls in the ports.[18] Hence, her confusion could signify the disparity between the man who purports he wants to marry her and make her an integral part of his life and the words of the song which gives sailing the ocean priority over any emotional ties.

Eveline can only speculate that "perhaps" Frank will give her love (D, 26). Again, reading with knowledge of Attachment Theory, one can interpret her uncertainty through the use of the word "perhaps" as a reflection of her insecure avoidant attachment traits. Firstly in her acceptance of the possibility of being let down yet again by someone and secondly because there is an implication that she sees herself as unlovable.[19] Yet she is convinced that he will "give her life" which, having seen her mother's life as one "of commonplace sacrifices closing in final craziness," one could envisage would be of paramount importance to her (D, 25–26).

The reported disagreement between Eveline's father and Frank, with his comment regarding his knowledge of "these sailor chaps" serves only to create further uncertainty for the reader with regards to Frank's integrity. Is he to be viewed as a man with a girl in each port, or is there a simple and selfish explanation: that her father is a man who would oppose any relationship Eveline may embark upon to keep her (and her wages) under his control? Eric Bulson notes that many critics have suggested that Frank could be setting Eveline up for a life of prostitution.[20] David Pierce, although rejecting such suggestions regarding Frank's intentions, cites Jonathon Green's *The Cassell Dictionary of Slang*, which explains that "to go to Buenos Aires" in the nineteenth century meant "to start working as a prostitute."[21] This would explain why critics have interpreted Joyce as implying such a fate for Eveline, whilst also raising the issue of the sexual dangers to young women. Yet conversely, as Sidney Feshbach points out, Frank's story is plausible since the "Allan Line" was "a steamship line" which served England and North America and economic data shows that at the time Joyce was writing it would have been possible for Frank to have earned good wages and possibly buy a house in Buenos Aires.[22]

As Joyce carefully creates and layers such ambiguity, he also makes it increasingly difficult for the reader to agree or disagree with her plans. The doubt that has been slowly creeping into the narrative is also reflected in the admission that "now she was about to leave it she did not find it a wholly undesirable life" (D, 24). Although unspoken, there appears to be a partially understood realisation on Eveline's part that she will be severing all ties for what appears to be the answer to her problems, but which in reality is a step into the unknown and at worst could result in even less security than the little she has now.

Although Joyce relates how Eveline "stood up in a sudden impulse of terror" on recalling her mother's words, he does not describe her journey to the docks (*D*, 26). Thus, some critics have suggested that she may not have left the house at all but instead imagines what will happen at her arrival.[23] David Trotter notes that Joyce's "letters and memoirs" point to the fact that he "made a habit out of movie going" and one could therefore alternatively view Joyce as using a more cinematic approach to his writing, as though abruptly cutting to a new frame and a new location.[24] It is known that as early as 1897 films were shown in Dublin in the Star of Erin, later reopened as the Empire Palace.[25] Although many early films were made with a camera in a fixed point, in 1900 Cecil Hepworth filmed Queen Victoria's visit to Dublin "from a variety of positions" and by 1903 he produced an adaptation of Lewis Carroll's *Alice in Wonderland*.[26] It therefore seems a reasonable assumption to make that Joyce would have been familiar with films that cut from one scene to another. In his writing of "Eveline" the extra line space he leaves before the final scene can be seen as denoting a change of scene.

Whether the reader interprets Eveline's arrival at the docks to be actual or imaginary, the uncertainty regarding Frank loses all prominence at this point. A far deeper problem within her psyche is revealed: vacillating between the memory of her mother and her need for escape, the question of whether she can psychologically let go of her dying mother's request and physically leave Ireland, comes to the fore: "what was her duty?" (*D*, 26). Joyce's description of Eveline as being in "a maze of distress" at once implies extreme anxiety and an inability to see which is the right path to take (*D*, 26). Emotional episodes can often involve a bodily disturbance and here Eveline is no longer described as merely trembling; her anxiety has taken over her entire being as she experiences "a nausea in her body" (*D*, 26). In her psychological and physical turmoil, she is shown to turn to the only source of power she perceives as available to her, that of prayer. Yet she is portrayed as focusing her prayers on "her duty" rather than, for example, a supplication for courage in starting her new life, indicating that her mother's psychological hold is still strong (*D*, 26).

No longer able to focus on her hopes for a new life Eveline is instead paralysed with fear that Frank "will drown her" (*D*, 26). Although she has envisioned him as someone who offers both a new life and an escape from Dublin ties, it appears her mind is now very much with her mother's dying moments and she fears that against her hopes he could destroy her dreams just as her father had destroyed her mother's. Joyce's depiction of this scenario exemplifies the laws put forward by Alexander Shand, regarding the interaction of emotions and the correlation between hope and anxiety, two of which he states as follows:

> (132) *When Hope is present, the disposition to Anxiety is excited; and when Anxiety is present, the disposition to Hope is also excited.*
> [. . .]
> (135) *If Anxiety succeeds in destroying Hope it also destroys itself, and the new emotion of Despair takes the place of both.*[27]

Bowlby notes how Shand's theories of anxiety were very similar to Freud's, written a decade later, theories that he subsequently "adopted and elaborated" on when discussing grief and mourning. (*AL*3: 26–27). In the "laws" quoted above, Shand is not specifically relating them to grief, but is nevertheless proposing that when hoping for something, anxiety is produced for fear that these hopes might in some way be dashed. Should anxiety take over, hope is lost, and despair takes over. This is precisely what Joyce portrays as happening to Eveline as she yields to the influence of her mother, which is clanging like a "bell [. . .] upon her heart" (*D,* 26). With the possibility that her plans could fail, she cannot justify defying her mother's wish. The pull of the dead is shown to negate the demand for escape.

In a moment of realisation, knowing that it will be "impossible" for her to leave, she is portrayed as letting out "a cry of anguish" in her overwhelming despair as her hopes and dreams are abandoned (*D,* 26). Again, it is possible to see Joyce's writing technique taking on an almost cinematic approach, as he relates Eveline's recognition of her entrapment in no uncertain terms. Against the backdrop of the noise of the crowds, the soldiers with their luggage, the sounds of the boat preparing for departure, and Frank's inaudible words, he focuses closely on Eveline; facing the reader with her debilitating anguish as she stands "like a helpless animal" in a spotlight, unable to move. Not unlike the still from a film, he portrays her frozen in a moment in time. Paralysed by the pull of the dead, her "cold," "white face" takes on the aspect of a pale, inert cadaver (*D,* 26). Oatley discusses how emotion can be viewed as carrying out a communicative function, not only cognitively in the person who is experiencing that emotion, but to others in the social group.[28] As Joyce focuses on her still, incapacitated body, her anxiety and paralysing helplessness are shown to be communicated to Frank through her blank and expressionless eyes, giving "no sign of love, farewell, or recognition" (*D,* 26).

Reading from a Lacanian viewpoint, Josephine Sharoni argues that Eveline's momentary paralysis is a consequence of "her sexual desire never having been formed, leaving her incapable of responding," hence, the "helplessness (*Hilflosigkeit*) of the child before the resolution of the Oedipal complex" has been evoked.[29] Like Garry Leonard, Sharoni is arguing that Eveline's father is devoid of his patriarchal and masculine stance. Leonard puts this down to his alcoholism and slide toward poverty.[30] However, Sharoni appears to suggest that Eveline's father has always been "lacking" in the Lacanian sense, unable to take on the role of the symbolic father, hence the parental metaphor (the substitutive (metaphorical) character of the Oedipal complex) has failed.[31] This is quite a large assumption to make, especially as Eveline reveals that "her father was not so bad" when her mother was alive (*D*, 23).

Reading from an attachment perspective offers an alternative explanation to that of a problem with Eveline's psychosexual development. Joyce has portrayed Eveline as a young woman who has had to become self-sufficient, not only physically in terms of taking on her mother's role but also, with the lack of any emotional support, psychologically. As such there is a sense that, instead of coming to terms with her mother's death, Eveline has repressed her grief and continued as best she could with her life. Bowlby has argued that those who show a prolonged absence of conscious grieving, often seen in those who are self-sufficient, may still be influenced by the dead without the person realising, but may also break down due to certain events or triggers.[32] Joyce portrays such a scenario showing how Eveline, at an extremely crucial moment in her life, is unable to contain the emotion she has suppressed for so long. At the very point she is to put her plan for a better life into action, Joyce depicts her heart, the symbol of love and affection, not only as feeling her mother's words clanging upon it, but also as experiencing the tumult of "all the seas of the world" (*D*, 26). With her despair and yearning made evident, there is an implication that she is regressing into the phases of grief that have hitherto been unresolved. Her portrayed state of fearful inertia illustrates that, until she can relinquish the hold of her mother's words, she will, like Dilly in *Ulysses*, drown in the paralysis of Dublin life and her own emotional needs for a secure base will not be realised.

Ironically, it is not Frank that is causing Eveline to "drown" but her self-sufficiency and the containment of her grief have which lead to the grief process not being fully resolved. In discussing epiphany in *Dubliners*, Hélène Cixous states that "reality seems to break under the strain of misfortune, just long enough for us to perceive the abyss below."[33] Joyce's depiction of Eveline, who has created an internal narrative of how life could be, shows her close to losing her sense of reality as she becomes momentarily incapacitated at the dock. Her "misfortune" in being thwarted by her unresolved grief and the pull of the dead returns her to the "abyss" of the continued paralysing life with her abusive father.

Eveline is not the only character within *Dubliners* who has created a narrative that Joyce implicitly questions. In his final short story "The Dead" Joyce portrays a woman, Gretta, who through containing her grief has also created an internal narrative regarding a deceased lover. When this is finally vocalised the epiphanic moment rests with her husband rather than, as in "Eveline," with the bereaved protagonist; a realisation which carries the implication that it will henceforth influence their married life. This is the focus of my next chapter.

NOTES

1. Mikulincer and Shaver, "An Attachment Perspective on Bereavement," 94.

2. Suzanne Keen, *Empathy and The Novel* (Oxford: Oxford University Press, 2007), xxi.

3. Andrew Gibson, *The Strong Spirit. History, Politics and Aesthetics in the Writings of James Joyce, 1898–1915* (Oxford: Oxford University Press, 2013), 53–54.

4. Costello, *James Joyce: The Years of Growth*, 213.

5. See R. Brandon Kershner, *Joyce, Bakhtin and Popular Literature: Chronicles of Disorder* (Chapel Hill: The University of North Carolina Press, 1989), 69.

6. Donald T. Torchiana, *Backgrounds for Joyce's Dubliners* (Boston, Allen and Unwin, 1986), 72.

7. Nigel P. Field, "Whether to Relinquish or Maintain a Bond with the Deceased," in *Handbook of Bereavement and Research Practice*, 120.

8. Parkes, *Bereavement*, 7.

9. William York Tindall, *A Reader's Guide to James Joyce* (New York: Farrar, Straus & Giroux, 1959: repr. 1978), 22.

10. Leonard, *Reading Dubliners Again*, 98.

11. Wim Tigges, "Dervaun Seraun!: Resignation or Escape?" *James Joyce Quarterly*, 32 (1994): 102.

12. Tigges, "Dervam Seraun!," 102–3.

13. Brenda Maddox, *Nora: A Biography of Nora Joyce* (Hamish Hamilton, 1988; repr. London: Minerva, 1989), 33–35.

14. Maddox, *Nora*, 21.

15. Ulrich Schneider, "Titles in Dubliners," in *Rejoycing: New Readings of Dubliners*, eds. Rosa Bosinelli, M. Bollettieri, and Harold F. Mosher Jr. (Lexington: University Press of Kentucky, 1998), 198.

16. Also Holmes, *The Search for a Secure Base*, 37.

17. Mary D. Salter Ainsworth, "Attachment: Retrospect and Prospect," in *The Place of Attachment in Human Behaviour*, ed. Colin Murray Parkes and Joan Stevenson-Hinde (London: Tavistock, 1982), 26.

18. See Don Gifford, *Joyce Annotated: "Notes for Dubliners" and "A Portrait of the Artist" as a Young Man*, 2nd ed. (Berkley: University of California Press, 1982), 51.

19. Howe, *Attachment Across the Lifecourse*, 44.

20. Eric Bulson, *The Cambridge Introduction to James Joyce* (Cambridge: Cambridge University Press, 2006), 33.

21. Pierce, *Reading Joyce*, 89. With reference to Jonathon Green, *The Cassell Dictionary of Slang* (London: Cassell, 1998).

22. Sidney Feshbach, "Fallen on His Feet in Buenos Ayres (D 39): Frank in 'Eveline,'" *James Joyce Quarterly* 20, no. 2 (Winter 1983): 223–24.

23. See Brandabur, *A Scrupulous Meanness*, 60; Earl G. Ingersoll, *Engendered Trope in Joyce's Dubliners* (Carbondale: Southern Illinois University Press, 1996), 61.

24. David Trotter, *Cinema and Modernism* (Massachusetts: Blackwell, 2007), 87.

25. Trotter, *Cinema and Modernism*, 94.

26. Trotter, *Cinema and Modernism*, 97; Simon Brown, *Alice in Wonderland (1903)*, accessed July 2018, http://www.screenonline.org.uk/film/id/974410.

27. Shand, *The Foundations of Character*, 505–6.

28. See Oatley, *Best Laid Schemes*, 44.

29. Josephine Sharoni, "The Failure of the Parental Metaphor: A Lacanian Reading of James Joyce's 'Eveline,'" in *Journal of Modern Literature*, 39, no. 4 (Summer 2016), 45.

30. Leonard, *Reading Dubliners Again*, 99.

31. The "parental metaphor," according to Lacan, "involves the substation of one signifier (the Name of the Father) for another (the desire of the mother)." It "thus designates the metaphorical (i.e., substitutive) character of the Oedipus Complex itself." Dylan Evans, *An Introductory Dictionary of Lacanian Psychoanalysis* (Sussex: Routledge, 1986), 137.

32. See *AL3*: 152–72 for the effects of prolonged absence of grieving.

33. Cixous, *The Exile of James Joyce*, 612.

Chapter Eight

"The Dead"

Disenfranchised Grief, Idealisation of the Deceased, and the Effect on the Living

When discussing "The Dead" many authors have concentrated their critical interpretations on Garbriel. However, it is Gretta's expression of grief that is functional to her husband's moment of self-realisation and hence deserves further exploration. Through the loss of her friend and sweetheart Michael Furey as a young adult, Gretta can be read as having experienced disenfranchised grief and as having idealised his memory. Disenfranchised grief can be said to occur when, following "a significant loss [. . .] the resultant grief is not openly acknowledged, socially validated or publicly mourned."[1] Therefore, "although the individual is experiencing a grief reaction, there is no social recognition that the person has a right to grieve or a claim for social sympathy or support," which Bowbly notes as important in successfully negotiating one's grief (*AL3*: 193).[2] Gabriel's consequent reaction to Gretta's revelation of her loss can in turn be read as revealing his own assumptions and how certain of his portrayed behaviours can be interpreted as attachment related.

The reader is introduced to both Gretta and Gabriel as they arrive at a party hosted by Gabriel's aunts, Kate and Julia Morkan. It is a party at which death appears to be a pervasive guest, so much so that John Wilson Foster has interpreted the party as "a funeral ceremony with its ritual dancing, ceremonial feast, formal speech and ritual singing." He views "the corpse" as being played on many levels: "at one level of reference by all the named and unnamed dead, at another level by Aunts Julia and Kate, and yet another level by all the guests themselves, who represent Joyce's lifeless Dublin in a lifeless Ireland."[3] Yet, whilst the absent members of Gabriel's family are recalled throughout the party, Joyce leaves the reader, like Gabriel and the other party guests, oblivious to the fact that Gretta is still carrying with her the grief caused by the death of her childhood sweetheart.

Reminiscent of the effect that the playing of the street organ had on Eveline Hill, so the rendition of the song Michael "used to sing" to Gretta *"The Lass of Aughrim,"* evokes a phase of pining in Gretta (*D,* 158). Enwrapped in the song, such that after it is finished she is "unaware of the talk around her," she is psychologically transported to another time and place (*D,* 153). Gabriel's initial failure to identify the woman listening to the song in her "stillness" as his wife foreshadows his later realisation that he had failed to recognise her as an individual; a woman whose emotional life had not always been entwined with his (*D,* 151). As if to give emphasis to his ignorance, Joyce has Gabriel conflate artifice and reality as he wonders at her "grace and mystery" and puzzles over what "a woman standing on the stairs in the shadow, listening to distant music [is] a symbol of" (*D,* 151). That she is far more than a romantic symbol, but a sentient being whose grief has been brought to the fore, is made patent when she is alone with Gabriel in their hotel room.

Alan Friedman argues that because Gretta missed Michael's "proffered love, as well as his dying and funeral" that he "remains undead and unburied for her."[4] Phrasing this argument in terms of attachment and taking into consideration the different stages of the grief process put forward by Bowlby, it is possible to argue that Gretta has not successfully negotiated all the stages of that process. Indeed, her "outburst of tears," as she responds to her husband's questions and prompts about the boy "in the gasworks," which finally result in her becoming "overcome by emotion," represents a reaction reminiscent of the initial stages of grief (*D,* 157–60). Certainly, her inability to talk about her loss without being overcome, despite Michael's death occurring some years ago, can be seen to represent her unresolved grief. Taking into account the information provided within the text and reading with knowledge of Attachment Theory, it is possible to read the portrayal of Gretta as that of someone who has suffered from disenfranchised grief.

In studying disenfranchised grief, like Bowlby, Kenneth Doka has looked at the various cognitive, affective, behavioural, and physical effects of loss. Discussing this type of socially unrecognised grief from a cultural perspective when considering Western societies he notes that there are "grieving rules" which emphasise that "family members have a right to grieve the deaths of other family members" whilst others will show "sympathy and support" to the bereaved family. However, he also notes that "human beings exist in intimate networks, associations that include both kin and non-kin."[5] Questioning why the right to grieve is monopolised by family members, despite the complicated social networks in which humans exist, Doka turns to the work of J. Kamerman. Kamerman saw "a latent function" of the grieving rules as strengthening "the traditional family by denying recognition of other relationships outside the family, especially socially unsanctioned relationships, such as lovers or unmarried partner."[6] By depicting Gretta as outside Michael's family and a lover (by which I mean sweetheart), Joyce has created a scenario where recognition of her grief would have been negated. Furthermore, by placing Gretta in a convent at the time of Michael's death, Joyce has also created a situation in which her grief may not have been acknowledged by surrounding others at that time.

In convent life, thoughts of romantic love would not have been considered appropriate, and Joyce gives no indication that Gretta actually shared the fact that she had suffered a loss with anyone therein. However, looking beyond appropriate behaviour and convention one could also propose a deeper spiritual element behind her silence and containment. Paul Rosenblatt, through his research carried out on nineteenth-century diaries, concluded that: "To the extent that a diarist believed that God knew inner feelings, and to the extent that religious beliefs demanded acceptance of God's will, people might have thought that feelings that seemed to question God's wisdom had to be controlled."[7] Rosenblatt then goes on to give examples to support his conclusion. Joyce makes plain the religious belief of God being "Allseeing and Allknowing" and that one is on this earth "to do God's holy will" in *Portrait* (*P*, 111 and 118). Although he does not make this explicit in this short story, any reader with knowledge of the Christian faith would be aware of such religious tenets and how Michael's death at such a young age would have been interpreted as God's unquestionable will.

Yet the initial surge of emotion when learning of the death of someone who is loved cannot be totally denied. In Joyce's laconic style the reader only has Gretta's exclamation: "O, the day I heard that, that he was dead!" in order to imagine her original felt distress (*D*, 159–60). However, descriptive restraint can be seen as a device by which to elicit a greater emotional response than may possibly have been conveyed by an extended narrative. Oatley notes how the reader of a narrative "generates information," with each interpretation arising as a result of "a meeting of the text created by the writer" and "the simulation resources and preoccupations of each individual reader."[8] In addition to Culpeper and Keen, many other literary critics and philosophers have acknowledged how readers call on their own life experiences and hence emotional responses when interpreting novels and filling in any narrative gaps within the texts.[9] Here, Joyce's open statement of Gretta's grief provides the forum for such cognitive activity. To imagine being in a setting where one has to stifle that emotion, can only further increase the reader's sympathy toward Gretta and therefore create greater empathy with her felt distress.

With the lack of any indication of social support in dealing with her bereavement, Joyce creates a sense that Gretta has internalised her feelings of grief and in doing so simultaneously created an idealised narrative regarding

Michael's death. Although she can be read as ultimately accepting his death was God's will, she romantically states: "I think he died for me" (*D*, 159). However, one could surmise that had she not written to him until after she had left for the convent, he would not have made the journey to see her and hence a more accurate description would be: "he died because of me," or at the very least, "I hastened his death." Yet analysing the language used to describe his death elucidates why Joyce portrays her as wanting to romanticise it. Instead of saying, for example "isn't that a *sad* thing, to die so young," she uses the phrase "*terrible* thing" (my emphasis), which denotes something horrifying and hence more menacing (*D*, 158). Her idealisation of events can be viewed as gratification of a need to psychologically remove her contribution to his "terrible" death, albeit an unwitting one. It is telling that at no point does Joyce have Gretta express regret for writing to him when she did, thereby allowing her quixotic illusion to remain intact.

As in *Ulysses*, where Simon Dedalus and Martin Cunningham reinforce the goodness of Paddy Dignam following his recent death, Gretta's emotional and subjective memory of Michael appears to have gradually erased any perceived faults that he may have had. Parkes and Pigerson explain how grieving "becomes a creative activity" where "re-evaluation of the dead person, an activity sometimes termed "idealisation" "can occur in order to perpetuate "the happy memories and valued aspects of the relationship."[10] In this story Joyce has Gretta render an idealised vision of Michael himself, in addition to that of his actual death. From his "big, dark" expressive eyes, to his "good voice," his gentle personality and how they were "great together," her representation of him is of one who was talented and perfect (*D*, 158–59). His only discernable fault appeared to be his health, for which she expresses pity. Constructing such a romanticised vision of Michael and his death enables Joyce to fabricate a contrast between fantasy and real life. Michael, as an idealised memory, is a faultless young man, unlike the living with whom Gretta interacts.

That being said, Joyce does not appear to give any reason for the reader to deduce that Gretta's marriage to Gabriel has been an unhappy one, or equally that she has not been committed to her husband. Her relationship with him is represented as more mature, bringing with it the responsibility of children. Her young and relatively carefree feelings of first love experienced with Michael Furey, by their very nature, should be viewed as quite distinct from those experienced with Gabriel. Therefore, Richard Brown's description of Gabriel as "the wronged husband" and David James's comment regarding Gretta's "deception," both of which implicate bad or immoral behaviour on Gretta's part, appear inappropriate.[11] Firstly, Gretta's relationship with Michael had blossomed and tragically ended before she knew Gabriel, so she cannot be said to have been unfaithful to, or in Brown's terminology, "wronged"

Gabriel in the sense that he should be viewed as a cuckold. Secondly, literature on grief "uniformly reports" how "feelings of guilt and powerlessness" can be intensified in disenfranchising circumstances.[12] Gretta's previous silence about Michael Furey is not, therefore, necessarily confirmation of a sordid episode in her life enfolded in secrecy. It can equally be interpreted as being borne of a continued sense of guilt, believing as she does that Michael died for her. The portrayal of the emotion experienced by Gretta creates the impression that this is the first time that she has ever exposed her true feelings of loss to anyone and although she does not "answer at once" when Gabriel asks her what the matter is, neither does she brush away his question (*D*, 157). Her willingness to unveil her grief to him can be read as denoting that she is secure in his company and certain of his unconditional love.

By virtue of Gretta's conversation with the two aunts on their arrival at the party, Joyce ensures that Gabriel, for his part, can be viewed as someone who sees himself as taking his responsibilities with regards to his family's well-being seriously:

> He's really an awful bother, what with green shades for Tom's eyes at night and making him do the dumb-bells, and forcing Eva to eat the stirabout [. . .] O, but you'll never guess what he makes me wear now!
> [. . .]
> Whenever it's wet underfoot I must put on my galoshes. (*D,* 130)

That he sees himself as her protector is evidenced further by his romantic thoughts: "he longed to defend her against something and then to be alone with her" (*D,* 154). His longing for "something," anything, from which he can protect her before being "alone with her" supports Kershner's argument that "his potency is a function of his partner's helplessness," particularly his sexual potency.[13] Joyce's representation of Gabriel is, therefore, that of someone who confuses dominance with the notion of love and as such places importance in legitimising his patriarchal role in order to maintain his sense of worth. His view of himself as an academic with "superior education" also appears to go some way in helping him to mentally justify his dominance (*D,* 129). His mother obviously clearly reinforced that view, seeing her son, who liked foreign cycling holidays to "keep in touch with languages," as above his wife, whom she called "country cute" (*D,* 135–36). However, whilst Gabriel can at times appear to have an overinflated view of himself, he is also portrayed as anxious as to how others see him, as made evident by his deliberations over what to put in his speech.

Gabriel has created an internal narrative about himself regarding his education and his cosmopolitanism with his holidays abroad, although he "does not represent cosmopolitanism and Europeanism but rather a provincial flirtation with these ideas."[14] Similarly he can be viewed as having created his own distended and androcentric internal narrative with regards to his unique place and importance in Gretta's life. The "felt humiliation" that he describes on learning of the deceased Michael Furey can be interpreted as resulting from the dissolution of that narrative, which although erroneously created, had been believed in unreservedly in terms of his wife's past life and the depth of his own love for her (*D*, 158). He is forced to consider, ostensibly for the first time, Gretta's individual and sentient life before they met, as well as the emotional depth of his own relationship with her; specifically, whether he would willingly give his life for her. From the moment the painful process of dealing with his cognitive dissonance begins, Gabriel is portrayed as reevaluating his own view of himself. The speaker who had everyone's generous attention at the party now sees himself as "a ludicrous figure" and a "pitiable fatuous fellow" (*D*, 158).

Gabriel's own emotional response to Gretta's narrative is shown to result in him eventually succumbing to tears, which are described as "generous" (*D*, 161). However, the reliability of the narrator is in question here. Certainly, Gabriel is shown to accept her highly romanticised interpretation of Michael's demise; to absorb and become absorbed in her narrative, much like the reader of a novel. His ready identification and sympathy with her narrative could be viewed as relating to his passionate feelings toward Gretta throughout the evening, coupled with his own fertile and romantic imagination as evidenced on their arrival at the hotel. Here he is portrayed as being more than capable of creating his own story in which he wishes to immerse them both: "as they stood at the hotel door, he felt that they had escaped from their lives and duties, escaped from home and friends and run away together with wild and radiant hearts to a new adventure" (*D*, 155). Having abandoned his own romantic notions and sexual desires, one could view his tears for her tragic tale as "generous." Yet it could also be argued that his tears are due to the realisation that his feelings for his wife were not as deep as he himself had imagined. By his own admission he had never experienced feelings, such as Michael had for Gretta, "towards any woman, but he knew that such feeling must be love" (*D*, 161). In an attitude of self-debasement, he sees himself as merely a "well-meaning sentimentalist," with his earlier ardent thoughts as "clownish" (*D*, 158). Hence, Michael Furey's reported sacrifice becomes nothing short of heroic in its selflessness and in his own eyes he is left wanting, believing he has "played a poor part" in Gretta's life (*D*, 160). As Foster succinctly writes, "Gabriel is put in the shade by a shade."[15]

Brandabur's Freudian reading of Gabriel resists such a reading, deducing instead that Gabriel loves Gretta "in a neurotic way. Forbidden in this by a repressed injunction, possibly by his own mother's opposition, he must both express and feel affection in devious ways, by identification: by "feeling into" the experience of others, in this case Michael."[16] However, Gabriel's riot of thoughts seems to go against this reading. He initially experiences "anger," then "terror," only to finally transmute into needless self-pity (*D*, 157–60). Rather than feeling "by identification" with Michael as Brandabur argues, it is clear Gabriel believes himself to be the injured party, or in Brown's terminology, the "wronged husband." First, he is shown to expresses his belief that whilst "he had been full of memories of their secret life together [. . .] she had been comparing him in her mind with another" (*D*, 158). He then goes on to watch her sleep "as though he and she had never lived together as man and wife" (*D*, 160). Finally, as he casts his eyes toward "the chair over which she had thrown some of her clothes," there is a tacit implication that his thoughts are turning towards the likelihood of a physical aspect to her relationship with Michael, as he ponders the possibility that "she had not told him all the story" (*D*, 160). Such emotional overreaction can be interpreted as deriving not only from the loss of his own narrative, but overwhelmingly from concern regarding his own emotional support base in terms of Gretta's love for him.

Like Master Dignam, Gabriel adopts what could be termed an anxious/ambivalent strategy, although in this case it is not evident through his proposed actions but through his dialogue. Before learning of Michael's death, his rather sulky accusation that Gretta wanted to visit Galway in order to see Michael is devised to elicit a response: a denial of such a notion and affirmation of her love for him, her husband. Similarly when Gretta first disclosed she was thinking of someone she knew long ago Gabriel straight away asked "Someone you were in love with?" and in the absence of a denial, he continued to repeat the question: "O, then, you are in love with him?" and "I suppose you were in love with this Michael Furey" (*D*, 158). Again, what he is really asking for is her refutation and the relevant affirmation of her love as a form of reassurance of his position of importance in her life.

It seems worth noting that, in his portrayal of Gretta, whilst Joyce has set up a comparison between romantic idealisation and "real life" for the reader, he has not represented her as *consciously* comparing Michael with Gabriel, enabling the reader to maintain sympathy with her. She is portrayed as having recounted her teenage experiences to Gabriel innocently, unaware of their emotional impact on him, arguably relieved that she is able to express her grief openly to someone she believes will understand her. It is evident that for Gretta it is an old but painful event, a lasting sorrow, the intensity of which has been revivified by the playing of the song. However, for Gabriel this is a revelation, causing him to fight off the "impalpable and vindictive" being that is jealousy (*D*, 159). David Howe argues that for anxious/ambivalent individuals, "declarations of undying love and feelings of possessiveness are as likely as outbursts of mistrust and jealous anger" both resulting from "the anxious need to be loved, reassured and never be abandoned."[17] Although he is relatively restrained verbally, Joyce certainly represents Gabriel as mentally experiencing both aspects of the emotional spectrum throughout the narrative. Caught up in his own anxieties, it is perhaps then unsurprising that Gabriel resorts to mentally accusing Gretta of comparing him to Michael, when in fact it is he who is comparing his own feelings for his wife with those that Michael evidently carried for her.

Gabriel's mistrustful thoughts, which implied the possibility of a physical relationship between Michael and Gretta, also seem unfounded and again a symptom of his anxious/ambivalent tendencies, when one considers her narrative. She mentions twice how they used to go out walking together. However, on mentioning this the second time, she refers to her husband by name, at once placing emphasis on the fact that she wants to make sure that he is listening attentively and also signifying that she needs him to understand her explanation: "you know, Gabriel, like the way they do in the country" (*D*, 159). In contrast to her husband's deliberately ironic and manipulative questions, her statements are straightforward and do not indicate any duplicity. The continual references she makes to Michael's eyes suggest a relationship which consisted of furtive glances and loving looks. Unlike Joyce's portrayal of Frank from Eveline's viewpoint, where she sees safety in his arms, there is a distinct lack of any form of touch, envisaged or actual, in Gretta's narrative. Even her description of their last meeting is devoid of any form of physical contact; instead she again recalls his eyes. Thus, there is nothing within Gretta's narrative to substantiate Gabriel's suspicion that their relationship could have entered the physical realm.

As Gabriel lies down beside Gretta, he knows that the disclosure of her grief has created a new chapter in their life together. He must recognise her as a woman that needs to be loved rather than a possession to be fussed over: as an individual as well as his wife, which will challenge his exhibited anxious/ambivalent tendencies of possessiveness. Through relating his emotional overreaction and hence self-debasement, Joyce shows how Gabriel has come to acknowledge some of his faults. As his thoughts become calmer and less accusatory, he can also be seen as admitting to a modicum of admiration for Michael Furey: "Better to pass boldly into that other world, in the full glory of some passion, than fade and wither dismally with age" (*D*, 160). Perhaps he will be able to find some sympathy with the passion with which Miss Ivors defends his native Ireland, which he professes to be "sick of" (*D*, 137). Perhaps, rather than seeing his aunts as "two ignorant old women" he will see them as women that have followed their passion and love for music (*D*, 139). Joyce does not take the reader beyond Gabriel's epiphany of self-realisation to show precisely how deeply his inner being has been affected in terms of how he will now live his day-to-day life. Yet, as he lays down to sleep and the conscious world full of turmoil and uncertainties begins to fade, the snow which is "general all over Ireland," falling "upon both the living and the dead" can be seen as symbolic of an "inclusive sympathy" (*D*, 161).[18]

Through his narratives concerning both Gretta and Eveline Hill, Joyce has represented the continuing effects of grief due to bereavement suffered as a young adult. Although, unlike Gretta, the grief experienced by Eveline would have been socially validated, due to her avoidant traits she is nevertheless shown to be unable to reach the stage of cognitive reorganisation where she feels she no longer needs to answer to her mother. Pierce's description of "Eveline" as "an emigration story with a difference" is an apt one since her eventual inability to leave predominantly rests not with the emotional pull of the living, but with that of the dead.[19] Brian Cosgrove, taking his cue from the "Hades" episode of *Ulysses*, suggests that Gretta "valorises the dead over the living, preferring, perversely, the romantic memory of the deceased Michael Furey to the "warm fullblooded life" of her man-alive husband" (see *U*, 6.1005).[20] However, taking into account what I believe is the portrayal of Gretta's disenfranchised grief, I take a different view. Whilst admittedly Gretta is shown as having romanticised Michael's death and thus her vision of him, the fact that she does not "yield wholly" to Gabriel is a reflection of her felt grief and emotional state at that moment in time and expressed grief does not necessarily denote preference (*D*, 157). As I have already argued, there is nothing in the narrative to suggest that the reader is to interpret Gretta as loving Gabriel any less than she loved Michael, but much to indicate that Gabriel's feelings for his wife were not as strong as her dead lover's. Whereas Eveline was portrayed as making a definite and final choice between her dead mother and Frank, Gretta has momentarily allowed free reign to a grief that had previously remained hidden, giving the impression that perhaps now it has been acknowledged, it will finally begin to be resolved. Combining this with Gabriel's own self-realisation, one is left with a sense of hope for Gretta and Gabriel rather than the sense of despair that engulfs Eveline.

NOTES

1. Kenneth J. Doka, "Disenfranchised Grief in Historical and Cultural Perspective," in *Handbook of Bereavement and Research Practice*, 224.

2. Doka, "Disenfranchised Grief," 224.

3. John Wilson Foster, *Fictions of the Irish Literary Revival: A Changeling Art* (New York: Syracuse University Press, 1987), 146.

4. Friedman, *Fictional*, 134.

5. Kenneth J. Doka, "Disenfranchised Grief," 225–26.

6. Doka, "Disenfranchised Grief in Historical and Cultural Perspective," 226 referring to Kamerman "Latent function of enfranchising and the disenfranchised griever" in *Death Studies,* 17 (1993), 281–87.

7. Rosenblatt, *Bitter, Bitter Tears*, 107.

8. Oatley, *Best Laid Schemes*, 245–46.

9. For example, see: Marguerite Harkness, *A Portrait of the Artist as a Young Man*, 53; Peter Lamarque and Stein Haugom Olson, *Truth, Fiction and Literature: A Philosophical Perspective* (Oxford: Clarendon Press, 1994), 89–90.

10. Parkes and Prigerson, *Bereavement*, 81.

11. Richard Brown, *James Joyce and Sexuality* (Cambridge: Cambridge University Press, 1985), 17; David James, "Modernist Narratives: Revisions and Rereadings," in *The Oxford Handbook of Modernisms*, eds. Peter Brooker, Andrzej Gasiorek, Deborah Longworh, and Andrew Thacker (Oxford: Oxford University Press), 95.

12. Kenneth J. Doka, "Disenfranchised Grief," in *Disenfranchised Grief: Recognizing Hidden Sorrow*, ed. Kenneth J. Doka (New York: Lexington books, 1989), 7. Doka lists several studies to support his argument.

13. Kershner, *Joyce, Bakhtin and Popular Literature*, 143.

14. Foster, *Fictions of the Irish Literary Revival*, 152.

15. Foster, *Fictions of the Irish Literary Revival*, 160.

16. Brandabur, *A Scrupulous Meanness*, 122.

17. Howe, *Attachment Across the Lifecourse*, 140.

18. Peter K. Garrett, "Introduction," in *Twentieth Century Interpretations of Dubliners: A Collection of Critical Essays*, ed. Peter K. Garrett (New Jersey: Prentice-Hall, 1968), 15. Garrett writes: "The image of the snow likewise suggests death, or frozen paralysis, but also, as it joins all the parts of Ireland, living and dead, past and present, suggests inclusive sympathy."

19. Pierce, *Reading Joyce*, 89.

20. Brian Cosgrove, *James Joyce's Negations: Irony, Indeterminacy and Nihilism in Ulysses and Other Writings* (Dublin: University College Dublin Press, 2007), 60.

PART III

Character Traits and Individual Expressions of Grief: Stephen Dedalus, Leopold Bloom, and Molly Bloom

Part III

Introduction

Arnold and Gemma, in their discussion of bereavement, state that: "The experience of loss erupts feelings associated with previous losses and previous pain. We reach into the past to childhood and feel hurts of long ago."[1] Part 3 will show that the grief reactions exhibited by the main protagonists of *Ulysses,* that is to say Stephen Dedalus, Molly Bloom and Leopold Bloom, can be read as an expression of their portrayed attachment history and past hurts of childhood. However, to access the childhood experiences of Stephen Dedalus one also needs to return to *Portrait*. In both *Ulysses* and *Portrait*, Joyce includes many self-referential elements and can be seen as making sense of his own life experiences in addition to the various responses to grief. Indeed, Mark Shechner views Joyce's books as "the records of his analytic transaction with his own unconscious." He links Joyce's propensity to self-analysis to his "Catholic upbringing" and "Jesuit education."[2] (Joyce's relationship with religion will be discussed in detail in Chapter 11.)

When coming to understand our past experiences, hurtful or otherwise, philosophers, psychologists and attachment theorists all agree on the importance of the form of narrative. Philosopher Peter Goldie states that "when we seek to understand our own and others' lives backwards, reflecting on earlier thoughts, feelings and emotions, and responding emotionally to them [. . .] what we think, feel and do is in narrative form."[3] Such reflections relayed by novelists and poets, whom Alexander Shand regarded as "good observers of human emotion" enabled Shand to develop his theories on emotion and character that "were clearly ahead of his time."[4]

In his work on grief, Bowlby built on the concepts put forward by Shand. Jeremy Holmes explains the link between the narrative form and self-knowledge from an attachment perspective:

> Attachment Theory has shown that self-knowledge in the form of narrative is associated with a core state characterised by secure attachment. Narrative turns experience into a story which is temporal, is coherent and has meaning. It

objectifies experience so that the sufferer becomes detached from it, by turning raw feeling into symbols. It creates out of fragmentary experience an unbroken line or thread linking the present with the past and future. Narrative gives a person a sense of ownership of their past and their life. (*JB*, 150)

Attachment therapists therefore aim to weave "a known and ownable narrative out of the unconscious attitudes, assumptions and affects which the patient brings to therapy" (*JB*, 158).

Many critics have acknowledged the psychological insight shown within Joyce's fictional narratives. In describing *Portrait* as a "picture of my spiritual self" to his friend Adolf Hoffmeister, Joyce highlighted that he called on his own narrative of his inner self in order to create Stephen Dedalus.[5] Chester G. Anderson argues that Joyce "came to understand more about the self than any other person of his time" but he adds that he chose "not to become a Freudian about it, but rather to create fictions about it."[6] Existential psychologist, Rollo May describes the creative act as an encounter between two poles, a "subjective pole," which he describes as "the conscious person in the creative act itself" and the objective pole, which he describes as "the artist's or scientist's encounter with his *world*." He goes on to explain: "World is the pattern of meaningful relations in which a person exists and in the design of which he or she participates." It is something that "is interrelated with the person at every moment. A continual dialectical process goes on between the world and self and self and world; one implies the other and neither can be understood if we omit the other."[7] Therefore, when reading a book as world "we start to apply our knowledge of the world to the book" and hence "characters come alive and we treat them as real people."[8] In other words a humanising approach is taken as attempts are made to fill in the narrative gaps, or as H. Porter Abbot refers to them, "shadow stories [. . .] the sensed possibilities of what *might* be the case, what might link the dots, however likely or unlikely," that are so much a part of Joyce's narrative technique.[9]

Kristian Smidt advocates a humanising approach by making the point that the character of Stephen Dedalus "cannot be understood without reference to the psychology of the real individual whom he portrays."[10] This view can be further supported if one takes into account Ellmann's claim that in writing *Portrait* "Joyce plunged back into his own past, mainly to justify, but also to expose it. The book's pattern, as Joyce explained to Stanislaus, is that we are what we were; our maturity is an extension of our childhood, the courageous boy is father to the arrogant young man."[11] That Joyce acknowledged our mature selves relate to our childhood resonates with Bowlby's theory and I will argue that the removal from the family home had a profound effect on the fictional character of Stephen (as well as on the young James Joyce). There is textual evidence that Joyce's portrayal of Stephen becoming a "courageous boy" at Clongowes Wood directly relates to the absence of having any one to rely on but himself. Thus, his subsequent aloofness can be read as not only being due his "arrogance" but also his fear of being hurt; that his portrayed behaviours can be connected to his insecure attachment traits and ultimately how he grieves.

Bowlby argued that an individual's past life, particularly the responsiveness of parents and carers, had consequences for future confidence, sense of self-worth, ideas about identity and ultimately expressions of grief (*AL*1: 378).[12] Holmes explains that Bowlby viewed "the neurotic patient as basing his relationship to the world on outdated assumptions, for example that he will be ignored or let down by people, or that his feelings will be dismissed or ridiculed." He adds that:

> While these are, in his [the patient's] view, fairly accurate reflections of the way the person has been treated as a child, they do not necessarily bear any relation to current reality, and can lead to poor adaptation in the form of avoidant or ambivalent relationships.
>
> Two factors are at work in maintaining these outmoded models. The first is defensive exclusion of painful emotions [. . .]. The second, related, phenomenon is the need to preserve meaning and to order incoming information from the environment in *some* kind of schema, however inappropriate. (*JB*, 170)

It must be acknowledged that no individual can be neatly fitted into a particular psychological box and, furthermore, that there are several factors that affect how one grieves. However, due to the work carried out by Bowlby and consequent studies that have built on his ideas, it is possible to make some general comments regarding expressions of grief and attachment behaviour; specifically, those individuals who form ambivalent attachments "might be more prone to chronic mourning," whereas "avoidant individuals might claim to experience fewer reactions in the face of a loss as they defend against feelings of distress, sadness or anger."[13]

With the responsiveness of parents and carers being of importance to one's sense of self, it is notable that Joyce was sent to Board at Clongowes Wood and therefore away from his parents, at the young age of six and a half. Although in *Portrait* Stephen's age is not given, critics tend to read him as around the same age when entering the college due to the prominence given to sensory inputs and evident limitations in his vocabulary and understanding. In representing Stephen from his childhood (in *Portrait*) to adulthood (in *Ulysses*) Joyce explores how life experiences and prototypical memories contribute to one's psychological being.[14] Holmes explicates prototypical memories as follows:

> Just as language is infinite but based on a finite number of simple grammatical rules, so, despite the potentially limitless capacity of memory, most people have a small number of prototypical memories that epitomise their fundamental relationship to others and to the world. These often concern important transition points in the life history—the birth of a sibling, a first day at school, and so on. They might be called 'nodal memories' in the sense that they represent a concentration of the assumptions, fantasies or working models about the self in relation to others. They may be actual or imagined. The individual usually 'reads' a particular meaning into them which acts as an organising principle around which they organise their present-day experience.[15]

Chapter 9 discusses the relationship Joyce creates between Stephen's prototypical memory of being sent to boarding school and lack of access to his mother, his sense of identity and increasing insularity, and how these factors relate to his consequent reaction to her death.

Leopold Bloom is depicted as the son of Ellen Higgins, a "half Irish and half Hungarian Jewess" and Rudolph Bloom, a Hungarian Jew who appears to have some Austrian ancestors.[16] This adds a certain complexity to how he negotiates his own cultural identity, seeing his nation as Ireland, whilst also being aware of his Jewish ancestry, although adhering to no particular faith (see *U*, 12.1430–31). However, his position as an only child of increasingly vulnerable parents is also shown to play an important role in his sense of self. The text reveals that, by the age of twenty, Bloom had lost both his parents, possibly within a week of each other, although Joyce maintains a certain vagueness in regards to how soon after his mother's death his father committed suicide. Whilst Molly comments that he poisoned himself "after her" and attributes this to him feeling lost, she gives no temporal frame (*U*, 18.162).

Joyce has Bloom recall only snippets of the suicide note, including the following: "Tomorrow will be a week that I received . . . it is no use Leopold to be . . . with your dear mother . . . that is not more to stand . . . to her . . . *das Herz . . . Gott . . . dein*" (*U*, 17.1883–85). The initial phrase could be implying that it is a week since he received news of his wife's death, although the ellipsis leaves this in doubt. If this is the case, the word "receive" points to them being apart at the time, although Joyce does not reveal how or where she died. The ambiguity created through the ellipses leaves room for alternative interpretations of the initial phrase. Bernard Benstock suggests that it "sounds ominously like a notice of financial disaster," the implication being, therefore, that his "business venture with the ownership of the Queen's Hotel in Ennis was doomed to bankruptcy."[17] Acknowledging Joyce's comment regarding his father in his *Trieste notebook*: "He is an Irish suicide," Bennett argues that Joyce drew inspiration from the letters he received from his father, which sounded almost suicidal and commented on his "miserable existence" since his wife died as well his dire financial situation.[18] Whether the actions of Bloom's father are read as being due to unbearable financial pressures, unbearable grief, or even a combination of both, what is made plain is that he took his own life on June 27, 1886, and not many years later Bloom was again to suffer a close family bereavement when his only son, Rudy, lost his short battle for survival on January 9, 1894.

On the day of Paddy Dignam's funeral, June 16, 1904, remembrances of past losses are aroused within mourners; relatives who were loved and public figures such as Parnell that were admired are recalled and acknowledged. For Leopold Bloom, memories of his father's suicide and his son's short life continually resurface, although as noted by Paul Schwaber, Bloom's mother is "almost totally missing from his thoughts."[19] With the lack of information regarding the circumstances of the passing of Bloom's mother, there is an implication that this was a less traumatic death to come to terms with in comparison to his father's suicide and the loss of his child. His father's death will be discussed in Part 4 of this book. In Part 3 I will concentrate on how Bloom has been affected by the death of his son and the impact it has had on his relationship with his wife, Molly.

Molly's internal monologue, which often flows into a stream of consciousness, has the effect of raising many questions regarding her parents. Events and memories become conflated and entwined, thus resulting in various contradictions, which Raleigh chronicles particularly well.[20] For example, Molly's various references to her father causes Raleigh to question whether he should actually be read as a Major, or rather as a Sergeant Major who has playfully elevated his status among drinking friends.[21] However, Joyce leaves no doubt that Molly should be viewed as having no memory of her biological mother ("my mother whoever she was") and also creates the impression that she has grown up without the comfort of a close female attachment figure (*U*, 18.846–87). The apparent lack of female friends in her adult life can be read as a reflection of that absence, which for her has been the norm.

Whilst Molly had various housekeepers, the only female she mentions with fondness is her friend Hester, whom she remembers as being like a cousin to her (see *U*, 18.641). When Hester left Gibraltar, Molly became acquiescent to the fact that "people were always going away," just as her mother had done before them (*U*, 18.668). Devoid of any permanent friendships, her sense of self has developed and thus been dependent upon the admiration bestowed on her by the men of the military which, from her recollections, seems to have been particularly forthcoming. But it was Bloom, whom she perceived as someone who "understood or felt what a woman is," that she chose to marry (*U*, 18.1579). Bloom, as a nonmilitary person, would not necessarily be required to continually go away. Thus, with the birth of their daughter, Milly, Molly was ostensibly able to gain her first memorable experience of complete family life. Although Joyce creates the sense of a once settled and secure home life through the recollections of Molly and Bloom, he also poignantly portrays how the death of their son, Rudy, has had a profound impact on their marital relations.

With the evidence of close family losses and memories of the dead pervading *Ulysses,* James Maddox argues that "the most terrible opiate of all" within the novel is that "the living are drugged by their allegiance to the dead," with Joyce's characters carrying their ghosts of the past about with them.[22] What Maddox appears to be noting in his description of bereavement as some kind of drug, is that the grief of the main characters appears not to be fully resolved, thereby affecting their everyday lives. Inextricably linked with this is another condition the main protagonists all share: a lack of close friends in whom they could confide and hence turn to for emotional support, especially when coming to terms with their respective bereavements. The importance of social support in dealing with grief was described by Shand and has been expanded upon since in various studies and texts.[23] Molly's comment that they get "no visitors or post ever" implies an intense psychic interdependence within the Bloom's marital relationship, with only each other for support through the vagaries of life (*U,* 18.715).[24] Yet when it comes to dealing with the loss of their son, Joyce portrays them as emotionally distant from each other, with their individual thoughts contained rather than shared. Equally, Stephen is represented as keeping himself aloof from his acquaintances and appears to have no true close friends with whom he can discuss the loss of his mother in a meaningful manner. It is with Stephen Dedalus that I will begin my detailed discussion on the main protagonists of *Ulysses* and their respective expressions of grief.

NOTES

1. Joan Hagan Arnold and Penelope Buschman Gemma, *A Child Dies: A Portrait of Family Grief* (Maryland: Aspen, 1983), 9.
2. Mark Shechner, *Joyce in Nighttown: A Psychoanalytic Inquiry into Ulysses* (Berkley: University of California Press, 1974), 18.
3. Goldie, "Narrtative and Perspective," 202.
4. Archer, *The Nature of Grief,* 14–15.
5. Adolph Hoffmeister, "Portrait of Joyce," in *Portraits of the Artist in Exile,* 132.
6. Chester G. Anderson, "Introduction" to Part III, in *The Seventh of Joyce,* ed. Bernard Benstock (Bloomington: Indiana University Press, 1982), 56.
7. May, *The Courage to Create,* 50.
8. Thomas, *James Joyce's Ulysses,* 14.

9. H. Porter Abbot, "How Do We Read What Isn't There to Be Read? Shadow Stories and Permanent Gaps," in *The Oxford Handbook of Cognitive Literary Studies*, ed. Lisa Zunshine (New York: Oxford University Press, 2015), 104.

10. Kristian Smidt, *James Joyce and the Cultic Use of Fiction*, rev ed. (Oslo: Oslo University Press, 1959), 7.

11. Ellmann, *James Joyce*, 306.

12. Also see Howe, *Attachment Across the Lifecourse*, xiii–xi; Archer, *The Nature of Grief*, 177.

13. Howe, *Attachment Across the Lifecourse*, 85.

14. As discussed in the Introduction, information available from both Joyce's manuscripts and also his stipulations regarding the publication of translations of *Portrait* and *Ulysses* invites one to read the character of Stephen across both texts.

15. Holmes, *The Search for a Secure Base*, 88.

16. Raleigh, *The Chronicle of Leopold and Molly Bloom*, 17.

17. Bernard Benstock, *Narrative Con/Texts in Ulysses* (Urbana: University of Illinois Press, 1991), 75.

18. Andrew Bennett, *Suicide Century: Literature and Suicide from James Joyce to David Foster Wallace* (Cambridge: Cambridge University Press), 2017, 103–5. With reference to: Robert Scholes and Richard M. Kain, eds, *The Workshop of Daedalus: James Joyce and the Raw Materials for a Portrait of the Artist as a Young Man*, ed. Robert Scholes and Richard M. Kain (Illinois: Northwestern University Press, 1965), 103; *Letters of James Joyce*, ed. Richard Ellmann, 3 vols. (London: Faber and Faber, 1966), 2: 221–223.

19. Paul Schwaber, *The Cast of Characters: A Reading of Ulysses* (New Haven: Yale University Press, 1999), 112.

20. Raleigh, *Chronicle*, 17–19.

21. Raleigh, *Chronicle*, 78–80.

22. James H. Maddox Jr., *Joyce's Ulysses and the Assault Upon Character* (Sussex: Harvester Press, 1978), 53.

23. See Shand, *The Foundations of Character*, 355–36; Archer, *The Nature of Grief*, 14–15. For discussions on studies of the benefits of social support see, for example: Sheila Payne, Sandra Horn, and Marilyn Relf, *Loss and Bereavement*, Health Psychology Series (Buckingham: Open University Press, 1999), 40; Colin Murray Parkes, *Love and Loss: The Roots of Grief and its Complications* (London: Routledge, 2006), 183–91.

24. Although on the day in which *Ulysses* is set, Boylan has provided both for Molly, her comment here refers to the lack of personal friendships held by her and Bloom as a couple.

Chapter Nine

Stephen Dedalus

It is of relevance that the date of June 16, 1904, is only ten days before the first anniversary of the burial of Stephen's mother, Mary Dedalus. Joyce chooses not to divulge Stephen's immediate reaction to his mother's death apart from the fact that he "wept alone" (*U,* 9.224). However, via access to Stephen's stream of consciousness, the psychological impact of his bereavement and consequent grief is elucidated as his emotional dissonance steadily manifests itself throughout the day. Of considerable significance is Stephen's remorse of conscience, or as he refers to it, his "agenbite of inwit," for refusing his mother's request to pray for her at her deathbed (*U,* 1.481). This is a good example of where Joyce referred to his own life experience for artistic inspiration but changed certain aspects for dramatic effect. His brother Stanislaus recalls how, when their dying mother had passed into a state of unconsciousness, their uncle asked them to pray for her; a request they both denied.[1] In *Ulysses*, however, Joyce makes this a singular appeal to Stephen directly from his conscious mother, thereby intensifying his emotional predicament. In her conscious, although rapidly deteriorating state, she can be read as having been all too aware of his denial and as taking the knowledge of his action with her to her grave. The conflict between Stephen's intellectual beliefs and the indoctrination of the Church with regards to his grief will be discussed in Chapter 12. The current chapter focuses on how Joyce develops Stephen's character as one that can be read as exhibiting insecure avoidant attachment traits and thus a certain emotional expression of grief.

When Stephen first appears in *Ulysses* it is on the top of the Martello Tower, where he repeatedly recalls how his dead mother "in a dream [. . .] had come to him" (*U,* 1.103–4; 1.270). Although Stephen's later vision in the "Circe" episode can be clearly related to his sense of remorse, this particular dream, with his mother "mute" yet speaking "secret words" appears to additionally gesture toward an earlier trauma depicted in *Portrait*: that of being parted from his mother at a young age (*U,* 1.105; 1.272).

The Stephen of *Portrait* has been described as "a fictionally modified version of the author's younger self in experiential interaction with the world."[2] Ellmann makes a very relevant comment regarding the young James Joyce: "That a boy of his age, suddenly removed from his family, could have been untroubled is hardly conceivable."[3] Attachment theorists would be in agreement with Ellmann since research has shown that insecurely attached "avoidant subjects were more likely than others to report having experienced a lengthy period of separation from their mothers during childhood."[4] Joyce's portrayal of his "fictionally modified" self, at the time of being sent away to board at Clongowes Wood College, is one of a young child with an inquisitive mind, particularly with regard to language. That Stephen's dream features his mother silently speaking "secret words" can be interpreted as a reflection of his prototypical memories and the emotional effect of her inability to communicate to him both words of comfort and the meanings of words he perceived the other schoolboys as knowing, yet were undisclosed to him, as he tried to deal with the emotional difficulties of school life (see "Emotional Traumas in an Alien Landscape" section below) (*U,* 1.272).

Bowlby's one time colleague, Mary Ainsworth notes that Bowlby disbelieved "early infant-mother interaction sets the pattern of an infant attachment for all time; he reported evidence that events occurring throughout childhood may have a profound effect on the anxiety versus security of relationships experienced with attachment figures."[5] Joyce's representation of Stephen's time at Clongowes Wood shows that if he had previously held a belief in the reliability and helpfulness of others, which Bowlby has since argued was so important in the ability to form secure attachments, this working model appears to have been updated to one where others cannot be relied upon to give support or act justly; that they will let him down (*AL*1:378). His lack of perceived security is of consequence when considering how Joyce portrays Stephen's later relationship with his mother and other family members, as well as the formation of future affectional bonds. One therefore needs to look initially to the earlier novel of *Portrait* and how Joyce develops Stephens sense of self, as this is fundamental to the understanding of how he subsequently portrays Stephen's later reaction to his mother's death in *Ulysses.*

EMOTIONAL TRAUMAS IN AN ALIEN LANDSCAPE: STEPHEN'S SEPARATION FROM HIS MOTHER AND THE CONSEQUENT NEED FOR SELF-RELIANCE

In *Portrait* the "small and weak" Stephen is sent away to board at Clongowes Wood for approximately one year although, as Bruce Bradley S. J. points out, Joyce himself was actually there for over three years (*P,* 4).[6] Joyce's representation of Stephen when he initially joins the college is one of a child who views his world in mainly sensory terms of smells, bodily sensations and visual cues; his short, simple sentences demonstrating that, despite his precocity, his understanding of language is still in its infancy, as is his sense of self in relation to others. Patrick Hogan, in his discussion of desire, attachment and dependency in relation to romantic spaces, proposes that "our sense of both time and space is structured by feeling."[7] Following this argument, spaces will therefore seem very large if physically away from those we love and similarly the time until we are again reunited with them will seem interminably long. Hogan argues that for a child space can be thought of more simply as "'with Mom' and . . . everything else," thereby indicating the close association between attachment, space and separation anxiety.[8] Hence, for Stephen (and for the young Joyce himself), any landscape without his mother, including Clongowes Wood, would be seen as "alien."[9]

Joyce demonstrates Stephen's perception of the vastness of the landscape and his smallness within it by virtue of his writing on the geography flyleaf: "*Stephen Dedalus / Class of Elements / Clongowes Wood College / Sallins / County Kildaire / Ireland / Europe / The World / The Universe*" (*P,* 12). Contemplating everything "big"—the universe, God, even the boys in trigonometry with "big voices and big boots"—serves only to reinforce his sense of being "small and weak" (*P,* 14), whilst the unattainable goal of being "at home" with "his head on his mother's lap" transmutes into sadness (*P,* 9). It is significant when considering Stephen's behavioural traits, that he is portrayed as having a propensity to keep his true feelings to himself and his emotions under control. In this instance, although hankering for the comfort of his mother's lap, he combats his urge to cry by taking comfort in the sensory world he knows and the auditory effects of opening and closing "the flaps of his ears" (*P,* 10).

Represented as unsure of himself in formal surroundings and among unfamiliar people, Stephen's yearning for home is further reinforced by the description of the paper he has stuck inside his desk lid which has the number of the remaining days until the Christmas vacation written on it; a number he changes in a daily ritual. Joyce gives prominence to the emotional impact that Stephen's experiences at the college will have on him by representing his time there through the recollection of three events that were both confusing and hurtful to him. Since these situations provide Stephen with internal working models (or in cognitive terms schema), which are shown to affect his relation to the external world, it is worth taking time to consider each of them.

Firstly, the narrator relates the psychological bullying that Wells subjects Stephen to. Whilst Stephen comments how previously Wells had been "mean" to him by pushing him into the "cold slime of the ditch," it is the probing question as to whether he kisses his mother before going to bed, followed by the public ridicule he experiences, that is initially shown to cause him greater emotional distress (*P*, 11). Deriding Stephen, regardless of whether he answers the question in the positive or negative, Joyce compels the reader to consider whether there is a certain age where one should desist in engaging in such demonstrative acts of affection. Of course, there is no correct answer, but Stephen believes that there must be and what is more that "Wells must know" (*P*, 11). The anxiety he feels when having his private world held up for public ridicule is shown to translate into physiological signifiers, with his "whole body" becoming "hot and confused in a moment" (*P*, 11). However, notably, rather than reveal his inner turmoil to his peers Stephen is shown to choose to laugh at himself along with them, again containing his true feelings as an apparent form of defence.

As Joyce allies Stephen's negotiation of his sense of self with his negotiation of language, it is evident that he needs to acquire the cognitive capabilities to complement his sensory understanding of the world. Endeavouring to understand why a particular word is used ("His mother put her lips on his cheek; [. . .] they made a tiny little noise: kiss") and the significance of what it is denoting ("Why did people do that with their two faces?") Stephen finds himself unequipped to deal with such questions (*P,* 11–12). Feeling that his understanding of language and subjects such as politics are inadequate contributes to his sense of being "small and weak" and his exasperation is described as being such that it "pained him" (*P*, 14).

This description of Stephen's frustration in relation to his lack of knowledge, leading to a growing sense of difference from those around him, creates the image of a child in need of maternal reassurance. Hence the narrator relates Stephen's view of himself as "sick in his heart if you could be sick in that place" (*P*, 10). Here Stephen is thinking of his heart on a symbolic level, as a signifier of love and affection and registering the emotional upset he feels without his main attachment figure to turn to. Mark Shechner notes that Joyce's "public stance toward psychoanalysis was never friendly," oscillating as it did "between indifference and downright hostility" and here one has to acknowledge Joyce's adroit use of phraseology.[10] His use of the term "sick" negates any suggestion of an Oedipal complex in a way that, for example, the term "broken hearted" would not. Instead the implication is that this is a person who is ailing and is consciously aware for his need of responsive attention or, in terms of attachment, with a need for emotional support and security.

Whilst Stephen's mother remains absent and hence "mute" there is no one to relieve him of his pain. However, the capability of his mother to provide support to him, even if she were close by, has inevitably been brought into question since his last memory of her, before leaving him at the college, was when she was crying. To realise the vulnerability of the person one relies on can prove to be disconcerting, especially to a child. Indeed, the narrator describes Stephen's face as "terrorstricken" when Mr. Casey "sobbed loudly and bitterly" and "his father's eyes were full of tears" following their exchanges with Dante at Christmas (*P*, 39). That Stephen thinks of his mother as "not so nice" when she cries makes explicit his propensity to view her differently in such situations (*P*, 5). Marguerite Harkness notes that with the young Stephen "only two elements can be compared at any one time," and that *Portrait* "forces us to interact with such dualism, such juvenile distinctions. It seems to assume that we will draw the inferences that permit us to 'make sense' of the world by weaving our own constructs of the word into those overtly presented in the novel, adding our own to the voices of the novel."[11]

When interpreting and making sense of Stephen's views of his mother crying, if we consider his thoughts with the synonym of "nice," "good": "She was a nice [good] mother but she was not so nice [good] when she cried" (*P*, 5) it takes us to the realm of Freud with "good" and "bad object" and consequently to Attachment Theory. As discussed in Chapter 1, "good" and "bad object" can be equated with "a working model of an attachment figures who is conceived as accessible" and "helpful" or one that provides "uncertain accessibility" and helpfulness respectfully (*MB*, 140). With Stephen's lack of proximity to his main attachment figure and the reliability of any support she would be able to provide in question, one can read Joyce as presenting the reader with a portrait of a lonely and increasingly insecure child.

Although throughout his time at Clongowes Wood Stephen is portrayed as a child who has a limited knowledge of self, he also appears to exhibit certain awareness that concealment of weakness can avoid further hurt. The hiding of his emotions is seemingly prudent, but whether this should be viewed as an entirely conscious decision is difficult to ascertain. Yet his agreement with Fleming that whatever is wrong "will go away," is confirmed without any hesitancy, an almost intuitive response, despite his state of anxiety at that moment in time (*P*, 10). However, Joyce leaves no doubt that, as Stephen matures, his emotional concealment has developed into a desired and hence fostered psychological state. For example, during his attendance at a party long after leaving Clongowes Wood, the narrator comments that a "silent watchful manner had grown upon him" and tells of his desire to withdraw "into a snug corner of the room" where he could "taste the joy of his loneliness" (*P*, 71). This description of his behaviour appears to denote that his emotional defence mechanisms have developed such that he has reached a state of mind where maintaining his distance from others is preferable and even pleasurable.

At Clongowes Wood, however, Joyce shows that what Stephen essentially craved was the reassuring comfort of his family being readily accessible to him. The second traumatic event he suffers there, his illness and hence time in the infirmary as a consequence of being pushed into the ditch by Wells, is intensified on a psychological level by his perceived physical and emotional remoteness from them. With Attachment Theory being "in essence a *spatial* theory," it is possible read their absence ("How far away they were!") as exacerbating his anxiety (*P,* 21).[12] Stephen's angst is such that he is shown to be in fear that he may not live to see his mother again. Robert Spoo comments that the rhyme regarding Wolsey's death that Stephen recalls "yields a child's overview of illness and death—plants, animals, humans—all cobbled together from mnemonic jingles in grammar."[13] However, more importantly for a child who is away from his attachment figure, Spoo also argues that it hints "at an unarticulated worry: if canker kills plants and cancer animals, what did Wolsey die of, and will Stephen, too, be felled by some mysterious ailment?"[14]

Unwell, within an alien landscape and with such possible latent worries, Joyce shows how severe anxiety gives primacy to the imagination, as Stephen contemplates his own death. His imagined demise and funeral clearly signify his fear, but this fictitious scenario is also shown to transmute into a cathartic act of revenge, with the sorrow and hence evident guilt of Wells being compounded by his ostracisation: "no fellow would look at him" (*P*, 22). Ironically this could be read as a foreshadowing of Stephen's own situation in *Ulysses* as one can view him as effectively becoming a version of the imagined Wells following the death of his mother, not only through his own feelings of guilt but also through the condemnation by his relatives: "The aunt thinks you killed your mother [. . .] That's why she won't let me have anything to do with you" (*U*, 1.88–89).

Of further significance is the association Stephen makes with intelligence when thinking about the death of animals, as compared to the death of humans: "But the minds of rats could not understand trigonometry. When they were dead they lay on their sides. Their coats dried then. They were only dead things" (*P,* 20). Stephen's thought association implies that, being devoid of intellectual capabilities, death is final for the rat; it is just a dead thing. Yet in comparison, his own death, imagined partly through a rhyme, results in his soul being carried away by angels. Although presented as random and childish thoughts of death, they prefigure the offence taken by Stephen as young man to Mulligan's comment that his mother was *"beastly dead"* (*U,* 1.198–99).

As Stephen matures, so too do his thoughts of human capabilities, specifically the artist, such that he begins to view the artist not only as intelligent but also, as evidenced by his conversation with Lynch, as "like the God of the creation" (*P*, 233). With his conversation with Lynch in mind and his portrayal in *Ulysses* as someone who has built his self-image on his vocation as an artist, William Schutte notes how Stephen is depicted as viewing "[a]esthetic and material creation [as] merely different manifestations of the same mystical process."[15] This is a concept Joyce continued to represent throughout his work to *Finnegans Wake*: "He lifts the lifewand and the dumb speak" (*FW*, 195.5). Schutte goes on to argue that "if man *is* merely a highly developed beast, then the life of the individual, as Stephen sees it, has no meaning at all" thus undermining his "heroic vision of himself" as "a priest of the eternal imagination."[16] Put simply, Mulligan's comment has the potential to destroy the tenet to which Stephen has dedicated himself and should such dissolution occur, he would again be as the young Stephen of Clongowes Wood, without a sense of self in relation to the external world.

The final traumatic event that Joyce uses to portray Stephen's time at Clongowes Wood is the pandybat episode where Farther Arnall fails to stop Stephen from being punished for "not writing [his] theme" although he had told him "not to study" until his new glasses arrived (*P*, 58). That the prefect of studies is shown to take great pleasure in meting out the chastisement illustrates that Stephen's experience of the college was one in which he not only had little protection from bullying peers and frightening illnesses, but also from some of the priests.

Prior to the pandybat incident taking place, Stephen had already been made aware of the trepidation of his fellows with regards to corporal punishment, although at that point he had no reason to suspect he would be a participant in such an event. Standing among the group of fellows as they discussed the possible transgression committed by some pupils (had they drank the alter wine or were they caught "smugging in the square"?), Stephen is shown to have no comprehension of words such as "smugging" and finds himself again feeling "weak" and "afraid to speak" (*P*, 40–42). However, still highly reliant on sensual inputs, he is aware of the fear within the laughter of the fellows when discussing corporal punishment. The anxiety the boys convey to Stephen evoke a physical response within him, much as the anxiety caused by the bullying he received from Wells had done, but on this occasion he feels "shivery" and "cold" as he contemplates the pain that could be inflicted (*P*, 45).

Edward Boyd Barrett, who attended Clongowes Wood not long after Joyce and who for a time was a Jesuit priest himself, explains how sadism and masochism were "common in the Order" with some Jesuits lashing boys "in a state of passionate excitement."[17] Joyce had obviously become aware of sexual tensions among the priests as he wrote in his Trieste notebook that the Jesuits "are erotically preoccupied."[18] If corporal punishment was used as a form of sexual release, as Barrett claims, one can see why Joyce chose to represent a transgression committed by a few boys being translated into an excuse to punish others. The prefect of studies is portrayed as roaming the college looking for someone to chastise, specifically entering the classroom to see if "any boys want flogging," his heightened state of agitation possibly signifying his state of arousal and excitement (*P*, 49). The tension his entrance creates—the "quick whisper" followed by "an instant silence"—signifies the cognisance of most of the boys as to what could be expected (*P*, 49). However, just as Stephen is shown to be too young to understand the implied sexual actions of the boys, he is also shown to be too young to interpret any sadistic tendencies of the prefect of studies and is therefore left bewildered by the "unjust and cruel and unfair" treatment he received at the hands of Father Dolan, the humiliation of which he suffers "time after time in memory" (*P*, 54). For Stephen this provides another reason to be distrustful of others.

The corporal punishment received by Stephen is shown to become a turning point for him in terms of his self-reliance. With his sense of injustice enraged, he summons the courage to complain to the rector. Although the subsequent success of his protest leaves him feeling "happy and free" from the prospect of further punishment from Father Dolan, he is represented as being fearfully aware that when making his protest he was very much alone (*P*, 60). Joyce makes the solitude of Stephen's action evident by having a multitude of eyes follow him. Leaving the refectory he knew "without turning his head to look, that all the fellows were looking after him"; as he walked down the corridor to the rector's room he noticed all the portraits "looking down on him silently" and the old servant "looked after him" as he went toward the rector's door (*P*, 57).

Taking a Freudian stance, Sheldon Brivic has argued that Stephen's action is "an assertion of his masculinity" and as such Joyce's repeated description of the "dark narrow corridor" he walks down can be viewed as representing "an entrance into the female."[19] However, at such a young age and his action being that of protest, one could alternatively interpret the repeated use of this image of darkness and confined space as denoting the oppression that Stephen feels after being unfairly punished. In addition to carrying the weight of being "called a schemer before the class," most significantly he carries with him the cruel knowledge that, although Father Arnall knew the truth about his glasses, he failed to support him and protect him from punishment (*P*, 53). Alone in an alien landscape, without a figure who could provide a sense of security and yet seemingly watched by so many people, it is therefore unsurprising that, in the absence of any certainty that those in authority will behave justly, "his heart jumped when he heard a muffled voice say:—Come in!" (*P*, 58).

Reading Joyce in the light of Attachment Theory, one can see that, through his representation of Stephen's experiences at Clongowes Wood, he has provided an illustration of a prototypical memory acquired by Stephen; that people can behave unjustly and in such circumstances there is no guarantee that those to whom he would naturally turn for support would actually be there for him. Joyce described his youth as "painful and violent" and the portrayal of Stephen's teenage years in *Portrait* and also in his young adult life in *Ulysses* can be read as an illustration that the painful experiences of Clongowes Wood are retained in Stephen's schematic memory, thus affecting his relationship with his mother and also future relationships.[20]

In *Portrait* Joyce allows more information to emerge with regards to Stephen's isolation and psychological well-being when, now older and travelling on the train with his father, memories of his childhood resurface:

> Nothing moved him or spoke to him from the real world unless he heard in it an echo of the infuriated cries within him.
> [. . .]
> He had not died [in the infirmary] but he had faded out like a film in the sun. He had been lost or had wandered out of existence for he no longer existed. How strange to think of him passing out of existence in such a way, not by death but by fading out in the sun or by being lost and forgotten somewhere. (*P,* 98–99)

Stephen's lack of attachment figure to give comfort and reassurance whilst in the infirmary had a profound effect. Without his mother's presence and with his anxiety such that he was in a state of acute despair, it is unsurprising that he saw himself as emotionally "lost" and "forgotten" by her. Thinking of himself here in the third person represents not only a certain distancing of Stephen from his younger self, but also an understanding that when he entered Clongowes Wood he was psychologically very different to when he departed it and in that respect the young boy who said goodbye to his crying mother "no longer existed." Thus, the "infuriated cries within" can be interpreted as a result of his need for affection which he is unable to express; a consequence of having wrapped himself in a self-reliant world in order to avoid further hurt. Yet anything that echoes those cries has the ability to move him, since their resonance with his engrained memories causes his anguish to resurface.

In *Ulysses*, one sees the entrenched memory of the pandybat episode resurface in "Circe." Stephen has difficulty in lighting a cigarette, seemingly unable to judge the distance between the cigarette end and the match as he had broken his glasses the day before. With the brief thought "Sixteen years ago" his mind appears to be returning to his time at Clongowes Wood (*U,* 15.3629). When soon after he "*extends his hand*" to the prostitute, Zoe, she must turn it palm upwards as she offers to "read" his hand (*U,* 15.3469–56). This action, combined with the sound of Lynch slapping Kitty's behind causes the drama of the unjust treatment by Father Dolan and the sympathetic hearing Stephen received from Father Conmee to be replayed in his mind, albeit in a conflated manner:

> FATHER DOLAN
> Any boy want flogging? Broke his glasses? Lazy idle little schemer. See it in your eye.
> *Mild, benign, rectorial, reproving, the head of Don John Conmee rises from the pianola coffin)*
> DON JOHN CONMEE
> Now, father Dolan! Now. I'm sure that Stephen is a very good little boy! (*U*, 15.3670–76)

As Zoe examines Stephen's palm he murmurs: "Continue. Lie. Hold me. Caress" (*U*, 15.3680). The need he felt for affection and protection as a child whilst at Clongowes, a need he still continues to have, is made evident. His inebriated state allows his emotional anxieties, including his past hurts of childhood, to come to the fore; his self-containment and aloofness have momentarily lapsed.

PORTRAIT OF AN AVOIDANT INDIVIDUAL

With Stephen's sense of isolation, his general containment of emotion and vulnerability, Joyce has depicted what attachment theorists would term the development of an insecure avoidant personality, where others are seen as potentially hurtful but "the self is modelled as strong" and "in control."[21] Hence, as noted at the beginning of this section, when Stephen did weep for his mother's passing, it was in private, thus maintaining his outward persona of one who is emotionally strong. A letter written by W. B. Yeats to Lady Gregory again evidences how Joyce was calling on his own narrative of his inner self when creating Stephen: "I saw Joyce in Dublin; he said his mother was still alive and it was uncertain whether she would die or not. He added "but these things really don't matter."[22] This seemingly dismissive response to the potential death of his mother illustrates how Joyce regulated any display of emotion to give the impression of being "strong" and "in control."

Before going on to discuss the emotional impact of the death of Stephen's mother, it is worth considering how, reading with a knowledge of Attachment Theory, one can discern textual evidence for reading Stephen as exhibiting avoidant traits and how his perceived lack of support from his mother has affected his attachment to her, which in turn has influenced his grief response.

When at Belvedere College, where Joyce studied following his removal from Clongowes Wood due to lack of funds, he "won honour for himself and the college" for his "English composition."[23] In *Portrait* Joyce depicts Stephen similarly winning a prize through his academic achievements, which leads to a "swift season of merrymaking" with his family, by virtue of the money received (*P*, 104). The portrayal of Stephen's generosity and the pleasure he gains from this also provides an example of what Jeremy Holmes and David Howe later argued, respectively: that an avoidant individual, in order to be in control and maintain self-esteem, will keep intimacy at bay and at most "can only feel good about himself when giving to others" and for such individuals to be "seen as competent and successful by other people feels safer than being intimate and open."[24] When Stephen's money eventually runs out Joyce reveals the motivational element to his generosity via an epiphanic moment which shows that Stephen, in his relaxed and relatively affluent state, had allowed his defence mechanisms to lapse as he attempted to get close to his family again only to find an unbridgeable gulf:

> He saw clearly [. . .] his own futile isolation. He had not gone one step nearer the lives he had sought to approach nor bridged the restless shame and rancour that divided him from mother and brother and sister. He felt that he was hardly of the one blood with them but stood to them rather in the mystical kinship of fosterage, fosterchild and fosterbrother. (*P,* 105)[25]

In his "Introduction" to the draft of *Portrait*, *Stephen Hero,* Theodore Spencer comments that "even when the same incidents are mentioned" the text of *Stephen Hero* "treats them in a different manner—a more direct and dramatic manner—than that used in the *Portrait.*"[26] For this particular incident the text of *Stephen Hero* makes explicit how all parties have contributed to his emotional isolation: "She was called his sister and his mother was called his mother but there had never been any proof of that relation offered him in their emotional attitude towards him, or any recognition of it permitted in his emotional attitude towards them" (*SH,* 131). Whilst Stephen clearly perceives that he has been rejected on an emotional level by his family, for his part, the use of the term "permitted" is significant. It implies that he had not *allowed* himself to get emotionally close to them, at least for some time.

Dettmar expresses his own interpretation of such a distance between Stephen and his mother stating that "Stephen seems not to have been especially close to his mother."[27] A simple yet telling example of the emotional distance between them is evident in *Portrait* when Joyce relates how financial difficulties had resulted in the relocation of the family and how during the process of moving Stephen "sat with his redeyed mother" in the "railway carriage" (*P*, 68). Quite often what Joyce does not say is very revealing and here there is no mention of him trying to comfort her, or of feeling sorry for her, or any other emotion toward her; merely that he sat next to her in the train looking out of the window.

Indubitably it is possible to read the perceived distance from his family from a Freudian perspective. Patrick Parrinder reads Stephen's epiphanic moment in *Portrait* as "mentally disowning his family" and thus reflecting the psychic manifestation that Freud termed the "family romance"—a need to replace one's parents with those, usually, of better standing.[28] However, if viewed from an attachment perspective, an alternative explanation becomes evident. David Howe explains that for avoidant individuals, whilst "the lid is normally kept on too much emotional display, it is during moments when control is in danger of being lost that aggressive behaviour is most likely to surface."[29] Although Stephen is not described as acting aggressively he nevertheless reports a feeling of "rancour," dividing him from his mother and siblings. Through Stephen's admittance that he had "sought to approach" their "lives" Joyce creates the impression that Stephen, in a happier and perhaps more confident state, had tried to relinquish his fear of rejection and had permitted himself an attempt to regain some emotional stability and *rebuild* the diminished affectional bonds, rather than sever them. However, he finds he has been unable to restore what has long since faded.

Furthermore if, as Parrinder's reading would suggest, Stephen's emotional response can be associated with his family's economic decline, his anger would have been aimed toward his father. However, as it is directed toward his mother and siblings, his resentment can be read in light of their emotional distance. In Chapter 3 I discussed how readers make "meaningful connections" and here, piecing together the emotional traumas of Clongowes and the consequent development of Stephen's insecure attachment traits it is possible interpret his anger as a consequence of the imposed distance, both physical and emotional, from his mother when sent away, whilst his siblings remained in her protective proximity. Critics reading this from a Freudian standpoint may argue that this interpretation would indicate that Stephen is subject to Oedipal fantasies, but given the presentation of Stephen's avoidant traits—his self-reliance and, "his habit of psychological withdrawal"—it is possible to read this from an attachment perspective.[30]

Although both Freudian and attachment theories focus on the psychology of parent/child relationships, attachment theorists consider how certain types of parenting and separations from an attachment figure can produce certain internal working models. Having been removed from his family home at a young age to board at Clongowes Wood, although Stephen is shown to recognise that what had been denied to the younger children "had been given freely to him, the eldest" he nevertheless suffered psychologically for his privileged education (*P,* 176). Not only had he been troubled by "[t]he coming of September" knowing that he was to be sent away, but when actually at college, he had been forced to contemplate the possibility of his own death in an alien landscape (*P,* 66). Moreover, as the Stephen that left to go to college "no longer existed" he was also predestined to ostensibly return home a stranger (*P*, 99). Therefore, what Joyce has brought into focus with Stephen's epiphanic moment is not that his psychosexual development was arrested at a certain stage, but rather the propensity for physical abandonment to cognitively transmute into emotional abandonment and, having become detached, how difficult it is to regain the affectional bonds that previously existed. This could be seen as a contributing factor as to why he is represented as only offering his sister, Dilly, sympathy when coming face to face with her in the street in the "Wandering Rocks" episode of *Ulysses*, despite having money in his pocket (see *U*, 10.862–80). The portrayal of this meeting again reinforces Stephen's sense of filial distance and his realisation that no amount of money will bring him nearer to Dilly, despite the fact that he can see so much of himself in her. Instead, she could drown him, not only in the paralysis of everyday life, but also in a sea of emotion, resurrecting the "restless shame and rancour" the narrator of *Portrait* described him as feeling (*P*, 105).

Although thus far I have argued that Stephen's avoidant traits are a result of his prototypical memories of Clongowes Wood and the absence of his mother, there is also textual evidence to suggest that Stephen may have had an insecure attachment relationship with his father, if not originally with his mother, as it is possible to have different attachment strategies with different parents.[31] Suzette Henke has noted the divergence in how Stephen's thoughts are represented depending on whether he is contemplating the house of his father or the home of his mother: " 'He longed to be at home with his head on his mother's lap' (*P*, 9) but he differentiates between this mental sanctuary and "his father's house," "cold and dark under the seawall" (*P*, 14–15).[32] The disparity in Stephen's thought when he first arrives at Clongowes Wood tacitly implies two things that are not mutually exclusive: firstly that when Stephen joined the college there was already a certain emotional distance between himself and his father. Secondly, recalling how Stephen laughed at himself along with Wells and the other boys, he seemed to know how to hide his emotion, which could be viewed as reflecting insecure attachment traits. Later, at Belevdere, even the mention of his father by Heron "put his calm to rout in a moment," highlighting the distance and discomfort between father and son (*P*, 80).

Being sent away from home at such a young age, which in a patriarchal society would have been the decision of his father, suggests at the very least that his father viewed him as old enough to no longer require the presence of paternal figures on a daily basis when he delivered him to the college. However, the anxiety Stephen experiences whilst boarding there demonstrates that such a view was erroneous. Reading with a knowledge of Attachment Theory it is possible to surmise that any avoidant behavioural traits that had previously developed before entering Clongowes were exacerbated and gradually became the norm as he began to lose any sense of the reliability and helpfulness of others and updated his internal working model of his mother who had previously been present for him as his protector and comforter; his secure base.

Toward the end of *Portrait* Stephen's proclivity for isolation is commented on by his friend, Davin: "—You're a terrible man, Stevie, said Davin, taking the short pipe from his mouth. Always alone" (*P,* 218). Although removed from *Portrait*, Stephen's own sense of isolation and his self-dependency are reinforced in *Stephen Hero* when he tells Emma, (the girl with whom he wishes to unite his body and who in *Portrait* becomes the more abstract E—C—) "I live such a strange life—without help or sympathy from anyone" (*SH,* 202). In *Portrait*, Joyce uses his discussion with Cranly, which takes on the form of a confession, to indicate the contributing factors to his remoteness. The answers to Cranly's probing questions regarding Stephen's mother provide a comparison to his conversation with Wells, although Cranly's intent is not to ridicule. Just as Wells made him contemplate the word "kiss," he is now forced by Cranly to consider what is meant by the word "love." Seeing himself in terms of his creative ability and vocation as an artist, Stephen is now supremely confident in his use of language, yet his answer is found wanting. In describing how he "tried to love God," Stephen relates his attempt to "unite his will" with that of God rather than, as one would expect based on theological teachings of an all loving father figure, how he developed an emotional relationship with him (*P,* 261).

Lee Kirkpatrick argues that religion can be seen in terms of attachment by referring to the five criteria that Mary Ainsworth (once a member of Bowlby's research team) claimed characterised an attachment relationship: "(1) the attached person seeks proximity to the caregiver, particularly when frightened or alarmed; (2) the caregiver provides care and protection (the haven of safety function) as well as (3) a sense of security (the secure base function); (4) the threat of separation causes anxiety of the attached person; and (5) loss of the attachment figure would cause grief in the attached person."[33] Using Ainsworth's criteria, Stephen's attempted combining of wills cannot be interpreted as an affectional bond. With the work of Oatley in mind (see Introduction to Part 2), at best it could be viewed as trying to create a joint goal, the failure or success of which would create an emotional response. Stephen's response to Cranly therefore serves to reinforce how he has effectively deactivated his emotions and hence attachment responses.

Stephen's emotional distance from his family, coupled with his disbelief in the religious institution on which his mother heavily relies and which he perceives as restrictive in terms of creativity, enables him to leave his family and country and put to one side his religious teachings. Jean Paul Riquelme argues that: "Rather than being captive to the confessional" Stephen is taking "important steps towards achieving greater freedom."[34] Yet Stephen's comment to Cranly that he is not afraid "to make a mistake, even a great mistake, a lifelong mistake and perhaps as long as eternity too" demonstrates his continued awareness of the words of the priest at the retreat who warned: "In Hell all laws are overturned: there is no thought of family or country, of ties, of relationships" (*P,* 269; 131). Ironically, he is unable to leave his religious indoctrination as far behind as he thinks, particularly his propensity to introspection; something which Joyce develops as being of major psychological significance in *Ulysses* with regards to negotiation of his bereavement (see Chapter 12).

The loss of an attachment figure can create disorder and chaos in both the internal and external life of the bereaved individual, instantaneously shattering any perception of stability and replacing it with a feeling of vulnerability. Overcoming the psychic disorganisation caused by one's grief is a long process and hence, when Stephen emerges on the top of the Martello Tower in *Ulysses*, it is as a young man who has, as yet, been unable to come to terms with the loss of his mother and whose pursuit of becoming an artist on foreign soil has been thrown into disarray.

As Mulligan links arms with his sleepy companion to walk around the tower, Stephen's thought: "Cranly's arm. His arm," is a phrase that imparts much but needs further reflection at a later point in the novel (*U,* 1.159). Often it is when Joyce is at his most laconic that most information is imparted, particularly in terms of emotion and equally as often one finds the full significance of a phrase or thought as the novel progresses. This particular thought provides a good example of Joyce's technique. The reference to Cranly provides an intertextual link to *Portrait* and the detached dismissiveness of this thought succinctly signifies that the Stephen of *Ulysses* is still to be read as self-contained and hence still affected by his childhood memories. Demonstrating his continued emotional distance from those who have shown friendship toward him, it is therefore unsurprising that, just as he parted company with Cranly, he will soon part from Mulligan. Whilst Mulligan has chastised Stephen for refusing to pray at his mother's deathbed, arguably this is not the major cause of his distancing. Reading from a Jungian perspective, Jean Kimball interprets Stephen's consideration of separating from Mulligan as part of the individuation process and the "necessary dissolution of the Persona."[35] However, taking into account Stephen's avoidant traits his estrangement can be read as a reflection of the perceived need for self-reliance due to mistrust of others. Support for this interpretation comes from when the thought occurs to him again on Sandymount Strand, although this time it is expressed slightly differently: "His arm: Cranly's arm" (*U,* 3.451). The punctuation has the effect of conflating Mulligan and Cranly, thereby implying that to Stephen it is of little relevance whose arm it is because his internal working models will not allow him to trust either of them to be there for him.[36] This is something that Mulligan is clearly becoming aware of, hence his question: "Why don't you trust me anymore?" (*U*, 1.161).

Jonathan Culpeper, in his discussion of the interpretation of fictional characters, has argued that textual factors and cognitive factors (the reader's prior knowledge) help to provide a "particular impression of a character" and I have shown how knowledge of Attachment Theory provides a particular reading of Stephen.[37] Joyce can be said to have created a character, who if read in terms of his depicted attachment behaviours, seems unable to change, as Stephen's constant aloofness can be viewed as self-perpetuating. Unable to get close enough to anyone to experience behaviours that would disconfirm his view (based on past experience) that others will always let you down, he is unable to update his internal working models.[38]

The self-reliant world in which Joyce has trapped his protagonist offers an explanation of the comment he made to Frank Budgen regarding his composition of *Ulysses*, stating his interest in Stephen had lessened because he had "a shape that can't be changed."[39] It is therefore seen as entirely within character when, later in the day, Stephen rejects Bloom's offer of friendship. Brian Cosgrove, in comparing what he sees as the more "protean" character of Bloom in comparison to Stephen, although not discussing Stephen in terms of attachment, picks up on this trait:

> As the first three episodes in *Ulysses* suggest, Stephen in his immaturity, and reeling under the impact of feelings he cannot surmount, is involved in the business of establishing a stable centre of self; too preoccupied, it seems, to have anything left over for the kind of easygoing extraversion toward the world and society in which a mature Bloom can so readily though cautiously indulge.[40]

The only way Stephen feels he can maintain "a stable centre of self" is by being self-reliant, untrusting and therefore aloof. He cannot risk having this fragile equilibrium damaged by trusting in others, only to be let down.

THE EMOTIONAL IMPACT OF BEREAVEMENT: STEPHEN'S AVOIDANT TRAITS EXPRESSED IN HIS GRIEF

Bowlby argued that those who had been brought up in a family where "the attachment behaviour of a child is regarded unsympathetically as something to be grown out of as quickly as possible" tended to "stifle" their grief (*MB*, 117–18). That Stephen was forced to abandon certain of his attachment behaviours by virtue of his removal from his parents and has become emotionally contained, or in Bowlby's terms, "avoidant," is therefore of major importance when considering Stephen's grief reaction in relation to his past hurts of childhood.

Mark Shechner describes Stephen's mourning as "a constitutional melancholy disguised as fresh grief," but it is also possible to interpret Stephen's behaviour as reflecting an emotional response to his bereavement that hitherto had remained repressed and is hence manifesting itself for the first time.[41] As I argued in my discussion of "Eveline" (see Chapter 7), Joyce appeared to reflect what Bowlby had later observed in his work: that containment of emotion and avoidance of conscious grieving may lead to a strong emotional response triggered by certain events (*AL3*: 158–59). With June 16 being very close to when May Dedalus was buried, the approaching anniversary could be seen as such a trigger, exacerbating Stephen's feelings of grief and remorse and hence his waking visions of her. Indeed, critics have commented on the importance of the forthcoming date in terms of increasing his grief.[42] Joyce reflects Stephen's emotional response by continually evoking May Dedalus's presence, providing an apparent link to her in almost every episode in which he appears. This is achieved through Stephen's thoughts, through his visions and through the observation of others. For example, as those gathered at the hospital waiting for news that Mrs Purefoy had given birth, notice "how hard it was for him to be reminded of his [. . .] recent loss" (*U*, 14.1124–25).

The nineteenth-century Catholic Church "insisted the individuality of each soul is an essential presupposition of personal immortality" and it seemed that Joyce had not totally closed his mind to the existence of the soul, since after the death of his mother, he is known to have consulted "the newly published book by Frederic Myers" as soon as it became available in the library in 1903.[43] Entitled *Human Personality and Its survival of Bodily Death,* it is a philosophical report that tries to prove scientifically the possibility of the survival of the human soul independent of the human body and that humans can be inhabited by different spirits who utilise the bodies of the living in order to communicate with other living persons.[44] Yet what Joyce portrays Stephen as seeing in nighttown is not his mother's soul as a spiritual manifestation but rather an hallucination or vision; that is, something that he thinks he is seeing but is not actually there; a visual expression of his "agenbite of inwit" (*U*, 1.481). If one were to read the appearance of May Dedalus as a true manifestation it would make Stephen an object of an actual haunting rather than being haunted psychologically by his own remorse and guilt.

Whilst there is a clear illustration of the continued influence of the dead on the living, the primacy given to Stephen's inner being throughout his portrayal in *Ulysses* suggests that such influence should be seen in cognitive terms. Moreover, as often happens in dreams, there are elements from throughout Stephen's day incorporated into his vision in "Circe," such as his conversation with Sargent, where he appeared to question the sagacity of the words Cranly had spoken to him whilst still a student, as if giving them serious consideration of the first time: "Was that then real? The only true thing in life" (*U,* 2.143, Cf. *P,* 263). This resurfaced thought regarding a mother's love (see *U,* 15.4192–4204) which I will discuss further below, along with the theatrical way in which his mother appears, rising "*stark through the floor,*" like an actor emerging through the trap door in a stage, reinforces that what Joyce is portraying is to be viewed as fantastic rather than transcendent (*U,* 15.4157).

That Stephen gave primacy to his intellectual beliefs rather than his mother's last wish has clearly resulted in him feeling remorseful. Peter Randall describes remorse as "the emotional expression of personal regret experienced by individuals after they have perpetrated some behaviour that they know to be shameful or have failed to do something that they should have done."[45] Joyce, himself, can be said to have experienced such feelings over his mother's death whilst also taking some responsibility for her demise, as is evidenced by his letter to Nora in which he stated: "My mother was slowly killed, I think, by my father's ill-treatment, by years of trouble, and by my cynical frankness of conduct."[46] Furthermore he had also experienced his "own nightmares about his own mother, coming to him wrapped in her grave-clothes."[47]

In the most recent edition of his book on adult bereavement, Colin Parkes, when discussing bereavement support, states: "Hallucinations are so well known as a sign of madness that it can be most alarming to experience the hypnagogic hallucination of a dead husband. Fortunately it is easy to reassure people of the normality of such a phenomena."[48] Although, as one can see from the comments Parkes makes regarding grieving widows, current thinking suggests that sensing the deceased, dreaming of them and even hypnagogic (half-waking) hallucinations should be viewed as part of the normal grieving process, which as late as the 1940s, "were thought to be pathological."[49] Whilst Joyce had referred to *Portrait* as "the picture of my spiritual self" he explained that in *Ulysses* he had "transformed individual impressions and emotions to give them general significance."[50] With the obvious link between Joyce's own emotional response to his mother's death and the way in which he has portrayed Stephen's dreams and vision, plus the fact that at that time they would have been thought of as "pathological," I would argue that the extremely disconcerting and ghoulish representations of Stephen's mother are to be interpreted as signifying the emotional difficulty in dealing with grief when one is consumed by remorse and guilt, rather than a perfectly normal reaction to loss. Indeed, Bowlby has claimed that whether or not the bereaved find dreams comforting "seems likely to be a reliable indicator of whether or not mourning is taking a favourable course" (*AL*3: 98).

As bereavement can often feel like abandonment Stephen can be seen as having been abandoned by his mother twice—firstly by leaving him at Clongowes Wood and then through her death. In order to relinquish his remorse and consequently move forward toward resolving his grief, Stephen needs to be reassured of his mother's unconditional love. Therefore, in the "Circe" episode when he visualises his mother in front of him, he pleads: "Tell me the word mother if you know it now. The word known to all men" (*U*, 15.4192–93). Having recalled his conversation with Cranly regarding a mother's love during the day, in nighttown his imagination modifies his statement whilst simultaneously answering the question he originally posed. Whereas Cranly had said: "Your mother brings you into the world, carried you first in her body. What do we know at what she feels?" (*P*, 263), the vision of his mother states: "Years and years I loved you, O, my son, my firstborn, when you were in my womb" (*U*, 15.4204–5).

Similarly, Stephen also visualises his mother recalling the private time they shared, which can be interpreted as a reflection of his hope that she had also recognised his understanding of all she had done for him. The ethereal May Dedalus utters: "You sang that song to me. *Love's bitter mystery*" (*U*, 15.4189–90) which refers to when Stephen was "alone in the house" and sang *Who Goes with Fergus* to her, "holding down the long dark chords" (*U*, 1.250). Earlier in the day Stephen had recalled a very private moment that followed the song: "Silent with awe and pity I went to her bedside" (*U*, 1.250–52). The words "awe" and "pity" convey a sense of respect and also sorrow for what she had had to endure. Indeed, Joyce's choice of song for Stephen to sing to his mother is significant in its theme of sacrifice and also in its irony. From the play *The Countess Cathleen,* it was portrayed as having been written to "hold her [the Countess] back from sacrifice" and instead yield to "the triumph of dream."[51] His mother had yielded to her dream of romantic love and family life, only to have it result in her own sacrifice.

The feelings that Stephen reports experiencing at his mother's beside creates the impression that, although the cognitive effects of being sent away from her had persisted, just as he recognised the siblings from whom he was distanced had suffered sacrifice for what had been "freely given to him," so he had also come to recognise the many sacrifices his mother made for her family (*P*, 176). Hence, when he had been talking to his pupil, Sargent, his thoughts had turned from how Sargent's mother had prevented him from being metaphorically "trampled [. . .] underfoot" to his own mother: "His mother's prostrate body the fiery Columbanus in holy zeal bestrode. She was no more: the trembling skeleton of a twig burnt in the fire, an odour of rosewood and wetted ashes. She had saved him from being trampled underfoot and had gone, scarcely having been" (*U*, 2.141–47).

At the end of *Portrait* she had prayed that Stephen may understand "what the heart is and what it feels" and whilst it cannot be said that her prayers were unequivocally answered, it does appear that he is to be seen as having matured enough to lose his rancour, although not his emotional insecurities (*P*, 275). Yet despite his apparent understanding of all she had done, whilst she could sacrifice so many things for her children, he could not sacrifice his intellectual beliefs at her point of death. His inability to yield, even momentarily, to a system that he is attempting to abandon has created his remorse and guilt and is portrayed as playing a major part in his inability to resolve his grief (see Chapter 12).

NOTES

1. Stanislaus Joyce, "Extracts from James Joyce: A Memoir," in *James Joyce: Critical Assessments*, 1: 126–27.
2. Gregory M. Downing, "Diverting Philology: Language and Its Effects in Popularised Philology and Joyce's Work," in *James Joyce: The Study of Languages*, ed. Dirk Van Hulle, New Comparative Poetics Series No. 6 (Bruxelles: PIE-Peter Lange, 2002), 137.
3. Ellmann, *James Joyce*, 27.
4. Judith Feeney and Patricia Noller, *Adult Attachment*, Sage Series of Close Relationships (London: Sage, 1996), 34.
5. Ainsworth, "Attachment: Retrospect and Prospect," 12.
6. See Bruce Bradley S. J., *James Joyce's Schooldays* (Dublin: Gill and Macmillan, 1982), 5.
7. Patrick Colm Hogan, *What Literature Teaches Us About Emotion*, Studies in Emotion and Social Interaction, Second Series (Cambridge: Cambridge University Press, 2011), 76.
8. Hogan, 77; See also Jeremy Holmes, *John Bowlby*, 67
9. Hogan, 77–78, argues: "the child's geography is not unlike that of the ancient cartographers who distinguished between the known world, centered in their own capital, and the unknown world, marked by the legend "There Be Monsters." For the child, there is the safe space of home, centered in mother's arms, and, surrounding it on all sides, an alien space marked with the same legend as those yellowing maps."
10. Shechner, *Joyce in Nighttown*, 16.
11. Harkness, *A Portrait of the Artist*, 34.
12. Holmes, *John Bowlby*, 67.
13. Robert Spoo, *James Joyce and the Language of History: Dedalus's Nightmare* (Oxford: Oxford University Press, 1994), 41.
14. Spoo, 41.
15. William M. Schutte, *Joyce and Shakespeare: A Study in the Meaning of Ulysses* (Yale University Press, 1957; Connecticut: Archon Books, 1971), 93.
16. Schutte, *Joyce and Shakespeare*, 96–97.

17. Barrett, *The Jesuit Enigma*, 146.

18. *The Workshop of Daedalus: James Joyce and the Raw Materials for A Portrait of the Artist as a Young Man*, eds. Robert Scholes and Richard M Kain (Illinois: Northwestern University Press, 1965), 102.

19. Brivic, "James Joyce: From Stephen to Bloom," 131.

20. Power, *Conversations*, 46.

21. Howe, *Attachment Across the Lifecourse*, 104. With reference to Cooper et al., "Attachment Styles and Intrapersonal Adjustment: A Longitudinal Study from Adolescence to Young Adulthood," in *Adult Attachment: Theory, Research and Clinical Implications*, ed. W. S. Rholes and J. A. Simpson (New York: Guildford Press, 2004).

22. *The Letters of W. B. Yeats*, ed. by Allan Wade (London: Hart-Davis, 1954), 399.

23. Gordon Bowker, *James Joyce: A Biography* (London: Weidernfeld & Nicholson, 2011), 46–47.

24. Holmes, *The Search for a Secure Base*, 10; Howe, *Attachment Across the Lifecourse*, 102.

25. Parkes, *Love and Loss*, 99. Parkes explains that the avoidant individual "may struggle to find ways to get close to people despite their fears."

26. Theodore Spencer, "Introduction," in *SH*, 17.

27. Dettmar, *The Illicit Joyce of Postmodernism*, 125.

28. Patrick Parrinder, "A Portrait of the Artist," in *James Joyce's A Portrait of the Artist as a Young Man: A Casebook*, ed. Mark A. Wollaeger (Oxford: Oxford University Press, 2003), 105–6

29. Howe, *Attachment Across the Lifecourse*, 111.

30. Riquelme, *Teller and Tale*, 163.

31. See Feeney and Noller, *Adult Attachment*, 95. Feeney and Noller state: "[T]here is [. . .] some evidence that individuals may develop different models in different relationships. For example, an individual may be secure with mother but insecure with father."

32. Suzette Henke, "Stephen Dedalus & Women: A Portrait of the Artist as a Young Misogynist," in *Women in Joyce* eds. Suzette Henke and Elaine Unkeless (Urbana: University of Illinois Press, 1982), 85.

33. Lee A. Kirkpatrick, *Attachment*, 56. Kirkpatrick is referring to Mary Ainsworth, "Attachments Across the Lifespan," *Bulletin of the New York Academy of Medicine*, 61 (1985), 792–812. He goes on to discuss each of the 5 characteristics in terms of an attachment to God.

34. John Paul Riquelme, "Desire, Freedom, and Confessional Culture in *A Portrait of the Artist as A Young Man*," in *A Companion to James Joyce,* ed. Richard Brown (Oxford: Blackwell Publishing, 2008), 38.

35. Jean Kimball, *Odyssey of the Psyche: Jungian Patterns in Joyce's Ulysses* (Carbondale: Southern Illinois University Press, 1997), 62; "Individuation is a process rather than a state; it is never completed in a person's lifetime." It can be defined as "wholeness [. . .] of personality by integrating the conscious and unconscious parts of the personality. Individuation leads also to uniqueness, which results from differentiating oneself fully from other persons." Mary Ann Mattoon, *Jungian Psychology*

in Perspective (New York: The Free Press, 1981), 179–80; "Persona" is an example of what termed an "Archetype" and is "a need or drive to present yourself in the best possible light." Julie Winstanley, *Key Concepts in Psychology*, Palgrave Key Concepts Series (Basingstoke: Palgrave Macmillan, 2006), 135.

36. "His arm" is interpreted as still referring to Mulligan as Stephen immediately goes on to think; 'He will leave me,' which could only be Mulligan as he has already left Cranly. Also, he then goes to think about whether he is to blame for his mother's death, which Mulligan has accused him of, as reflected in the link to Stephen's words and those of Ibsen's Brand (see Gifford, *Ulysses Annotated*, 64.

37. Jonathan Culpeper, *Language and Characterisation*, 11. Culpeper defines the reader's prior knowledge as "the past knowledge and experience stored in the mind,' particularly the 'long term memory," 28.

38. See Howe, *Attachment Across the Lifecourse*, 224. Howe states that "Internal working models will create their own experience and bring about the social environments they expect."

39. Budgen, *James Joyce*, 107.

40. Cosgrove, *James Joyce's Negations*, 93

41. Shechner, *Joyce in Nighttown*, 28.

42. For example, see Robert H. Bell, *Jocoserious Joyce: The Fate of Folly in Ulysses* (New York: Cornell University Press, 1991), 29; Schwaber, *The Cast of Characters*, 62.

43. Mary Lowe-Evans, *Catholic Nostalgia in Joyce and Company*, The Florida James Joyce Series (Gainesville: University Press of Florida, 2008), 2; Costello, *James Joyce*, 212.

44. See Fredric W. H. Myers, *Human Personality and Its Survival of Bodily Death*, ed. Richard Hodgson and Alice Johnson, 2 vols. (London: Longmans Green, 1903; repr. 1915)

45. Peter Randall, *The Psychology of Feeling Sorry: The Weight of the Soul* (London: Routledge, 2013), 96.

46. *Selected Letters of James Joyce*, ed. Richard Ellmann (London: Faber and Faber, 1975), 25.

47. Costello, *James Joyce*, 212.

48. Parkes and Prigerson, *Bereavement*, 216.

49. Payne et al., *Loss and Bereavement*, 70.

50. Hoffmeister, "Portrait of Joyce," 132.

51. Harold Bloom, *Yeats* (Oxford: Oxford University Press, 1970), 119.

Chapter Ten

Leopold and Molly Bloom

From an attachment perspective, secure individuals believe themselves "to be of value and worth" thus equipping them a certain "resilience," whereas those who are insecure, when in challenging and stressful situations find that "negative memories flood their thoughts and feelings. A feared sense of helplessness resurfaces."[1] I have already discussed how Stephen's insecure attachment traits, can be seen to affect his relationship with his family and how he grieves, but he is not the only protagonist in *Ulysses* who is shown to be insecurely attached. Leopold and Molly Bloom, although different characters in many ways, do both appear to be endowed with anxious/ambivalent traits. These are evident through the representation of their marital relations, both past and present, which in turn can be related to information Joyce provides and makes implicit within the text regarding their respective childhood experiences.

In their discussion of interpersonal relationships, Mikulincer and Shaver describe the experience of anxious individuals as "likely to be negatively biased by their hypersensitivity to rejection" and go on to explain:

> Interpersonal exchanges involving emotional closeness and affection may cause them to experience positive emotions, arouse feelings of optimism and hope [. . .]. But anxious people are unlikely to sustain positive emotions over time, because even minimal signs of partner unavailability, lack of interest, betrayal, or rejection will reactivate attachment-related worries, fears, and hyperactivating defences.[2]

I believe there is a strong argument to made that the events of June 16, 1904, enable Leopold Bloom to exert greater control over his emotional defence mechanism and exhibit more objectivity. To support this argument, it is first necessary to look to Bloom's childhood experiences in order to understand his internal working models and portrayed attachment behaviours.

BLOOM'S RELATIONSHIP WITH MOLLY: THE CONSEQUENCE OF A FRAGILE MOTHER?

Discussing Bloom's character, Erwin Steinberg describes him as "interested in a wide variety of ideas and eager to understand them."[3] Through the childhood memories that Joyce has Bloom recall, the inference is that this has been the case from an early age. For example, Bloom reminisces how, at the age of six, his father would talk to him of "migrations and settlements" and commercial matters, whilst he "accompanied these narrations by constant consultation of a geographical map of Europe (political) and by suggestions for the establishment of affiliated business premises in the various centres mentioned" (*U*, 17.1907–15). Seemingly precocious from a young age, one can view Bloom as being aware from quite early on in his life of his own social surroundings and of having a relatively elderly father. (John Henry Raleigh has calculated that he was "between fifty and fifty-nine years old" when Leopold was born.[4]) As noted with Stephen Dedalus, the recognition of vulnerability in one's attachment figures, on whom one relies for protection, can be unsettling for a child and by virtue of Bloom's waking dream in the "Circe" episode, there is an implication that if he had felt concern for his father's advancing years, there were also reasons for the young Leopold to feel concern for his mother's well-being.

Joyce provides the only glimpse of Bloom's mother to the reader in "Circe" where Bloom enters what can be described as a dream state. Kiberd argues that Joyce uses the dream state to "bring out what has been depressed or denied" during the day, enabling examination of the "sicknesses (and more positive yearnings)" of the characters.[5] Here Bloom's mind creates several narratives, bringing out among other things his desire for power and success, something which has been noted in those with anxious/ambivalent attachments (see *U*, 15.1354–710).[6] Joyce's narrative technique in this episode allows him to succinctly emphasise certain character traits of Bloom's mother, with Bloom imagining her as a pantomime dame, a parody of herself. The fact that he is portrayed as envisioning her in this particular guise rather than any other, whilst also furnishing her with somewhat melodramatic language, can be read as an indication that in Bloom's eyes she had a strong personality (pantomime dames are usually unpredictable, brusque, and abrasive) and was prone to overreaction. Her envisioned need for smelling salts to stop her from fainting additionally infers a degree of emotional and physical fragility.

Recalling how moments before Bloom visualised his mother he had visualised Molly in Turkish dress, Paul Schwaber poses the question: "Does Molly, who figures as male and female to him, often camouflage and cover his mother in his thoughts?" He goes on to reason:

He has very few memories of mamma but repeated thoughts of Molly and a ready fascination with women generally. His relation to them may suggest its beginnings with his mother—at some level terrified and terrifying, superstitious, explosive, very fragile, and yet very powerful, at least in the hold such a mother can have on a child, requiring of him precocious care, attention, cooperation, patience, and no answering explosiveness: the very qualities Bloom displays in the present crisis with Molly.[7]

Schwaber, a Freudian clinician, reads Joyce from a specific psychoanalytical perspective, interpreting his character as having not "sufficiently secured his adult masculinity before it was doubly traumatised" by the loss of his father and his son.[8] However, his observation is also useful when considering Bloom's early attachment. It can be seen that the qualities required of him in relation to his mother (care, attention, and patience) are those that one would normally expect to find in a mother when dealing with her child. In other words, their roles appear to have been reversed; something that Bowlby has argued often results in anxious/ambivalent attachment (see *MB*, 163). By virtue of Molly's interior monologue and her remembrance of the behavioural traits exhibited by Bloom the text further provides a link between the attachment relationship Bloom had with his mother and his later attachment behaviour exhibited with Molly.

Of particular significance is Molly's recollection of what happened when she refused to let him "lick" her: "he slept on the floor half the night naked the way the jews used when somebody dies belonged to them and wouldnt eat any breakfast or speak a word wanting to be petted" (*U*, 18.1245–48). One can translate his reaction as being related more to his feelings of rejection (something an anxious/ambivalent person would be very sensitive to) than the fact he was unable to perform the desired sexual act. Bowlby has argued that rejection arouses both anxious and angry behaviour which is "directed towards the attachment figure" in order to retain "maximum accessibility" to that figure and also as a form of "reproach," so as to prevent a repetition (*AL2*: 292–93). The similarity between Bloom's reaction to his unmet sexual desires and those of Gabriel Conroy, in "The Dead," as discussed in Chapter 8, with his sulky behaviour toward Gretta and ensuing feelings of anger, are evident.

Yet what is also of note is Joyce's acknowledgment of the association between feelings of emotional abandonment or rejection and those of bereavement, which is demonstrated by virtue of the link Molly makes between Bloom's behaviour following her refusal and that seen following the death of a loved one. This behavioural association seems to exemplify the assumption Bowlby later made as to why anger is often seen in the early stages of grieving:

> A bereaved person usually does not believe that the loss can really be permanent; he therefore continues to act as though it were still possible not only to find and recover the lost person but to reproach him for his actions. For the lost person is not infrequently held to be at least in part responsible for what has happened, in fact to have deserted. (*AL*2: 287)

Bowlby goes on to conclude that "although expressed towards the partner, such anger acts to promote, and not to disrupt, the bond" (*AL*2: 287). Molly's interior monologue describes not only how, following her refusal, Bloom made his anger toward her known by his own refusal to talk to her, but also how he sought reassurance of their affectional ties through his need to be "petted." Shechner argues that "Molly serves two purposes in her husband's life: excitation and reassurance" and one can see that in this instance the refusal of the former increased his need for the latter.[9]

With Bloom's emotional need for Molly's positive regard laid bare it makes his self-control throughout the day of June 16, 1904, and the early hours of the following morning all the more remarkable and his feelings of sadness and loneliness all the more poignant. Research has shown that those with anxious/ambivalent attachment styles tend to avoid discussing sexual betrayal with the transgressor and will often stay with them.[10] However, with Molly's revelation regarding Bloom's past behaviour and also her admittance that "he used to be a bit on the jealous side" (*U*, 18.183–84) one would perhaps not predict that a protagonist with such traits would be represented, as he is in the "Ithaca" episode, as reacting with "more abnegation than jealousy, less envy than equanimity" with regards to Molly's adultery (*U*, 17.2195).

Intimate relationships are based on the "need to belong" and "betrayal may be the ultimate dissolution of belonging," threatening the psychological comforts and reassurance that the relationship brings.[11] Yet by virtue of the adoption of the question and answer format in the "Ithaca" episode, which allows a certain amount of ironic distancing, Joyce has Bloom reflect sardonically on Boylan's actions: "that each one who enters imagines himself to be the first to enter whereas he is always the last term of a preceding series even if the first term of a preceding series even if the first term of a succeeding one, each imagining himself to be the first, last, only and alone, whereas he is neither first nor last nor only nor alone" (*U*, 17.2127–30). However, Joyce also illustrates that Bloom's poise and reasoned response does not come easily through the production of the long list of lovers his wife may have had, although Bernard Benstock notes, "the list has little basis in psychological reality" (see *U,* 17.2133–42).[12] His lack of objectivity here can be read as reflecting the emotional turmoil he is fighting hard to overcome. Similarly, he also finds it necessary to create a narrative for himself, by considering a catalogue of worse behaviours, in order to reach such a tolerant state (see *U*, 17.2180–2194).

Although gaining his equanimity takes a good deal of effort, Bloom is nevertheless able to remain composed rather than exhibit the type of reproachful behaviour that Molly recalls. This can be comprehended as a consequence of his psychological journey that day. He "has travelled" not just physically around Dublin but mentally, facing certain aspects of his grief in relation to Rudy and the state of his marital relations, seemingly leading to a better sense of self and hence a more confident self (*U*, 17.2320). He is now able, as Marilyn French states, to accept "the impossibility of ownership of another human being."[13] From an attachment perspective, he has not allowed negative memories to overwhelm his thoughts and feelings.

Before further discussing Bloom's relationship with his wife, it is worth considering Bloom's cognitive journey in more detail. That is, his realisation that his chronic grief is partly due to his lost aspirations and the continued need for a father/son relationship in addition to his own feelings of guilt.

BLOOM'S CAUSATION GUILT FOR THE LOSS OF HIS SON: THE NEED FOR A FATHER/SON RELATIONSHIP

By making the reader privy to Bloom's inner world, Joyce shows that Bloom has been unable to reach the reorganisation phase of the grief process following the loss of his son, even though it is almost eleven years since his death. In order reach this phase, according to Bowlby, one has to accept one's loss and cognitively reorganise how one views the relationship with that person, so that a symbolic and continuing attachment can be maintained (see *AL3*: 94). As already noted, those with anxious/ambivalent attachments often tend to exhibit chronic mourning, but Bloom's grief appears to have been further exacerbated due to the additional burden of causation guilt. This is one of the forms of guilt often felt following the death of a child whereby, as the terminology suggests, the parent feels that they had "a role in the death."[14]

That Bloom can be viewed as suffering from such guilt first becomes evident to the reader when his thoughts are revealed whilst travelling in the carriage to Dignam's funeral. Thoughts of Rudy had already been invoked by virtue of the occasion and also by Simon Dedalus's comments regarding his own son. However, as a child's white coffin flashes by, Bloom's mind turns to the image of his own offspring's tiny cadaver lying in the coffin: "A dwarf's face, mauve and wrinkled like little Rudy's was. Dwarf's body, weak as putty, in a whitelined deal box. [. . .] Meant nothing. Mistake of nature. If it's healthy it's from the mother. If not from the man" (*U*, 6.326–29). With Bloom's thought that Rudy was a "mistake of nature" further embellished by

Molly's description of him in the "Penelope" episode as "neither one thing nor the other," Joyce appears to be signifying that their son had some kind of congenital defect or deformity (*U*, 18.1308). Initially the narrative suggests that Bloom accepted this defect as a natural anomaly. Yet when his thoughts turn to "the ancient Jewish belief that the health of a child is a reflection of the virility of the male," the inference narrows from the general to the particular; from nature per se to Bloom as the bearer of the responsibility for Rudy's death.[15]

Whilst Bloom does not follow the Jewish faith, there is evidence within the text that his thought association regarding this belief is more than just a passing thought; that it resonates with how he has construed the death of his son. His concern that he may have played a role in the death of his son manifests itself in many ways. Firstly, throughout the day Bloom's penchant for scientific explanation of various phenomena has been made apparent and in the "Oxen of the Sun" episode he can be read as seeking such an explanation for the death of Rudy when, at the maternity hospital, he turns the conversation to causes of infant mortality (see *U*, 14.1240–42). Whilst Mulligan "blames sanitary conditions," Crotthers points to "abdominal trauma in the case of women workers subjected to heavy labours in the workshop and to marital discipline" and also "neglect" (*U*, 14.1242–60). Yet these theories cannot be applied to Molly and Bloom's perceived burden of responsibility for the death of his son remains undiminished at this point in the narrative.

Secondly, situated between the initial appearance of Bloom's causation guilt in "Hades" and his visit to the hospital in "Oxen of the Sun" the "Sirens" episode also provides an illustration of Bloom's apparent causation guilt coming into his conscious thought. As he sits in the bar listening to Ben Dollard sing *The Croppy Boy* his mind wanders to Molly being aware of admiring glances, then to his failure to produce a son: "Last of my race [. . .] Well, my fault perhaps. No son. Rudy" (*U*, 11.1066–67). Yet here one must recognise the ambiguity that is embedded within Bloom's reflection on his "fault." As well as echoing his guilt, he could also be acknowledging that it has been "10 years, 5 months and 18 days during which carnal intercourse had been incomplete, without ejaculation of semen within the natural female organ" (*U*, 17.2282–84). (I will return to the effect Rudy's death has had on the connubial relations of Molly and Bloom, but for the moment I wish to remain with Bloom's thoughts of his son.)

Thirdly, and most persuasively, in the "Circe" episode where Bloom physically finds himself in nighttown through acting on his paternal instinct toward Stephen Dedalus, in his waking dream he momentarily transmogrifies into a mother, producing eight boys. Bloom's transformation into the female form allows him to rid himself psychologically of any responsibility for their health should it be poor. However, in this cathartic state he imagines all the boys turning out not only healthy, but also *"handsome"* and *"well conducted"* and *"immediately appointed to positions of high public trust"* (*U*, 15.1823–29). The success of his imagined offspring not only reflects his own wish for power but also provides a link to his earlier thoughts of Rudy whilst travelling in the coach to the funeral: "If little Rudy had lived. See him grow up. Hear his voice in the house. Walking beside Molly in an Eton suit. My son. Me in his eyes. [. . .] I could have helped him on in life. I could. Make him independent. Learn German too" (*U*, 6.75–84). The desire to "help him on in life" and provide him with knowledge of German for business ("Germans making their way everywhere") indicates that Bloom had commercial and social ambitions for his son, thus enabling him to become his own "independent" person (*U*, 8.555). With his thoughts of Rudy's potential for achievement and his subsequent dream of producing several successful sons, there is an implication that part of Bloom's grief is bound up in his lost aspirations.

Acknowledging Ellmann's claim that Nora's miscarriage helped Joyce portray Bloom's grief at the loss of his infant son Rudy, Joyce appears to be relating what current health professionals have since documented.[16] Nurses who have spent their careers dealing with the bereaved, argue that: "Children embody the hopes and dreams of their parents. They are the parents' link to their past childhoods and their future existence."[17] Joyce clearly portrays that Bloom's now vanished ambition was to provide Rudy with the knowledge to succeed, to triumph where he had failed, becoming a highly successful businessman who was not seen as "other" due to his Jewish ancestry.

In the "Hades" episode Simon Dedalus's angry comments regarding his son's acquaintances had caused Bloom, by association, to consider what may have been had Rudy lived. Acutely aware of his failure to produce a healthy son, when later encountering Stephen at the maternity hospital in the "Oxen of the Sun" episode the narrator reports how: "Leopold that had of his body no manchild for an heir looked upon him his friend's son and was shut up in sorrow for his forepassed happiness and as sad as he was [. . .] so grieved he also in no less measure for young Stephen for that he lived riotously with those wastrels and murdered his goods with whores" (*U*, 14.271–76). "Oxen of the Sun" not only depicts the birth of Mina Purefoy's child, but also the birth of modern language, and in this section, Joyce uses the style of Thomas Malory. In T. S. Eliot's "English 26" notes on Joyce, he makes the suggestion "that allusions are an organic part of the modernist writer's synchronizing procedures, in which 'memories, both from reading and life' are 'charged with emotional significance.'"[18] The allusion to Mallory here romanticises Bloom, having already presented him as "sir Leopold," he becomes Stephen's white knight (*U*, 14.264). For although unable to help his own son, Bloom is nevertheless aware that Stephen is in need of fatherly advice and guidance, something the "noisy selfwilled" Simon Dedalus had apparently thus far failed to give in any meaningful way (*U*, 6.74).

Stephen's father is all too willing to look superciliously down on others and pass blame to them for any failings in his son, signifying a distancing from his own parental behaviour and hence any attributed blame (see *U*, 6.63–71). Margot Norris describes Simon Dedalus as "someone whom [Stephen] has learned not to rely [on] for protection or support."[19] Although not using Bowlby's terminology her description perfectly sums up an insecure avoidant relationship. In nighttown it is Bloom who establishes contact with Stephen, taking on a protective role toward him by safeguarding his finances from the money grabbing Bella and protecting his physical person after his fight with Private Carr.

Following the fight Stephen lies before Bloom, momentarily as helpless as Rudy been during his short life. Seeing Stephen curled in the foetal position at his feet causes him to have a vision of his son. Although imperfect in his behaviour, Stephen is seemingly perfect anatomically (weak eyes and bad teeth excepted) and as Ellmann points out, the ethereal Rudy is "altered from the misshapen dwarflike creature who dies at eleven days, and re-embodied as a perfect eleven-year-old boy."[20] However, there are other similarities that Joyce evokes between Stephen and Rudy. As a "changeling" Rudy is linked to the world of faery and with his studious attitude, the Tuatha De Danann.[21] Similarly, Maria Tymoczko argues that Stephen, with his surname, many skills, learning and aloofness, can be seen as "a representative of the Irish invaders with a Greek heritage, particularly the Tuatha De Danann."[22] Also, just as Stephen's surname links him to Greek mythology, so Rudy's attire, his cane, helmet and lambkin, links him to the Greek god, Hermes.[23] The suggested similarities and links between Stephen and Rudy, combined with Joyce's portrayal of how Bloom visualises his son (studious with evident wealth as symbolised by his *"diamond and ruby buttons"* on his Eton suit) at once reflects the aspirations he had for Rudy whilst tacitly implying that he sees in Stephen the same potential for success (*U*, 15.4965–67).

Arguing against the speech made by Diotima of Mantineia, which Socrates used in his discourse on immortality in Plato's *Symposium*, Martin Hägglund states that the ambition to live on through one's children is "not a desire for immortality" (i.e., a desire "to repose in a state of being that is eternally the same") but a desire "to *survive* as a mortal being for oneself and/or for others" (i.e., "to live on in a temporal process of alteration, where one is always becoming other than oneself, as one's children will also be exposed to death").[24] Joyce appears to have Stephen relate a similar philosophy in his discussion in the library: "That which I was is that which I am and that which in possibility I may come to be. So in the future, the sister of the past, I may see myself as I sit here now but by reflection from that which then I shall be" (*U*, 9,382–85). The argument of a wish for survival, of the past and future united, albeit in a changed state, is of considerable significance when considering Bloom's vision of Rudy. If, as Goldberg suggests, at that moment "Bloom is probably as close as he ever gets to understanding the significance Stephen has for him," he would have gained some sense that he is grieving for his lost aspirations and future existence in the form of his son.[25]

Karen Lawrence acknowledges that "Bloom does not recover his son Rudy in Stephen; rather he acts like a father to him."[26] This distinction is important as it appears that it is the possibility of being able to have a father/son type relationship ("Something to hand on") that Bloom requires to help fill the emotional void he has admitted feeling (*U*, 6.74–75). In aiding Stephen and showing paternal-like care to him, perhaps something of Bloom will live on in him, albeit only his ethics (business and/or personal), thus providing Bloom with a way to, at least partially, breach that particular emotional gulf.

Taking this argument forward, one has to question the plausibility of Stanley Sultan's suggestion that, in showing Molly's photo to Stephen, Bloom is "subtly offering" her to him in so much as he actually wants an affair to take place.[27] Whilst admittedly he may be using her image to make his invitation an attractive proposition, given the emotional turmoil he has been shown to suffer throughout the day due to Molly's relationship with Boylan, the likelihood that he would want any admiration on Stephen's part to progress to what could be considered a quasi-incestuous relationship seems somewhat remote. Joyce leaves no doubt that in Bloom's eyes Molly is still an attractive woman, even if "distinctly stouter" than when the photo he cherishes and has proudly shown to Stephen was taken (*U*, 16.1480). However, it is worth taking a few moments to consider Bloom's thought "And why not?" in relation to Stephen's apparent comment that Molly's picture "was handsome," as it can provide a clue to Bloom's actual intentions (*U*, 16.1480).

Rather than Bloom condoning a possible relationship, the comment could simply be interpreted as his discernment that there is no reason why Stephen should not express this opinion about such an appealing woman. But taking into account Bloom's sometimes wily behaviour throughout the day, he could also be viewed as considering that there is no reason why he shouldn't use Molly's picture as a lure despite, in his view, there being nothing physical on offer; especially as Stephen had spent his time with "profligate women who might present him with a nice dose to last him his lifetime" (*U*, 16.1555–56). In other words, he could be seen as mentally justifying his devious use of the photograph. This side of Bloom's character had been made evident in "Lotus Eaters" when he pretended to remove his hat due to the heat, when in fact he was retrieving card from his hatband that would enable him to claim the letter from his secret female correspondent at the post office (see

U, 5.20–28). Similarly, the more astute side of his character had also surfaced in the "Circe" episode where he prevented Bella from relieving Stephen of too much money, which she acknowledged by calling him "a slyboots" (see *U*, 15.3583–86). It also appears that Stephen has already mentally questioned how truthful Bloom is being with him when, earlier on in their conversation "he looked up and saw the eyes that said or didn't say the words" (*U*, 16.1146–47).

By his own admission the death of Rudy has had a detrimental effect on his connubial relations with Molly. Walking between Adam Court and Grafton Street earlier in the day, Bloom had thought: "Could never like it again after Rudy," although it was not entirely clear at that point to whom this thought referred (*U*, 8.591–610). However, as the text progresses, revealing the inner thoughts of both Bloom and Molly regarding Rudy and their subsequent relationship, it appears that Bloom was thinking of himself; particularly in the light of Molly's thought "O thanks be to the great God I got somebody to give me what I badly wanted" following her sexual encounter with Boylan (*U*, 18.732–33). Yet Bloom's admission does not necessarily imply that he would encourage other men to take his place in the marital bed. Marilyn French has noted that, whilst Molly "carries the implicit suggestion [regarding Stephen] to completion in her imagination," the same cannot be said for Bloom.[28] It is possible to read Bloom's goal as to provide little opportunity for Molly's liaisons with Boylan to continue, both through Stephen's presence in the house and also through Molly's preoccupation with her singing and Italian lesson with him. Additionally, Molly's deduction that Bloom sent Milly away to allow for her liaison with Boylan is only a supposition and therefore cannot be seen as a reliable indicator of how one is to interpret Bloom's motivations. His awareness of the tension Molly reports between herself and Milly allows for an alternative reason for his actions, such as maintaining good long-term family relations (see *U*, 18.1004–14).

That Bloom's scheme could, however, run the risk of Stephen and Molly actually embarking on an affair has not passed him by, as demonstrated by his mental deliberations as to why women take younger lovers (see *U*, 1542–52). Yet, relishing Stephen's company and with a need to breach the gulf left by Rudy's death, he is shown to continue with his strategy. Stephen has revealed himself to be "educated, *distingué* and impulsive into the bargain," and what's more, Bloom, as is typical of his commercial and business reveries, has an idea of managing Stephen and Molly's singing career, thereby creating a quasi-family business (*U*, 16.1476–77). Of course, whether Molly would go along with the "hash" is another matter (*U*, 16.1604). Ultimately, however, the plan is doomed to failure as Stephen's depicted inability to trust anyone means that any offer of further help from Bloom will be refused. Neil R.

Davison picks up on Stephen's avoidant traits when he describes his departure from Bloom: "He walks away, enveloped by the night; but it is the darkness of his self-imposed isolation that truly swallows his departing figure."[29] Until he is able to update his working models (or schema) he is doomed to metaphorically walk in the shadows.

MOLLY'S LACK OF A MOTHER FIGURE: THE NEED FOR ADORATION

Bowlby comments that anxious persons are more likely than others to have had daily care from a succession of different people or parents that have separated and exhibit increased demands for attention or affection (*AL*3: 218–19). Molly's need for attention in the form of adoration and the anxious/ambivalent traits that appear inherent in her relationship with her husband are important to understand as they in turn are reflected in the marital relations following the loss of their son.

After spending time with Stephen in the early hours of the morning, "Bloom rests. He has travelled" (*U*, 17.2320) but not before making a demand on Molly, in the form of a request for breakfast in bed, something which he has not done since they were residing at the City Arms Hotel some years previously (see *U*, 18.2). This was their home from 1893–1894 and where Rudy spent his short life from 29 December 1893 to 9 January 1894.[30] There is a tacit implication here that, having confronted his feelings of guilt and inadequacy, along with his realisation of his latent yearning for a father son relationship, this is a tentative step toward the happier times and pre-Rudy days. However, unaware of Bloom's psychological journey, his request is shown to have astounded Molly, her anxiety made evident by the representation of her thoughts running in several directions.

Frederick Hoffman, reading from a Freudian perspective, regards Molly as "a literary demonstration of naïve desire" and the absence of punctuation in her reverie as "point[ing] to a release of the slight hold which the social amenities ordinarily have upon her."[31] However, following Bloom's unexpected and unexplained request, one can also draw a parallel between Molly's interior monologue, which often flows into a stream of consciousness, and how anxiety is expressed in the conversation of those who form anxious/ambivalent attachments:

> [W]hen aroused, anxious and preoccupied people find it difficult to collect their thoughts, assess their feelings, and be mentally organised. This anxious pattern can be picked up in speech and conversation when one thought or memory leads uncontrollably to another and another in a free-ranging, incoherent ramble.

Caught up, *enmeshed* and *preoccupied* with their anxious feelings and memories, they fail to "monitor their own discourse."³²

Joyce represents Molly's thought process in an opaque manner, due to the undiscriminating use of the pronoun "he." This obscurity and the combined lack of punctuation, allowing thoughts to drift from one person to another and one scenario to another, in turn creates a sense that she has lost a certain amount of coherence due to her involvement in her own feelings of uncertainty, guilt and jealousy, which gradually unveil themselves as her thoughts flow. Making the connection between the technique Joyce uses to represent Molly's thoughts and the textual information he provides regarding her lack of a permanent mother figure, Molly can be read as someone that would have a tendency to form anxious/ambivalent attachments and as such a particular need to be noticed and responded to positively (*AL3*, 218–19).

With the portrayal of Molly as someone who has built her sense of self on an internal narrative based on male admiration, there is an implication that, as a young adult in a military enclave, she was responding to her need for attention and affection in the only way she knew how and this has since become something that she continually requires in order to define herself. With her sensitivity to any lack of attention, Molly is shown to have interpreted Bloom's decreased libidinal drive as a reflection of her waning allure: "I suppose he thinks Im finished out" (*U*, 18.1022); "I suppose Im nothing anymore" (*U*, 18.1244). Without her husband's positive regard Molly is potentially in danger of losing her sense of self and hence amenable to Boylan's advances.

Throughout *Ulysses* Joyce does not develop Boylan's character, more often than not any description given by the narrator concentrates on his attire. Although Boylan becomes Molly's lover Joyce makes plain she has no emotional attachment to him, with Molly's thoughts regarding her adultery being totally devoid of any romantic inclination: "anyhow its done now once and for all with all the talk of the world about it people make its only the first time after that its just the ordinary do it and think no more about it" (*U*, 18.100–102). On a personal level Molly perceives Boylan as having "no manners nor no refinement nor no nothing" and with a poor intellectual capacity: "the ignoramus that doesnt know poetry from a cabbage" (*U*, 18.1368–71). His admittance to her bed has been purely to satisfy her physical needs.

However, Joyce also implies that her ability to entice carries at least as much importance as her physical satisfaction. Although she spends time thinking of the sexual pleasure Boylan gave her, she is also shown to gain pleasure from her recollection of how she attracted him, from their initial encounter in the café when he noticed her feet, to their recent tryst where "he couldnt resist" her "plump and tempting" breasts (*U*, 18.1378–79) and how he wouldn't have seen "a better pair of thighs" (*U*, 18.1144–45). Similarly she dwells on how she had attracted and excited her various lovers in Gibraltar, as well as how on her first meeting with Poldy they just "stood staring at one another," which she puts down to her "jewess" looks (*U*, 18.1183–84). Further to her own reminisces, the men of Dublin are shown to talk and think of her in a sexualised way and there is abundant evidence that she has sought to be noticed through her choice of clothing (e.g., see *U*, 11.496–97, 11.1056–60, 18.1033–34).

Joyce therefore invites a reading of Molly's sense of security, in terms of her marriage, as requiring substantiation through both physical affirmation and constant admiration. With such defining needs, Bloom's request for breakfast is shown to have had a far greater effect in terms of potentially bringing Molly closer to him than had Stephen been willing to accept his offer to stay. Of course, Bloom is unaware of the disquiet he has caused. It is not the request for breakfast in itself that appears to have caused her consternation, but rather that this constitutes a change in their usual domestic arrangements and hence a change to the existing dynamics of their relationship. She is now required to be attentive to Bloom in the morning as opposed to Bloom responding to her needs. But the origin of this change, Bloom's psychological journey, is not within Molly's realm of knowledge. She is therefore left wondering what, or more to the point who, has brought this change about and consequently begins to reassess her relationship with her husband.

That Molly still holds Bloom in deep affection is made clear as she thinks fondly of him preparing breakfast for her: "I love to hear him falling up the stairs of a morning with the cups rattling on the tray and then play with the cat" (*U*, 18.933–34); and expresses appreciation his knowledge: "if I only could remember the 1 half of the things and write a book out of it the works of Master Poldy" (*U*, 18.579–80). But her love for him is most clearly demonstrated when she allows herself to consider having another child: "supposing I risked having another not him [Boylan] though still if he was married Im sure hed have a fine strong child but I dont know Poldy has more spunk in him yes thatd be awfully jolly" (*U*, 18.166–68). These reflections are portrayed as leading her to consider who Bloom's supposed lover may be, following his arrival home in the early hours of the morning. Her ensuing thoughts reveal that she too can be "a bit on the jealous side" (*U*, 18.183–84). Whilst Molly declares not to "care two straws now who he does it with," her use of pejorative and damning language, indicates that this claim does not represent her true feelings (*U*, 18.54–55).

The anger that Molly feels is made evident through her repeated reference to "some little bitch" (*U*, 18.45 and 18.1256) and the description of their ex-servant, Mary Driscoll as "that slut Mary" (*U*, 18.55–56). However, it is her considered threat to "tell him every scrap" of her activities and her passing of blame to Bloom for making her "an adulteress" which are most revealing, especially as this is at a point in her thought processes where she is shown to be gradually moving more positively toward Bloom (*U*, 18.1515–16). Should she turn her thoughts into action, just as with Bloom's past behaviour (following Molly's refusal to let him lick her), her outburst followed by a reproach can be seen as devised to keep him close to her. Indeed, she later comes up with another strategy in which she states this to be her aim: "Ill let him do it off on me [. . .] then Ill go out Ill have him eyeing up at the ceiling where is she gone now make him want me" (*U*, 18.1527–39). As well as bringing to the fore Molly's propensity for anxious/ambivalent behaviour, Joyce is highlighting the coercive way in which romantic relationships can be carried out, particularly with those who are in constant need of reassurance.

GRIEF AND THE CONNUBIAL RELATIONS OF LEOPOLD AND MOLLY BLOOM

Those researching various aspects of the grieving process have argued that "involvement in one's own grief may make it difficult to appreciate another person's perspective," a situation Joyce, himself, may have experienced.[33] Edna O'Brien reports that after Nora's miscarriage at three months, Joyce "said that he was the only one in the household who had dwelt on the truncated foetus and mourned it."[34] This does not necessarily mean, however, that Nora did not grieve her loss. In her study of grief and poverty in Britain between the late nineteenth and early twentieth century, Julie Marie Strange cites several cases where mothers stayed composed when an infant died although they were distraught; their "pragmatism and economy with words reflect[ing] a desire to make grief manageable and to look forward."[35] In his portrayal of Molly, however, Joyce shows that she has indeed grieved for Rudy. She recalls how his death "disheartened [her] altogether"; how she was "crying" as she buried him in a "little woolly jacket" that she had knitted for him (*U*, 18.1447–49). Her desire to protect Rudy from the cold by burying him in his woolly jacket reflects the continuation of parenting tasks, often seen with grieving parents.[36] Now, eleven years on, she thinks in a more practical manner; of how she could have saved the jacket and given it "to some poor child" (*U*, 18.1449).

According to Nora's biographer, Brenda Maddox, it is not known how Nora reacted to her miscarriage. Therefore, it is not known whether there was a lack of communication between herself and Joyce regarding their respective grief.[37] However, in *Ulysses* Joyce focuses on the effect losing a child has had on the marital relations on Molly and Bloom. The sexual relations of bereaved parents are an area which has been researched quite fully. In discussing why there can be a breakdown in sexual relations following the loss of a child, Doka and Martin have made the following observations from the reports of various studies:

> For many, the very act of intercourse was problematic—it meant inappropriate pleasure, evoked memories of the deceased child, or created anxiety over the prospect of a new child. In other cases, sexual intimacy was welcomed for the emotional comfort it offered, for the affirmation of life it provided, or for the creation of a new child. These meanings were not necessarily shared with the partner in the relationship.[38]

As already noted, via the individual thoughts of Molly and Bloom, Joyce evidences a mutual wish, although unexpressed to each other, for another child. Moreover, they have both expressed a desire to return to "happier" days, before they knew what it was to grieve for their own child (*U*, 8.608). Molly admits: "we were never the same since" (*U*, 18.1450). The disparity between Molly's need for affection and affirmation of life and Bloom's anxiety with regards to his ability to create a healthy son appears to have created a communicative gulf in their relationship. Although unconsidered by Molly, there is an implication that Bloom fears possible conception, as he could not cope with the pain of losing another child. However, as Margot Norris comments, "concealment is the property of narration," and the narrative silence Joyce maintains as to exactly why Bloom "Could never like it again after Rudy," means this is something that cannot be confirmed (*U*, 8.591–610).[39]

Whilst it is evident that Bloom has been too engulfed in his grief to understand Molly's physical needs, it must equally be acknowledged that Molly has not understood Bloom's preference to abstain from full sexual intercourse. She is shown to recognise that "hed go into mourning for the cat" (*U*, 18.1310). In other words, she acknowledges that he is prone to chronic mourning. Yet she appears to lack any comprehension or insight into her husband's deep and long-lasting grief for his only son. In her anxious state of uncertainty as to why their domestic arrangements are changing and who her love rival may be, she concludes that "he couldnt possibly do without it that long" (*U*, 18.77), thereby becoming convinced that he "came somewhere" (*U*, 18.34). Of course, her assumption is not entirely incorrect as Bloom did come somewhere, but this was through an act of voyeurism and self-stimulation, not through copulation as she suspects. Similarly, her additional deduction that he was writing covertly to another woman was also correct but, importantly, he has never seen the woman concerned. It is quite possible to read Bloom as having no intention of ever meeting her as psychologically he treats her like a literary character, preferring to use his imagination to create his own image of her.

Charles Peake interprets Bloom's masturbation and covert communications as mere "fantasy-substitutes for the sexual satisfactions which have been missing from his married life since the death of his son."[40] As the lack of such "satisfaction" has been through his own inability to reconcile his grief, the reader tends to forgive Bloom his indiscretions more easily than Molly's adultery. Certainly, the portrayal of Molly's sexual revelations, dominant in the obscenity trial against *Ulysses* in the United States, led critical descriptions of her character being frequently expressed in hyperbolic derogatory terms for some time.[41] Even in the 1960's, ironically seen as a time of sexual liberation and free love, Darcy O'Brien described her as "a thirty-shilling whore" and Forster Damon showed his emotional distaste by referring to her as "one of the most unpleasant characters in all literature."[42]

If one considers how Joyce portrays Molly's sexuality from a Lacanian perspective, as Colleen Lamos has done, Joyce appears to have represented a stance that is not typically feminine: "While 'Penelope' as a whole places Molly's body on display for its readers" viewing pleasure, she also possesses the power to look. Conventionally referred to as the male gaze, this spectatorial power, according to Lacan, signifies having the phallus, as opposed to being the object of the gaze—the supposedly feminine position."[43] One may read this as a reflection of her being raised in a predominantly male environment. However, with the textual evidence of what attachment theorists would term her anxious/ambivalent traits in mind, Joyce's representation of Molly's behaviour can actually be viewed as all too feminine and entirely within character.

Molly can be seen to embody the results of subsequent research investigating the relation between attachment and the expression of sexuality, which showed that "anxious-ambivalent females reported involvement in exhibitionism and voyeurism," amongst other activities, whilst anxious-ambivalent males tended to be more sexually reticent.[44] Portraying her style of dress as showing her ample bosom, along with her admittance that she used to be aware of "the fellow opposite" watching her dance about in her "short shift," Joyce makes her exhibitionism plain (*U*, 18.919–21). Voyeuristically she not only gains excitement from looking at Boylan's phallus and even that sculpted on the statue by her bed, but also from her own body: "they were so plump and tempting [. . .] they excite myself sometimes" (*U*, 18.1378–79). In need of adoration, she makes time to admire herself.

What is immediately obvious, however, is that Bloom is also partial to similar activities and cannot be described as more "reticent" in his sexual behaviour and as such can be seen, according to research, as having sexual preferences that were often seen in women. His masturbation on the beach whilst looking at Gerty and his awareness of "the sergeant grinning up" when he and Molly "came together when [. . .] watching the two dogs" from the window, are acts which simultaneously involved both voyeurism and exhibitionism (*U*, 6.79 and 18.1446). Further activities are also brought to light in the Circe episode (e.g., see *U*, 15.3340–70). Molly was attracted to "Leopold Paula Bloom" (*U*, 17.1855) because he "understood or felt what a woman is" (*U*, 18.1579). Furthermore, Bloom as a character was described in Joyce's notebooks as "ladylike" and in the "Circe" episode he has Dr. Punch Costello describe him as "a finished example of the new womanly man" (*U*, 15.1798–99).[45] It is also of note that Joyce appears to represent Molly's grief from what could be considered a more masculine perspective in so much as she seems to have accepted her loss more easily than her husband.[46] The representation of Molly's sexual behaviour, her dominance and her grief can be seen as feminine and masculine, respectively. Reflecting Schwaber's assertion that Molly "figures as male and female" to Bloom, this also serves to further signify he has formed the same type of attachment with Molly as he did with his mother, who could be seen as feminine in her fragility, yet dominant.[47]

Whilst Molly appears unashamed of her sexuality, she can be read as having experienced a form of so called "moral guilt"—a belief "that the loss of the child is punishment for the parents' moral transgressions"—if one considers her protest: "it wasn't my fault we came together when I was watching the two dogs" (*U*, 18.1446).[48] Furthermore, many nineteenth-century scientists held the belief that "maternal impressions and responses [could] produce certain clearly identifiable, "psychogenic" effects upon the unborn child."[49] Although she has no qualms in passing the blame to her husband, Bloom is shown to recall the occasion differently to Molly: "Molly wanting to do it at the window" (*U*, 6.761–72); "Give us a touch, Poldy. God I'm dying for it" (*U*, 6.80–81). This raises the question as to whether one is to interpret Molly's protest as an expression of her own internalised guilt or alternatively as a defence to an accusation made at some point by Bloom? Whilst I would argue for the former, Margot Norris has argued for the latter, positing that is Bloom who has actually "blamed Molly" for having "doomed" Rudy.[50] I find this unlikely given Bloom's thoughts regarding the fault being with the father and that in his waking dream state in "Circe" he needed to be in the female form in order to imagine the birth of his healthy sons. Moreover, such an argument would also imply that Bloom is somehow trying to punish Molly through their lack of full sexual relations which, given the obvious feelings and admiration he still has for her, again seems somewhat unlikely.

Although, as I have argued, Molly's thought implies she has experienced some personal guilt over how Rudy came to be conceived, she seems to have moved on in the grief process, refusing to think herself "into the glooms" anymore (*U*, 18.1451). Although Rudy is in her thoughts, the fact that Molly is no longer consumed by grief may have contributed to the less than positive stance taken toward her by some critics. Erwin Steinberg indubitably takes a negative view of Molly's maternal instinct, arguing that she has rejected both Milly and Rudy.[51] Certainly her reaction regarding Rudy's death ("what was the good in going into mourning for what was neither one thing nor the other the first cry was enough for me") does initially seem somewhat detached (*U*, 18.1307–9). Although, as already noted, Joyce portrays Molly's thought process in a somewhat opaque manner, the actual thoughts themselves are to the point and uncomplicated, in so much as there is little sophistication. One could, therefore, alternatively interpret that particular thought as a straightforward and hence seemingly stark reflection of her philosophical acceptance that, with his defect/deformity, Rudy was not meant for the mortal world. From an attachment perspective she could therefore be read as having been able to accept her loss and thus cognitively reorganise her relationship with her son. Hence, she is ready to reaffirm life in a way that sadly Bloom has as yet been unable to.

Despite their different grief processes, Joyce leaves no doubt that there has been some form of sexual activity between Molly and Bloom by having Molly recall "the last time he came on [her] bottom" (*U*, 18.77). Yet clearly Molly had felt physically unsatisfied and up to June 16, 1904, when she found someone in the form of Boylan to "give [her] what [she] badly wanted," this had not been fully acknowledged by Bloom (*U*, 18.732–33). Perhaps out of his sense of guilt due to his lack of consideration toward his wife's needs, Bloom is represented as complicit in Molly's adultery with Boylan, since not only is he portrayed as acting against his inclination to return home, but he also seems to acknowledge his own participation through his voyeuristic waking dream whilst in nighttown. Suzette Henke argues that with Bloom playing the role of both director and spectator in this "masochistic drama" he gains "artistic control over emotional trauma" which in turn grants him psychological catharsis.[52] Certainly one can see a parallel with Stephen in the infirmary in *Portrait*, confronting the trauma of his illness and possible death and his imagined cathartic revenge of Wells. Yet here, the anxiety Bloom has suffered all day in the knowledge of his wife's adultery is not purged by revenge but by acceptance.

Bloom's realisation of the link between Rudy's death, his decreased libido and ultimately Molly's adultery, can be seen as pointing toward what Jeremy Holmes terms "autobiographical competence."[53] In other words, a step toward owning his own narrative and consequently the tentative beginning of the resolution of his grief and in turn normal marital relations. The narrative format in "Ithaca" creates a certain distance that enables the depiction of experiential reflection; Bloom in the present analysing the events of the past day in order to gain such "competence" and equanimity.

Conversely, whilst Molly has derived a great deal of physical pleasure from her tryst, she has not gained any sense of inner calmness as a result of the day's events. Instead she is portrayed as experiencing a certain amount of guilt for breaking her marriage vows, as represented by her response to the thunderstorm: "that thunder woke me up God be merciful to us I thought the heavens were coming down about us to punish us when I blessed myself and said a Hail Mary" (*U*, 18.134–36). As "guilt may be conceptualised to be inturned anger" one could surmise that, despite her thought that she has done nothing uncommon ("doesn't everybody only they hide it"), she is angry with herself for betraying her husband (*U*, 18.1518).[54] This interpretation is further supported by her apparent need to pass blame to her husband for her actions in order to dissipate her guilt: "it's all his own fault if I am an adulteress'" (*U*, 18.1516). Her need to convince herself of her own martyrdom in so much as "hed never find another woman to put up with him" the way she does, could also be read in a similar light (*U*, 18.232–33). However, the latter comment could also be read as Molly convincing herself that she needs to stay.

Despite Molly's internal deliberations and notwithstanding Boylan's obvious virility, Joyce evidences how she would prefer the arms of her husband with whom she could shout "fuck or shit or anything" without the fear of looking "ugly" (*U*, 18.588–89). Blunt as Molly's comments are regarding her need for an active sex life, her narrative also reveals a romantic longing: she would like "somebody" to "write [her] a loveletter" (*U*, 18.734–35); she would like "some man or other" to give her "a kiss long and hot" so that it "almost paralyses" her (*U*, 8.104–6); and she purports that "a woman wants to be embraced 20 times a day" (*U,* 18.1407–8). If one considers her recollection of the letters from Bloom, referring to her "glorious Body" which had her at herself "4 or 5 times a day sometimes" (*U*, 18.1177–79); her remembrance of "the long kiss" when she passed the seedcake from her mouth to his and where she "near lost her breath" (*U*, 18.1575–76); and her complaint that Bloom never embraces her "except sometimes when he's asleep," one cannot help but conclude that the "someone" she is wishing for is in fact her Poldy of old (*U*, 18.1400–1401).

Unbeknown to Molly, Bloom has also joyously and sensuously recalled their kiss on Howth during the day (see *U,* 8.899–916). Yet despite their treasured memories, Molly and Bloom are also shown to have individually thought about divorce. However, in each instance it was with such transience that it could not be considered a serious contemplation (see *U*, 17.2202 and 18.846). This provides further textual evidence that, reading with a knowledge of Attachment Theory, Bloom and Molly can be read as exhibiting anxious/ambivalent attachment traits. Davila and Bradbury have found that anxious/ambivalent individuals are disinclined to give up on romantic relationships; their "[f]ears of being abandoned and alone make them more likely to stay in relationships, even when they are clearly unsatisfactory."[55] Yet despite the depicted anxious/ambivalent traits, the "rapid switch between the strong expression of positive and negative feelings, between threat and seduction" that both Molly and Bloom have been shown to display, Joyce also presents a deep mutual admiration and love, as well as their acceptance of each other's respective foibles.[56]

Much like Anna Livia Plurabelle in *Finnegans Wake*, Molly's ruminations "do not so much close the novel as provide it with an epiphanic vision of the eternal "yes" at once an end and a continuing."[57] The reader is left with some hope that, having faced his feelings of inadequacy and guilt in nighttown via his waking dream of producing healthy offspring and his vision of Rudy, that Bloom may start to reconcile his grief and renew his marital relations. That Molly is prepared to "give him one more chance" indicates that she would welcome such a change (*U*, 18.1498).

NOTES

1. Howe, *Attachment Across the Lifecourse*, 55.
2. Mikulincer and Shaver, *Attachment in Adulthood*, 271.
3. Steinberg, *The Stream of Consciousness*, 206.
4. See Raleigh, *Chronicle*, 15–16.
5. Declan Kiberd, *Ulysses and Us: The Art of Everyday Living* (London: Faber and Faber, 2009), 233.
6. See Holmes, *The Search for a Secure Base*, 39.
7. Schwaber, *The Cast of Characters*, 112.
8. Schwaber, *The Cast of Characters*, 112.
9. Shechner, *Joyce in Nighttown*, 208.
10. See Randall, *The Psychology of Feeling Sorry*, 31.
11. Randall, *The Psychology of Feeling Sorry*, 29.
12. Benstock, *Narrative Con/Texts in Ulysses*, 103.
13. Marilyn French, *The Book as World: James Joyce's Ulysses* (New York: Paragon House, 1993), 47.
14. John. H. Harvey, *Perspectives on Loss and Trauma: Assaults on the Self* (California: Sage, 2002), 42. Referring to C. A. Corr et al., *Death and Dying: Life and Living* (California: Brooks/Cole, 1994)
15. Gifford with Seidman, *Ulysses Annotated*, 111.
16. See Richard Ellmann, *James Joyce*, 278.
17. Arnold and Gemma, *A Child Dies*, 23.
18. Ron Bush, "'Intensity by Association': T. S. Eliot's Passionate Allusions," *Modernism/Modernity*, 20, no. 4 (2014): 719. Referring to T. S. Eliot: Unpublished Harvard English 26 lecture notes, "Contemporary English Literature (1890 to the Present Time)," notes for class on *Ulysses*, Tuesday, April 18, 1933. The MS version

of the lecture notes (ninety-two leaves) is in the Harvard University Houghton Library, MS Am1691.14(36).

19. Margot Norris, "Character, Plot and Myth," in *The Cambridge Companion to Ulysses*, ed. Sean Latham (New York: Cambridge University Press, 2014), 72.

20. Richard Ellmann, *The Consciousness of Joyce* (London: Faber and Faber, 1977), 70.

21. Dáithí Ó hÓgáin, *The Lore of Ireland: An Encyclopaedia of Myth, Legend and Romance* (Woodbridge: Boydell, 2006), 206–11.

22. Maria Tymoczko, *The Irish Ulysses* (Berkley: University of California Press, 2004), 30–31.

23. See Gifford with Seidman, *Ulysses Annotated*, 529.

24. Martin Hägglund, *Dying for Time: Proust, Woolf, Nabokov* (Massachusetts: Harvard University Press, 2012), 7–8; See Plato, *Symposium*, 211a, Trans. M. Joyce, Modified in *The Collected Dialogues of Plato*, referred to in Hägglund, 6.

25. Goldberg, *The Classical Temper*, 186.

26. Karen Lawrence, "Paternity as Legal Fiction in *Ulysses*," in *James Joyce: The Augmented Ninth*, ed. Bernard Benstock (New York: Syracuse University Press, 1988), 239.

27. Sultan, *The Argument of Ulysses*, 367.

28. French, *The Book as World*, 218.

29. Neil R. Davison, *James Joyce, Ulysses, and the Construction of Jewish Identity: Culture, Biography, and "The Jew" in Modernist Europe* (Cambridge: Cambridge University Press, 1996), 235.

30. See Raleigh, *Chronicle*, 12 and 273.

31. Frederick J. Hoffman, *Freudianism and the Literary Mind*, 2nd ed. (Louisiana: Louisiana State University Press, 1957), 139.

32. Howe, *Attachment Across the Lifecourse*, 137. In the final sentence, Howe cites M. Main et al., *The Adult Attachment Interview: Scoring and Classification system, Version 8*, Unpublished manuscript (University of California at Berkley, 2008).

33. Jane Littlewood, *Aspects of Grief: Bereavement in Adult Life* (London: Routledge, 1992; repr. 1993), 70.

34. Edna O'Brien, *James Joyce*, Lives Series (London: Weidenfield & Nicholson, 1999), 63.

35. Strange, *Grief and Poverty*, 254–55.

36. See Arnold and Gemma, *A Child Dies*, 58–59.

37. See Maddox, *Nora*, 116

38. Kenneth J. Doka and Terry L. Martin, *Grieving Beyond Gender: Understanding the Ways Men and Women Mourn*, Series in Death, Dying and Bereavement, rev. edn. (New York: Routledge, 2010), 129–30.

39. Margot Norris, *Virgin and Veteran Readings of Ulysses* (New York: Palgrave Macmillan, 2011).

40. C. H. Peake, *James Joyce: The Citizen and the Artist* (London: Arnold, 1977), 330.

41. See Kevin Birmingham, *The Most Dangerous Book: The Battle for James Joyce's Ulysses* (London: Head of Zeus, 2014).

42. Darcy O'Brien, *The Conscience of James Joyce* (Princeton: Princeton University press, 1968), 211; S. Forster Damon "The Odyssey in Dublin," in *James Joyce: Two Decades of Criticism* ed. Seon Givens (New York: Vanguard Press, 1963), 235.

43. Colleen Lamos, *Deviant Modernism: Sexual and Textual Errancy in T.S. Eliot, James Joyce, and Marcel Proust* (Cambridge: Cambridge University Press, 1998), 166–67.

44. Feeney and Noller, *Adult Attachment*, 120–21. With reference to C. Hazan, D. Aeifman, and K. Middleton, *Adult Romantic Attachment, Affection and Sex,* Paper presented at the 7th International Conference on Personal Relationships, Groningen, The Netherlands.

45. Philip F. Herring, *Joyce's* Ulysses *Notesheets in the British Museum* (Charltttesville: University Press of Virginia, 1972), 232.

46. Various studies have shown that mothers generally grieve more intensely and for a longer duration than fathers. See Archer, *The Nature of Grief*, 244–45; Doka and Martin, *Grieving Beyond Gender*, 128–29.

47. Schwaber, *The Cast of Characters*, 112.

48. John. H. Harvey, *Perspectives of Loss and Trauma*, 42. Referring to C. A. Corr et al., *Death and Dying: Life and Living* (California: Brooks/Cole, 1994).

49. R. Brandon Kershner, *The Culture of Ulysses* (Hampshire: Palgrave Macmillan, 2010), 220. Kershner is quoting from Susan Schoon Eberly, "Fairies and the Folklore of Disability: Changelings, Hybrids, and the Solitary Fairy," in *The Good People: New Fairylore Essays,* ed. by Peter Varvàez (New York: Garland, 1991), Kreshner links this "folk belief" to "Molly's worry that Rudy's death was a judgement" on how he was conceived.

50. Norris, *Virgin and Veteran Readings of Ulysses*, 259.

51. See Steinberg, *The Stream of Consciousness and Beyond*, 230.

52. Suzette A. Henke, *James Joyce and the Politics of Desire* (Routledge: London, 1990), 119.

53. See *JB*, 158 for how psychotherapy enables the patient to own their own narrative.

54. Payne, Horn, and Relf, *Loss and Bereavement*, 25.

55. Howe, *Attachment Across the Lifecourse*, 144. With reference to J. Da vilia, and T. N. Bradbury, "Attachment insecurity and the distinction between unhappy spouses who do and do not divorce," in *Journal of Family Psychology*, 15, 371–93.

56. Howe, *Attachment Across the Lifecourse*, 141.

57. John M. Warner, *Joyce's Grandfathers: Myth and History in Defoe, Smollett, Sterne, and Joyce* (Georgia: The University of Georgia Press, 1993), 155.

PART IV

Joyce, Religion, and the Portrayal of the Grief of Stephen Dedalus and Leopold Bloom

Part IV

Introduction

The role played by religion in the negotiation of the grief process is considered in the next two chapters by focusing on parental loss and the death of May Dedalus and Rudolph Bloom, respectively. Attachment Theory has been described by Jeremy Holmes as "a systemic theory in that it sees the individual not in isolation, but in reciprocal relationship; first to a primary attachment figure, then to subsidiary attachment figures within the family, then to the wider society."[1] Placing religion at the centre of the discussion enables consideration of the relationships (or lack of relationships) held by both Stephen Dedalus and Leopold Bloom with the wider religious communities in Dublin, in addition to their perception (or lack of perception) of a personal relationship with a particular deity, both of which have consequential effects when dealing with their bereavement.

Although Stephen has left the Catholic Church and Bloom, while of Jewish descent, follows no particular religious doctrine, there is nevertheless an undeniable but complex relationship that emerges in *Ulysses* between their expressions of grief, individual religious experiences, and the religious views of their fellow Dubliners. Joyce's own relationship with the Catholic Church was not straightforward, going through many phases from extremely pious to total rejection. His own views and experiences therefore served to influence his writing and will be considered before going on to discuss his two main protagonists.

Through his Jesuit schooling, Stephen is prone to intense introspection, which combined with his troubled conscience, accusations from relatives and avoidant traits, has left him racked with remorse and guilt regarding his treatment of his mother on her deathbed. Bloom, who has been endowed with ambivalent/anxious traits and is prone to chronic mourning, is portrayed as having his grief further exacerbated due to the religious indoctrination and hence strongly held views of his fellow Dubliners. Their belief system has a twofold effect on Bloom. Firstly, their perception of him as Jewish and hence "other" has left him on the outer edges of Dublin society with little support and secondly their views on suicide as a sin have led to self-initiated disenfranchised grief.

In Joyce's fiction, both Stephen and Bloom experience feelings of remorse regarding their behaviour toward their deceased loved ones, and in each case, religion plays a key role in the emergence of these feelings. The definition of remorse given in Chapter 9 was one of an "emotional expression of personal regret."[2] Forensic psychologist Michael Proeve and philosopher Stephen Tudor have distinguished the family of emotions to which remorse belongs:

> Remorse may be identified as one among a family or class of emotions which we shall call the "retractive emotions." Prominent members of this family are remorse, guilt, shame, regret, compunction, contrition and repentance [. . .]. These are all "retractive" emotions in so far as the self experiencing any one of these emotions in some way retracts of withdraws from something which is otherwise seen as belonging or associated with the self. That something may be an action, an omission, or simply a certain state or condition of being. In experiencing such emotions, the person retreats or resiles from their action or omission or state of being. The common thought is that "I wish I had not done that" or "I wish I was not like that," or a variation of this theme.[3]

Chapter 12 discusses Stephen's remorse in some detail. Unable to serve a God he claims to no longer believe in, he felt unable to compromise his intellectual beliefs and accede to his mother's request when asked; something he now suffers for psychologically. Bloom is also shown to have "experience[d] a sentiment of remorse," the reasoning for which is revealed in the "Ithaca" episode: "in immature impatience he had treated with disrespect certain beliefs and practices" (*U*, 17.1894–95). Although his "impatience" had been due to his own lack of belief, unlike Stephen who had to decide whether or not to go against his mother's wishes, he had not encountered any internal conflict at the time and this experienced emotion appears to be transient rather than something that could have a protracted psychological effect.

The decision by Joyce to portray both protagonists as lacking faith instantaneously isolates them in so much as they are removed from any support the religious community may offer, as well as the psychological support a belief system may afford. Attachment theorists Parkes and Prigerson have noted that having a faith, which will also involve certain rituals, acts to "provide an explanation from death and social support for the expression of grief, should reduce the confusion felt by the newly bereaved and might even be of psychological value in helping them to express their grief."[4] The element of confusion felt following bereavement is also commented on by literary critics Goodwin and Bronfen, who have argued that cultural constructs, including religion, "may be construed as a response to the disordering force of death.

Culture itself would then be an attempt to both represent death and to contain it, to make it comprehensible and thereby to diffuse some of its power."[5] It therefore follows that those with religious beliefs "may be more prepared than less religious persons to impose satisfactory meaning on a negative event such as bereavement."[6]

In discussing the psychology of religion, Lee Kirkpatrick explains that some aspects of religion, particularly Christian religion, such as perceiving "a personal relationship with a parent-like deity, can be well understood as manifestations of an evolved psychological system called the *attachment system*."[7] God, who is seen as ever-present and able to give comfort and protection, can be viewed as capable of providing all that is needed from an attachment figure, especially in end of life scenarios. Social psychologist Bruce Reed, whose study on religion as a social phenomenon acknowledges Bowlby's work and his suggestion that a religious group can act as subordinate or principal attachment figure (see *AL*1), notes that:

> [E]very form of attachment behaviour, and of the behaviour of the attachment figure, identified by Bowlby, has its close counterpart in the images of the relationship between Israel (or the worshipper) and God which we find in, for example, the psalms.
> [. . .]
> But be not far from me, O Lord: thou art my succour, haste thee to help me (Psalm 22:19).
> Yea, though I walk through the valley of the shadow of death, I will fear no evil: for thou art with me; thy rod and thy staff comfort me. (Psalm 23: 4)[8]

The words of the latter psalm exemplify the comfort that can be provided by a belief in God to the dying. As Elizabeth Nottingham states, holding "beliefs about death and afterlife cannot nullify death, of course, but they can help people to face it."[9] Similarly, such tenets also provide an attachment figure for the bereaved to turn to, as denoted in Psalm 22. In association with such precepts, the religious rituals in which the bereaved participate help to direct and orientate their behaviour, whilst those who attend the rituals—friends, relatives and the larger religious community—are available to provide support during the difficult transitional period of accepting one's loss.

Kirkpatrick, considers Attachment Theory to be "a good theoretical context for understanding religion" for several reasons, not least because it "purports to explain" how the differences in "orientation toward personal relationships" in people occur.[10] His examination of "the relationship between individual differences in religious belief and adult attachment styles" found that how one viewed God, and also whether one felt able to have a personal relationship with God, depended on internal working models of the self and of others.[11] As my argument has been that the portrayal of Bloom and Stephen is such that they can be read as demonstrating anxious/ambivalent and avoidant attachment traits, respectively, these differences will be referred to throughout my discussion.

The stance taken by attachment theorists on religion contrasts strongly with that taken by Freud, whose theories were based on instinctual drives as well as by Jung, whose thinking was more metaphysical. In *The Future of an Illusion* Freud argued that religion was "the universal obsessional neurosis of humanity" which "originated in the Oedipus complex, the relation to the father." In this paper he expressed the view that religious belief was an "illusion derived from men's wishes," which disregarded its "relations to reality," and originated as a result of "the adult's continuation" of "the child's helplessness," something which Kirkpatrick repudiates.[12] Whilst Kirkpatrick can agree with Freud to the extent that humans are concerned with finding a secure base that affords comfort and protection, he also points out that when viewed from the perspective of Attachment Theory, "there is absolutely nothing assumed to be 'infantile' or 'regressive' about any of this."[13]

Freud saw religion as a serious "enemy of science," with its strength deriving "from its readiness to fit in with our instinctual wishful impulses."[14] In the final lecture of his *New Introductory Lectures on Psycho-Analysis,* given in 1933, he describes religion as a *"Weltanschauung,"* a "specifically German concept" which he nevertheless does his best to define: *"Weltanschauung* is an intellectual construction which solves all the problems of our existence uniformly on the basis of one overriding hypothesis, which, accordingly, leaves no question unanswered and in which everything that interests us finds its fixed place." He goes on to argue that if attempts are made "to assign the place of religion in the evolution of mankind, it appears not as a permanent acquisition but as a counterpart to the neurosis which individual civilised men have to go through to their passage from childhood to maturity."[15]

Freud's one-time collaborator, Carl Jung, in "Psychotherapists or the Clergy," views religion not as a "counterpart to neurosis" but as positive force against it, arguing that as religious life declines, so does the frequency of neuroses. He criticised Freud's theories for "their exclusive concern with the instincts [which] fails to satisfy the deeper spiritual needs of the patient."[16] Jung did not define religion as a "creed" but rather as an "attitude peculiar to a consciousness which has been altered by the experience of the numinosum."[17] In other words religion is "an openness toward the transcendent self," which provides "a sense of the sacred in the everyday."[18] However, he did not discount the benefits of prescribing to a particular creed where the "numinous experience" can be shared in that community.[19]

In contrast to the theories of Freud and Jung, Attachment Theory is "inherently neither pro-nor anti-religious."[20] Kirkpatrick and Shaver explain that it is a theory that "emphasises the individual's active role in constructing, maintaining and negotiating close relationships (and mental models of these relationships) rather than viewing individuals as passive victims of internal and external forces beyond their control."[21] This means that Attachment Theory can be applied to religion without being burdened with what Kirkpatrick terms "evaluative baggage."[22] Bowlby's account of attachment deliberately avoids terms such as "regression" and "dependence," instead his model is based on "the 'need' for an available and responsive caregiver [that] remains with us throughout the lifespan."[23]

Kirkpatrick notes that experiencing the loss of a main attachment figure, such as a parent may cause the bereaved to "search for a *substitute* or *surrogate* caregiver, or at least increased reliance on a previously secondary figure" and therefore "one may turn to God or Jesus for this reason."[24] In *Ulysses* Joyce, despite having endowed Stephen and Bloom with insecure attachment traits, does not have them turn to a deity. Indeed, Stephen's rejection of religion is a major contributory factor in his difficulty in dealing with his grief. Bloom, perhaps due to his scientific bent, is shown to follow no particular creed and is used by Joyce to highlight much of what he disagreed with in the Catholic Church through the objective lens of someone outside of the community.

It is therefore perhaps surprising to the reader to find that in the "Ithaca" episode the narrator relates that this seemingly agnostic character of Jewish lineage, has been baptised as a Protestant twice (the second seems to have been merely a schoolboy reenactment) then as a Catholic (see *U*, 17.542–46). The reason he converted from Protestantism to Catholicism is revealed as follows:

> To Master Percy Apjohn at High School in 1880 he had divulged his disbelief in the tenets of the Irish (protestant) church (to which his father Rudolf Virag (later Rudolph Bloom) had been converted from the Israelitic faith and communion in 1865 by the Society for promoting Christianity among the jews) subsequently abjured him in favour of Roman catholicism at the epoch of and with a view to his matrimony in 1888. (*U*, 17.1635–40)

Having rejected precepts of Protestantism as a school child, Bloom finally took the step to change his faith to Catholicism in order to accommodate his marriage (although Luca Crispi points out that Bloom's notion that this was an actual requirement is an "erroneous idea").[25] However, in ascertaining the social standing of Bloom's family, the information provided within the brackets, in relation to the conversion of his father from Judaism to Christianity, is of greater import. A leaflet written in 1918 regarding the consequences of the degradation of the Jews states that: "Jews have been driven in increasing numbers to emigration, physical or spiritual. Vast numbers have sought refuge and betterment in Western Europe and America; many have given up the struggle and accepted baptism as a means of escape."[26] Taking this information to be correct, it is possible to interpret Rudolf Virag's baptism, along with his change of name to Rudolph Bloom, as an effort to integrate with the Dublin community and avoid prejudicial treatment.

The negative views that were held in Europe regarding the Jewish people are made plain in the writings of Otto Weininger, a contemporary of Joyce and described by Davison as "one of the most controversial psychobiologists in Vienna after 1903."[27] Of Jewish decent, Weininger converted to Protestantism and his work, which is both misogynistic and anti-Semitic, reflects the opposing traits he believed to be present in those who followed these respective religions. He expressed a view that:

> Judaism and Christianity [. . .] show the greatest, most immeasurable contrast. Of all forms of being, the former is most divided and most lacking in inner identity, while the latter has the firmest belief and utmost trust in God. Christianity is the highest degree of heroism; the Jew, on the other hand, is never integrated and whole. That is why the Jew is a coward, and the hero is his diametric opposite.[28]

Weininger sees the Jew as "lacking in inner identity" and not "integrated" due to their lack of belief in Christ and thus as having "forfeited the possibility of greatness." He therefore lists binary oppositions between Judaism and Christianity as the choice "between business and culture, between Woman and Man, between the species and the personality, between worthlessness and value, between the earthly life and the higher life, between nothingness and the deity."[29]

John McCourt suggests that, given the "interest in Weininger among Triestines, it would have been difficult for Joyce to have remained immune to his ideas and influence."[30] However, Davison goes further, stating there is reasonable evidence that Joyce had read Weininger's work, whilst simultaneously pointing out that certain of "Weininger's beliefs about "Jewish Nature" are both inverted and discredited" in *Ulysses*.[31] The most obvious example of such inversion is Bloom's position as a just "hero" in *Ulysses,* transcending the abuse, both verbal and physical, of the Citizen and the sexual transgressions of his wife; singly ascending from the pub in a manner representative of Elijah's ascension to heaven (2 Kings II:11) and retiring to his marital bed with a sense of forgiveness, recognising "the futility of triumph or protest or vindication" (see *U,* 12.1910–18; *U,* 17.2224–25).

By the end of *Portrait* Stephen is shown to have spurned the influences of his Jesuit education, culminating in his refusal to join the priesthood and his rejection of Catholic faith in order to respond to his need for uninhibited self-expression. Richard Ellmann relates how Joyce used his own experiences of the Catholic education system at both Clongowes Wood and Belvedere, including a nine-month period in which he became extremely pious, when portraying Stephen Dedalus in *Portrait*.[32] With such autobiographical elements in Joyce's work one can see how Stephen's eventual rejection of Catholicism reflects Joyce's own disillusionment. A letter Joyce wrote to his then girlfriend and future wife, Nora Barnacle On 29 August 1904 makes his rejection of the church plain: "Six years ago I left the Catholic Church, hating it most fervently. I found it impossible for me to remain in it on account of the impulses of my nature. I made secret war upon it when I was a student and declined to accept the positions it offered me. [. . .] Now I make open war upon it by what I write and say and do."[33]

Joyce had already started writing *Stephen Hero,* part of the first draft of *A Portrait of the Artist as a Young Man,* in 1904 and his condemnation of the church is evident when he describes Stephen entering the Church in Gardiner Street:

> Everywhere he saw the same flattered affection for the Jesuits who are in the habit of attaching to their order the souls of thousands of the insecurely respectable middle-class by offering them a refined asylum, an interested, a considerate confessional, a particular amiableness of manners which their spiritual adventures in no way entitled them to. (*SH*,125)

Despite Joyce's view of Catholicism, his total disbelief is questionable, since in the same letter to Nora he states: "No human being has ever stood so close to my soul as you stand" and according to the Catholic faith "the human soul begins to exist by a direct creative act of God."[34] Such ambiguity is also present in the character of Stephen Dedalus. With this in mind it is relevant to first explore Joyce's views on Catholicism and ascertain why he felt compelled to construct a "war" with the Catholic Church, before turning attention to his portrayal of the role of religion in his representation of the grief process in respect of parental loss.

NOTES

1. Jeremy Holmes, "Attachment Theory: A Secure Base for Policy?" in *The Politics of Attachment: Towards A Secure Society,* eds. Sebastian Kraemer and Jane Roberts (London: Free Association Books, 1996), 37.
2. Randall, *The Psychology of Feeling Sorry,* 96.
3. Proeve and Tudor, *Remorse,* 31.
4. Parkes and Prigerson, *Bereavement,* 210.

5. Sarah Webster Goodwin and Elisabeth Bronfen, *Death and Representation* (Baltimore: Johns Hopkins University Press, 1993), 4.

6. Hays and Hendrix, "The Role of Religion in Bereavement," 339.

7. Kirkpatrick, *Attachment*,16.

8. Bruce Reed, *The Dynamics of Religion: Process and Movement in Christian Churches* (London: Drayton, Longman and Todd, 1978), 14–15.

9. Elizabeth K. Nottingham, *Religion and Society*, Doubleday Short Studies in Sociology Series (New York: Random House, 1954), 30.

10. Kirkpatrick, *Attachment*, 18–19.

11. Kirkpatrick, *Attachment*, 108. With reference to Lee A. Kirkpatrick, "God as a Substitute Attachment Figure: A Longitudinal Study of Adult Attachment Style and Religious Change in College Students," in *Personality and Social Psychology Bulletin*, 24, 961–73.

12. Sigmund Freud, *The Future of an Illusion*, trans. W. D. Robson-Scott, The International Psycho-Analytical Library, ed. Ernest Jones, no. 15 (London: Hogarth Press, 1928, repr. 1953), 76

13. Kirkpatrick, *Attachment*, 19.

14. Sigmund Freud, "The Question of a *Weltanschauung*," in *The Freud Reader*, ed. Peter Gay (New York: Norton, 1989, repr. 1995), 785–91.

15. Freud, "The Question of a *Weltanschauung*," 783–88.

16. C. G. Jung, "Psychotherapists or the Clergy," in *The Collected Works of C. J. Jung*, trans. R. F. C. Hull, ed. Herbert Read and others, 2nd ed., 19 vols. (London: Routledge & Kegan Paul, 1969), 11: 330–35.

17. Carl Gustav Jung, *Psychology and Religion* (New Haven: Yale University Press, 1938; repr. 1968), 6. Earlier in the text Jung had defined "numinosum" as "a dynamic existence or effect, not caused by an arbitrary act of will; [. . .] either a quality of a visible object or the influence of an invisible presence causing a peculiar alteration of consciousness."

18. Tacey, *How to Read Jung*, 107.

19. See Jung, *Psychology and Religion*, 6;

20. Kirkpatrick, *Attachment*, 19.

21. Lee. A. Kirkpatrick and Phillip R. Shaver, "Attachment Theory and Religion: Childhood Attachments, Religious Beliefs, and Conversion," in *Journal for the Scientific Study of Religion*, 29 (1990): 319.

22. Kirkpatrick, *Attachment*, 19.

23. Kirkpatrick and Shaver, "Attachment Theory and Religion, 319.

24. Kirkpatrick, *Attachment*, 64.

25. Crispi, *Joyce's Creative Process*, 87.

26. Chaim Weizmann and Richard Gottheil, *What Is Zionism? Two Chapters from "Zionism and the Jewish Future"* (London: Zionist Organisation, 1918), 6.

27. Davison, *James Joyce*, 139.

28. Otto Weininger, *Sex and Character: An Investigation of Fundamental Principles*, trans. by Ladislaus Löb, eds. Daniel Steuer with Laura Marcus (Vienna: 1903; Bloomington: Indiana University Press, 2005), 295.

29. Weininger, *Sex and Character*, 927–300.

30. John McCourt, *The Years of Bloom: James Joyce in Trieste 1904–1920* (Wisconsin: The University of Wisconsin Press, 2000), 229.

31. Davison, *James Joyce*, 138.

32. See Richard Ellmann, *James Joyce*, new and revised ed. with corrections (Oxford: Oxford University Press, 1983), 30 and 47–50.

33. *Letters of James Joyce*, ed. by Richard Ellmann, 3 vols. (London: Faber and Faber, 1966), 2:48.

34. *Letters of James Joyce*, ed. by Richard Ellmann, II: 48; Bernard L. Marthaler and others, eds., *New Catholic Encyclopedia*, 2nd ed., 15 vols. (Detroit: Gale in Association with The Catholic University of America, 2003), 13:353.

Chapter Eleven

Joyce, Catholicism, and Family

Joyce's view on his spiritual life, which he defined in terms of his ability as an artist, would not have concurred with that espoused by the Catholic Church. His thoughts on the spirituality of the soul and on symbolism did take some of his views closer to those espoused by Jung, which I will discuss further in due course. He also placed significant weight on his relationship with Nora: "*Everything* that is noble and exalted and deep and true and moving in what I write comes, I believe, from you. O take me into your soul of souls and then I will become indeed the poet of my race."[1] Despite the dismissiveness often expressed toward his family ("my brothers and sisters are nothing to me"), which could be said to exhibit his own avoidant traits, he is clearly able to express his need for some form of spiritual union with Nora.[2] Holmes comments that "the avoidant may struggle to find ways to get close to people despite their fears" and here Joyce places their relationship in a more transcendent plane.[3] Rather than turn to God following his bereavement, Joyce turned to his main attachment figure.

Geert Lernout argues that Joyce "was an unbeliever from the start of his life as a writer," never returning "to the faith of his fathers" and therefore "his work can only be read properly if that important fact is taken into account."[4] His detailed account shows the complexity of this topic and how critics have interpreted Joyce's work in light of their own beliefs. What follows in this chapter discussing Joyce, Catholicism and family is therefore an overview. It points to what I believe are the most important factors for my consequent interpretation of Stephen's grief process in light of Attachment Theory. Firstly, the organisation of religion and the methods used by the Catholic Church. Secondly, how the specific actions of the priests contributed toward both James Joyce and his brother Stanislaus rejecting the organised religion of the church and the effect this rejection had on family relations. Thirdly, how religion influenced Joyce's own thoughts on death and the afterlife and his own response to his mother's death. Together these will provide a backdrop to the rendering of religion and its relation to grief and mourning within *Ulysses*.

THE ORGANISATION OF RELIGION

Former Jesuit priest Edward Boyd Barrett explains that the "Jesuit Institute is defined as *'the way of living and working peculiar to the Order'* and the arch-rule is that of uniformity, of thinking as speaking the same things." "In the Fourth Part of the Constitutions, the Order legislates concerning [. . .] 'Means to be taken to avoid dangerous Doctrines'" as follows: "*In general Superiors must carefully and constantly be on the watch to preserve Ours from the contamination of unrestrained study of new things (novitatum), and dangerous freedom in thinking (Paerculosa opinandi licentia).*"[5] It is of note that in *Stephen Hero* Joyce has Stephen's mother blame his loss of faith on his books (*SH*, 136–40) and in *Ulysses* he has Stephen describe himself to Haines as "a horrible example of free thought" when discussing religion (*U*, 1.625–26). The Catholic Church needed to maintain its influence over the religious community in general, not just those under its direct remit, and to do this, certain strategies were employed which will be discussed below.

Jacques Mercanton recalls how, when conversing with Joyce on matters of religion, it "always provoked him to mockery and excited a note of defiance in his laugh that it did not carry otherwise"; that he "spoke disdainfully about writers who portray priests without having known them, without having been subjected to them."[6] Joyce's thinking on spirituality (and that of his main protagonists) would have been seen as threatening and profane to the church, as sociologist Tom Inglis makes clear in his description of religion:

> It unites people into a community based on shared beliefs and values. Through engagement in collective rituals and practices, the community develops a shared way of reading, understanding and interpreting the world. [. . .] Everything that unites and protects the community—the beliefs, practices and symbols—is sacred. Everything that threatens or undermines the sense of community is profane.[7]

This sociological view of religion agrees with the argument previously put forward by David Sloane Wilson, who like Bowlby uses evolutionary biology for formulating his theories. Wilson draws an analogy between the workings of Christianity and an individual cell, with religion providing the cell membrane, allowing highly organised activities to take place within the cell amidst a larger chaotic world.[8] Thus, anything that threatened the membrane

(Christianity) would damage the entire cell (working structure of the religious community).

The "freethought or humanist movements," which were "an heir to the American revolution of 1766, to the French Revolution of 1789 and to the European Revolutions of 1830 and 1848," provided such a threat of damage to the Catholic Church. These movements "demanded from the established church freedom of expression and of religion, civil liberties for the individual, and the separation of church from state."[9] In a response to this Pope Puis IX introduced the infallible doctrine of the Immaculate Conception in 1854, followed by the doctrine of papal infallibility in 1869. Mary Lowe-Evans makes the point that:

> These two doctrines provide examples of the coercive and seductive strategies the papacy employed to maintain its position of authority. On the one hand, papal infallibility apparently required carte blanche, slavish adherence to official papal pronouncements. On the other hand, the doctrine of the Immaculate Conception responded to a popular, sentimental groundswell of affection for the Blessed Virgin Mary as evidenced in *Ad Diem Illum Laetissum,* an encyclical issued by Pope Pius X on February 2, 1904 (a date Joyce would have noted) in anticipation of the fiftieth anniversary of the dogma of the Immaculate Conception.[10]

"Seductive and Coercive" methods were not only used by the papacy according to Edward Boyd Barrett. He exposes how the Jesuit priests also resorted to such methods in order to: attract "suitable boys" to join the order; avoid doing charitable or "good work": obtain property from those who were about to enter the order; obtain government bonuses and flatter the rich.[11]

That Joyce became aware of at least some of these practices is evident from his Trieste notebooks where he noted the following regarding the Jesuits:

> They do not love the end they serve.
> [. . .]
> They flatter the wealthy but they do not love them nor their ways. They flatter the clergy, their half brothers.
> [. . .]
> Are they venal of speech because venality is the only point of contact between pastor and flock?[12]

Joyce appears to have encapsulated these perceived traits in the character of "the very reverend John Conmee S. J." in *Ulysses,* described concisely by Dennis Brown as "a religious hypocrite for whom self-satisfied inauthenticity has become a way of life" (*U*, 10.1).[13] His character does not provide a representation of the members of Jesuit order as those to turn to in times of need;

as those that would offer comfort or security. He is prepared to "Oblige" Mr. Cunningham in his attempts to help Master Dignam because he is "useful at mission time" and he will spend time conversing with "the wife of Mr. David Sheehy M.P.," but has no inclination to converse with, or financially help, an injured sailor (*U,* 10.5–11). Stephen Haag comments on how: "The flintiness of Father Conmee's worldview is evident in the fact that he does not even need to avert his eyes to shut the beggar out; he can look and bless and still not give."[14] The hypocritical behaviour of the clergy, which Joyce illustrates so clearly here, was undoubtedly a contributory factor to the rejection of the church by both his brother Stanislaus and himself. A further note from Joyce's Trieste notebook regarding the Jesuits is both damning and to the point: "They breed atheists."[15]

There were various incidences in the lives of Stanislaus and James where the clergy tried to drive a wedge between them and their family, which only served to drive a greater wedge between themselves and the church. Stanislaus relates how the rector of Belvedere managed to convince him to pass on some information regarding James, claiming their conversation was private, "as in a confessional," but the following day called for their mother and warned her of "the evil ways" of her eldest son.[16] He also recounts other occasions when the priests tried to estrange them from their mother. For example, when their mother was still grieving for the loss of her youngest son, the priest advised her to throw both Stanislaus and James out "before they corrupt[ed] the other children" and when James did leave the church the priest told his mother he was "very cowardly."[17]

The anger that Stanislaus felt toward the clergy and the negative impact they had on internal family relations, particularly between James and his mother, are laid bare in the following extract from his book, *My Brother's Keeper*:

> [T]he fact that my mother listened with docility to her clerical counsellors sank into his [James Joyce's] soul and gradually estranged him from her. In that her confessors succeeded. If my brother had abandoned his family to enter the Jesuit order, that would not have been cowardly; that would have been obedience to a higher call to a spiritual life—the spiritual life of the Jesuits! My brother had hearkened to a spiritual call, inaudible to their dull ears [. . .] but not without being assailed on occasion by sharp pangs of doubt.[18]

In considering Joyce's decision to leave the church, that he paradoxically felt to be a "spiritual call," is of major import. Mahaffey explains that for Joyce freedom "was primarily freedom of thought" and his detachment from church was therefore essential to his creativity.[19] According to Stanislaus, Joyce believed it to be "imperative that he should save his real spiritual life from being overlaid and crushed by a false one that he had outgrown" and that for him it was the "poets in the measure of their gifts and personality" that he saw as "the repositories of the genuine spiritual life of their race, and the priests were usurpers."[20]

It has been noted that "priests and other human spiritual figures" are often perceived as having a "distinct essence" and "special, internal qualities and powers that distinguish them qualitatively from other humans."[21] In viewing the priests as "usurpers" Joyce instead appropriates these qualities to the poet. This is illustrated in his portrayal of Stephen who has been described by Bonheim as aesthetically seeing himself as some kind of "secular saint."[22]

With art taking on a spiritualist aspect, one can see Joyce engaging with Arthur Symons' *The Symbolist Movement* (first published 1899), which Curran reported influenced Joyce no less than Ibsen.[23] In his "Introduction" to the book Symons wrote: "after the world has starved its soul long enough in the contemplation and the re-arrangement of material things, comes the turn of the soul: and with it comes the literature of which I write this volume, a literature in which the visible world is no longer a reality, and the unseen world no longer a dream."[24] There are two points of interest with regards to the language used here: Firstly, it clearly anticipates the work on dream symbolism by both Freud and Jung and how symbolic thought and theory permeated psychoanalytical movement. Secondly, the specific use of the word "soul," something Joyce continually refers to in both his letters and his texts, and its link to literature. As Symons espoused that: "Symbolism began with the first words uttered by the first man, as he names every living thing; or before them, in heaven, when God named the world into being," it can be assumed that, as someone who believed in God, he saw the soul as a as being created by God. With the association made between the soul and literary innovation, one can perceive why, as an artist who wanted to pursue his "genuine spiritual life," rather than be controlled by a specific dogma, Joyce found Symons so influential.

Later, Jung came to see the soul as a particular part of the psyche, as the collective personality of a person.[25] Perhaps Joyce had anticipated this thought when he linked the "gifts and personality" of poets with "spiritual life." Indeed, Maria Jolas, when questioned about the attitude toward Freud and Jung replied "it was as remarkable sign of his intelligence that he didn't fall for psychoanalysis when it was so current. He started beyond it."[26] In considering the attachment traits Joyce went on to give his protagonists, the conclusion drawn by Jolas does not seem unreasonable.

Having separated his spiritual life from the constraints of Catholicism, it is perhaps ironical that, sixteen days before Joyce wrote to Nora regarding his "open war" on the Catholic Church, Stanislaus made an entry in his diary listing the different views Joyce had taken toward it: "Catholicism he has appreciated, rejected and opposed, and liked again when it had lost its power over him."[27] "Liked" certainly seems contrary to the sentiment of his brother's letter to Nora. However, Stanislaus later claimed in *My Brother's Keeper*, Joyce actually had great respect for Catholic philosophy, seeing it as "the most coherent attempt to establish [. . .] intellectual and material stability," or as he has Stephen Dedalus describe it in *Portrait*, "an absurdity which is logical and coherent" (*P*, 265).[28] Nevertheless, for Joyce "freedom was a necessity: it was the guiding theme of his life" and incompatible with the rigidity of Catholicism.[29] Joyce instills this need for freedom in the character of Stephen, who in *Portrait* has Cranly repeat back to him what he had once told him he "wished to do in life": "To discover the mode of life or of art whereby your spirit could express itself in unfettered freedom" (*P*, 267).

For Joyce (and for the character of Stephen) therefore, the psychological need for liberty, affording the capability of responding to "the impulses of [his] nature," was the impetus for leaving the Church (see letter to Nora in Introduction to Part 4). The term "impulses of [. . .] nature" can be read as not only referring to artistic nature but also his views on human sexual nature. In the frequently quoted letter where Joyce draws an analogy between his writing and "put[ting] down a bucket into [his] own soul's well, sexual department" he writes: "I am nauseated by the lying drivel about pure men and pure women and spiritual love and love for ever: blatant lying in the face of the truth."[30] This statement, although quite general, can also be read as a specific reflection of his own experiences and loss of innocence; his visits to prostitutes in his teen years and his first date with Nora where she demonstrated her own lack of sexual inhibition.[31]

The influence exerted by the priests on his mother resulted in Joyce viewing her as "an accomplice of the Irish Catholic Church, the enemy of free thought and the joy of living."[32] The evident distancing of Joyce from his mother may have a bearing on another comment in his Trieste notebook, this time regarding Jesus: "His shadow is everywhere."[33] The ambiguity of what is meant by the metaphorical term "shadow" leaves this statement open to various interpretations. It could be a reference to the paralysis that he perceived in Ireland, as evidenced in his letter to Grant Richards, to which he believed religion was contributing.[34] However, it is quite possible that he was also thinking of the priests (as a representative of Christ) and the adverse effect their preaching of Catholic dogma could have on family life; something he recreated in *Stephen Hero*: "He argued no further with his mother, persuaded that he could have no satisfactory commerce with her so long as she chose to set the shadow of a clergyman between her nature and his" (*SH*, 214).

Joyce's portrayal of how the clergy touched Stephen's relationship with his mother reconstructs his own experience as related by Stanislaus, of how the clerics "gradually estranged him from her." I have already suggested that, from the biographical information available on Joyce, he appears to exhibit his own avoidant traits. It appears that the priests only helped to reinforce Joyce's internal working models, psychologically keeping him at a distance from her. From an attachment perspective, Joyce had a negative experience of religion whereas his mother, whose unfailing faith is undeniable, clearly felt she had a strong attachment with, and took comfort in, God. As Attachment Theory focuses on the individual in reciprocal relationships, one can appreciate why, unlike the theories of Jung and Freud, respectively, it is neither pro-nor anti-religious.

DEATH AND THE QUESTION OF AN AFTERLIFE

It was not only the "joy of living" that Joyce viewed the Catholic Church as interfering with; he also saw it as the reason that death is so feared, as he voiced to Arthur Power:

> [I]t is Christianity which has made us afraid of death, for men, nowadays, live in two halves in which their desire to live is tempered by their fear of death so that we no longer know which way to turn, and as a result both our public and private lives are smothered in hypocrisy. The pagans faced death as bravely as they faced life; "one life one death" was their philosophy.[35]

Here Joyce is referring to Catholic belief in the immortal soul, which denies the finality of death. After bodily death, it is said the soul will be judged by God and then will either go on to live in heaven, or to purgatory, or to damnation in hell, thus "retrospectively render[ing] meaning to the life that ended."[36] The fear of being judged in the next life, in Joyce's view, was affecting man's natural impulse to openly enjoy life, turning them into pretenders and hypocrites. Yet a letter Joyce wrote to Lady Gregory in 1902, when he had decided to abandon his studies in Dublin and go abroad, demonstrates that he continued to believe in the soul at that time: "All things are inconstant except the faith of the soul, which changes all things and fills their inconstancy with light. And though I seem to have been driven out of my country here as a misbeliever I have found no man yet with *a faith like mine.*"[37] I have emphasised the final words of this quotation because, as was always the case with Joyce, they appear to have been carefully chosen. He had not, for example written "a faith *as strong as* mine," which would have implied that he was still a devout Catholic. Kirkpatrick notes that however one tries to define Religion "there are always grey areas around the edges," giving rise to diverse "forms of thinking, belief, and experience," although the "cognitive processes underlying them are largely the same."[38] In his letter to Lady

Gregory I believe Joyce is referring to his own individual faith, his own way of thinking of religion, which appears to rest with the spirituality of the soul.

When it came to the subject of the continuation of the soul following death, Peter Costello states that "in his own mind" Joyce was "uncertain," hence his reading of the F. J. Myers book, *Human Personality and its Survival of Bodily Death,* when it came into the National Library (see Chapter 9).[39] Perhaps his choice of reading is also exposing his own avoidant traits, since it has been found that such individuals are "likely to fear the unknown nature of death," as opposed to secure subjects who generally experience less fear of death.[40]

Joyce's contemplation regarding the afterlife, even if present before his mother's demise, would have been enhanced by the recurrent dreams he had of her following her death. As Joyce felt he contributed toward his mother's death due to his "cynical frankness of conduct" and this no doubt played on his conscience.[41] The emotional effect of the recurrent dreams is reflected in a letter written to Nora at the beginning of September 1904. Following a night of unusually peaceful sleep he writes: "What a lovely morning! That skull, I am glad to say, didn't come to torment me last night. How I hate God and death!"[42] Unlike Freud and Jung, Bowlby did not focus on the interpretation of dreams since generally his work was focused on "observable behaviour rather than the inner world" (*JB*, 127). However, he did note that in terms of bereavement, if dreams were of the "traumatic aspects of the last illness or death" this could be an indicator that mourning is not taking a "favourable course" (*AL*3:98). The face of Joyce's mother "as she lay in her coffin—a face grey and wasted with cancer" evidently had a profound effect on him, as did the trauma of watching her slowly die of the disease.[43]

Although Bowlby did not choose to concern himself with dreams, the debate regarding their function and interpretation had been taking place for centuries before and attachment theorists following Bowlby have since gone on to make comment. In the sixteenth century, Michel de Montaigne, wrote: "I maintain that dreams are loyal interpreters of our inclinations [. . .] It is no miracle that men should find again in their dreams things which occupy them in their lives, things which they think about, worry about, gaze about and do when they are awake."[44] Montaigne's view anticipated that expressed by attachment-informed psychotherapist, Jeremy Holmes, who sees dreams as "a process of working through, of integrating material, of problem solving."[45] This is in contrast to Freud, who interpreted dreams in terms of wish fulfilment and Jung, who viewed them as compensating the conscious. From an attachment perspective one could therefore view Joyce's dream as not only indicating a problem in dealing with his grief, but also a concern with life after death, which obviously concerned his waking hours. Sensing the deceased, vivid nightmares and even hypnagogic hallucinations are now all seen as part of the normal grieving process.[46] However, in Joyce's time they would not have been and therefore, not uncommonly, he must have sought a logical reason from them, be it by questioning his own mind or questioning the continuation of the soul.

It is evident that the ambiguity Joyce felt toward the subject of eternal life and the rationality of such a belief translated into taciturn muteness when with his friends, as Arthur Power's recollection of his exasperation with Joyce illustrates. He relates how, when they were out walking Joyce's "determined silence on the subject of religion and on man's survival after death" caused his frustration to get the better of him:

> I [Power] pushed him [Joyce] into a corner of the street, and I asked him the straight question,
> Do you believe in a next life?
> [. . .] he answered,
> I don't think much of this life—and closed the conversation so that I realised that I would never get a direct answer on the subject from him.[47]

Whilst providing a typical example of Joycean wit, his response was also one that continued to leave the subject entirely open. Yet when Joyce represented the spectral appearances of May Dedalus in *Ulysses*, he chose to portray them as a vision or hallucination, not as actual hauntings. Despite this ambiguity and his rejection of Catholicism, Joyce chose to draw a parallel between what he was trying to do with his art and transubstantiation; seeing himself as "converting the bread of everyday life into something that has a permanent artistic life of its own" for the "mental, moral and spiritual uplift" of the people.[48] Here one can see a parallel with Jung, with art being connected to spiritual and mental well-being.

As I have made evident, Joyce's views on Catholicism and belief in God went through many phases. When he passed away a Catholic priest approached Nora regarding a religious funeral service and her response was unequivocal: "I couldn't do that to him."[49] Although a Catholic herself, she was aware of and respected her husband's views of the organised church. Yet it appears he had not totally rejected the concept of a human soul. Ellmann reports that in Trieste Joyce "intimated to his brother that he thought everyone retained some faith in a supreme being," which would have enabled him to keep faith in the existence and spirituality of the soul whilst he simultaneously rejected the specific dogma espoused by the Catholic Church.[50]

Joyce's difficult and complicated relationship with religion appears to be the result of an ineluctable tension between his Catholic indoctrination and his own life experiences and intellect. His self-referential portrayal of the interaction of Stephen Dedalus with the Catholic Church is also notable for its complexity. Like Joyce, he is depicted as going from spending his time with prostitutes, to living a life of extreme devotion, to then losing his faith and leaving the church. He "will not serve that in which [he] no longer believe[s]" in order to "express [him]self in some mode of life or art as freely as [he] can" (*P,* 269). In *Ulysses,* again like Joyce, Stephen is portrayed as having dreams of his dead mother, which, I will argue, are related to his unresolved grief.

NOTES

1. *Letters of James Joyce,* ed. Richard Ellmann, 2: 248.
2. *Letters of James Joyce,* ed. by Richard Ellmann, 2: 48.
3. Holmes, "Attachment Theory: A Secure Base for Policy?" 99.
4. Geert Lernout, *Help My Unbelief: James Joyce and Religion* (London: Continuum, 2010), 2.
5. *Jesuit Constitutions* in Barrett, *The Jesuit Enigma,* 88–89.
6. Jacques Mercanton, "The Hours of Joyce," in *Portraits of the Artist in Exile: Recollections of James Joyce by Europeans,* ed. Willard Potts (Seattle: University of Washington Press), 240.
7. Tom Inglis, "Religion, Identity, State and Society," in *The Cambridge Companion to Modern Irish Culture,* eds., Joe Cleary and Clare Connolly (Cambridge: Cambridge University Press, 2005), 60.
8. See David Sloan Wilson, *Darwin's Cathedral: Evolution, Religion and the Nature of Society* (Chicago: University of Chicago Press, 2002), 151.
9. Lernout, *Help My Unbelief,* 92–93
10. Lowe-Evans, *Catholic Nostalgia,* 32.
11. Barrett, *The Jesuit Enigma,* 86–87, 92, 132, 184, 316.
12. *The Workshop of Daedalus,* eds. Robert Scholes and Richard M. Kain (Illinois: Northwestern University Press, 1965), 102.
13. Dennis Brown, *The Modernist Self in Twentieth-Century English Literature* (Hampshire: Palgrave, 1989), 131–32.
14. Stefan Haag, "Listen and Be Touched: Aural Space in 'Wandering Rocks,'" in *Joyce's "Wandering Rocks,"* 117.
15. *The Workshop of Dedalus,* ed. Scholes and Kain, 102.
16. Stanislaus Joyce, *My Brother's Keeper,* 68–69.
17. Stanislaus Joyce, *My Brother's Keeper,* 190 and 230.
18. Stanislaus Joyce, *My Brother's Keeper,* 231
19. Vicki Mahaffey, "Darkening Freedom: Yeats, Joyce and Beckett," in *The Cambridge History of Modernism,* ed. Vincent Sherry (Cambridge: Cambridge University Press, 2016), 650.
20. Stanislaus Joyce, *My Brother's Keeper,* 107.
21. Kirkpatrick, *Attachment,* 282. With reference to Boyer, *The Naturalness of Religious Ideas: A Cognitive Theory of Religion* (Berkeley: University of California Press, 1994).

22. Helmut Bonheim, *Joyce's Benefictions*, Perspectives in Criticism Series (Berkley: University of California Press, 1964), 138.

23. See Michael Patrick Gillespie, *Inverted Volumes Improperly Arranged: James Joyce and His Trieste Library*, Studies in Modern Literature Series No. 10 (Michigan: UMI Research Press, 1983), 48.

24. Arthur Symons, *The Symbolist Movement in Literature*, 2nd ed. rev. (London: Constable, 1911), 4.

25. See Jung, "Psychological Types," in *Collected Works*, 4: 463–67.

26. "An interview with Carola Giedion-Welcker and Maria Jolas," ed. Richard Kain, *James Joyce Quarterly* 11 (Winter 1974): 120 quoted in Jean Kimball, *Odyssey of the Psyche*, 6.

27. *The Complete Dublin Diary of Stanislaus Joyce*, ed. by George H. Healey (London: Cornell University Press, 1971), 55.

28. Stanislaus Joyce, *My Brother's Keeper*, 108.

29. Stanislaus Joyce, *My Brother's Keeper*, 108.

30. *Letters of James Joyce*, ed. Richard Ellmann, 2: 191–92.

31. See Richard Ellmann, *James Joyce*, 65; Maddox, *Nora*, 42.

32. Stanislaus Joyce, *My Brother's Keeper*, 238;

33. *The Workshop of Dedalus*, ed. Scholes and Kain, 101.

34. *Selected Letters of James Joyce*, ed. Richard Ellmann, 83. Referring to *Dubliners*, Joyce wrote: "I chose Dublin for the scene because that city seems to me the centre of paralysis."

35. Power, *Conversations with James Joyce*, 83.

36. Zygmunt Bauman, *Mortality, Immortality and Other Life Strategies* (Cambridge: Polity Press, 1992), 26.

37. *Letters of James Joyce*, ed. Stuart Gilbert, 53 (my emphasis).

38. Kirkpatrick, *Attachment*, 291–95

39. Peter Costello, *James Joyce*, 212.

40. Feeney and Noller, *Adult Attachment*, 38. With reference to M. Mikulincer, V. Florain and R. Tolmacz, "Attachment Styles and Fear of Personal Death: A Case Study of Affect Regulation," *Journal of Personality and social Psychology*, 58 (1990): 273–80.

41. *Selected Letters of James Joyce*, ed. Richard Ellmann, 25.

42. *Letters of James Joyce*, ed. Richard Ellmann, 2: 50

43. *Letters of James Joyce*, ed. by Richard Ellmann, 2: 48.

44. Michel de Montaigne, "On Experience," in *The Complete Essays of Michel do Montaigne*, trans. M. A. Screech (London: Allen Lane, The Penguin Press, 1991), 1247.

45. Diana T. Kenny, *From Id to Intersubjectivity: Talking about the Talking Cure with Master Clinicians* (London: Karnac, 2014), 173

46. See Parkes and Prigerson, *Bereavement*, 216.

47. Power, *Conversations*, 59–60.

48. Stanislaus Joyce, *My Brother's Keeper*, 104.

49. Ellmann, *James Joyce*, 755, citing interview with George Joyce, 1953.

50. Ellmann, *The Consciousness of Joyce*, 50

Chapter Twelve

Stephen Dedalus
Grief, Guilt, and Remorse of Conscience

Attachment theorists, when discussing bereavement often refer to guilt as occurring either due to the mode of death, such as suicide, and/or due to the attachment relationship with the deceased (see *AL3*)[1] This chapter will focus on how Stephen's loss of faith and hence refusal to pray for his mother on her deathbed has led to profound guilt and remorse. In addition to Bowlby's work, that of Proeve and Tudor has also provided a useful reference point. Not only do their theories on the distortion of remorse dovetail with the work of attachment theorists, but their identification of the different *concepts* of wrongness, to which guilt and remorse belong, brings extra delineation to the discussion of Stephen's grief. Proeve and Tudor view remorse as being conceptualised as: "I have wronged another person" and guilt as being conceptualised as "I have broken a rule or disobeyed an authority." The latter can be "conceived in religious terms, as 'sin,' or alternatively in non-religious terms."[2] From a secular perspective Stephen can be read as having disobeyed the matriarch of the family. But the question remains as to whether one is to read his religious indoctrination as still playing a role, thereby effectively adding another layer to his guilt and enhancing his grief reaction (his emotional response to death) and consequently how he mourns (his public display of grief).

JESUIT INDOCTRINATION AND THE EXAMINATION OF THE CONSCIENCE

In *Ulysses* Joyce clearly shows Stephen's remorse through the ever-present spectre of his mother. He also portrays how Stephen's conscience plays an important role in his felt remorse and his continuing grief. Psychologist Peter Randall, who has explored the links between psychological research, feelings of sorrow and religious doctrine, describes the conscience as "more than Plato's rational facility for recognising good and more than Aristotle's virtuous clamp on self-indulgence. It is the moral essence of our being that passes judgement and can only be silenced by a great effort of will. It is not fooled by specious excuses or extinguished by convenient platitudes."[3] Although Joyce *shows* Stephen's remorse, he doesn't actually *tell* the reader by having Stephen verbalise or think "I wish I had not done that." He does, however, come very close. Consider Stephen's response to Haines following his request to "make a collection" of his "sayings": "Speaking to me. They wash the tub and scrub. Agenbite of inwit. Conscience. Yet here's a spot" (*U*, 1.481–82). Jeffrie Murphy interprets "Agenbite of inwit" as an "inconsolable bite of conscience," a type of remorse that "seems to involve the idea that the wrong one has done is so deep, has involved such a wanton assault on the very meaning of a person's human life, that one can in no sense ever make it right again."[4] Of course in *Ulysses*, with the death of Stephen's mother there is not only a "sense" he can never make it right again, it is absolute.

Only minutes before Stephen's conversation with Haines and following Buck Mulligan's accusation that there was "something sinister" in him for not praying for his mother, Stephen's conscience had made itself known (*U*, 1.94). Initially recalling a dream of his dead mother, he appears to experience a vision of her, which leaves him "trembling at his soul's cry" (*U*, 1.282). Joyce clearly illustrates to the reader, through his repeated reference to his conscience in Stephen's response to Haines ("Agenbite of inwit [bite of conscience]. Conscience,)" that his continuing grief and hence visions are very much connected with his sense of wrongdoing. This is further reinforced by Stephen's quote from *Macbeth*, "here's a spot" which is uttered by Lady Macbeth (V.i.32).[5] Comparable to Stephen's troubling visions, Lady Macbeth's conscience causes her to sleepwalk the castle, trying to wash the blood of the murdered king from her hands. Although she did not wield the knife herself (just as Stephen did not physically kill his mother), she was complicit in his murder and this intertextuality provides a tacit implication Stephen should be read as feeling some responsibility for his mother's death.

In order to understand the emotional weight that Stephen carries, one initially needs to return to his religious schooling as represented in *Portrait*. Through his education by the Jesuits at both Clongowes Wood and later at Belvedere College, it is possible to view Stephen as someone who would have been used to psychological self-examination. Joyce substantiates the role of introspection in the lives of Catholic students when he has Father Arnall define a retreat that Stephen and his fellow pupils from Belvedere are to attend as: "a withdrawal for a while from the cares of our life [. . .] in order to examine the state of our conscience" (*P*, 117). To enable them to carry out such an examination, the students would have taken part in various spiritual exercises, which were developed by St. Ignatius Loyla, the founder of the Jesuits.

An extract from the English translation of *The Spiritual Exercises* states as follows:

> GENERAL EXAMINATION OF CONSCIENCE
> *in order to purify oneself and to confess better (1),*
> (1) The principles and rules here expounded are intended for use when preparing for confession, where a general or an ordinary confession. They may also be used in our nightly self-examination. [. . .]
> [. . .]
> *There are two ways of sinning mortally. The first is, when a man gives consent to an evil thought with the intention of acting afterwards according to his consent, or with the desire of doing so if he could.*
> *The second way of sinning mortally is, when that sin is carried out in action; and this is a more grievous sin for three reasons: first, on account of the longer time (4); secondly on account of the greater intensity; thirdly on account of the greater injury to both persons.*
> (4) I.e., the longer time the soul entertains the thought of the sin, and adheres to it. [6]

The reader of *Portrait* is made aware that, before attending the retreat at Belvedere, Stephen had sinned mortally due to his frequent visits to prostitutes. As a consequence of his actions he had then sinned further as his "Devotion had gone by the board" due to his belief that "his offence was too grievous to be atoned for in whole or in part by a false homage to the Allseeing and Allknowing" (*P*, 111).

At the retreat Stephen reacted to the skillful oration of the preacher, or as Joyce describes it, the "preacher's knife" which "probed deeply into his diseased conscience," which had the effect of eventually leading him to a sense of "humility and contrition" (*P*, 123; 135). Hélèn Cixous comments that, as an artist who believes in "the evocative power of words" Stephen finds that the sermon touches "on the raw of his imagination." The words of the preacher "have affected his actual vision of the world [. . .] and he sees everything through his own disgust."[7] Consequently he finds himself wondering "how he could have done such things without shame?" as he looks to find a church in which to confess (*P*, 151). Theologian Lewis Smedes makes clear the demarcation between guilt and shame: "We feel guilty for what we do. We feel shame for what we are."[8] The narrator relates how, in reacting to his shame, to the sinner he had become, Stephen attempts to change who he is by going on to adopt an extremely pious stance; "not allow[ing] himself to desist from even the least or lowliest devotion" (*P*, 162). However, he is shown to find his relationship with God to be untenable.

How Stephen conducts his relationship with God can be read not only in terms of his artistic temperament but also in terms of avoidant attachment traits. Prior to the retreat Stephen is portrayed as only relating to God via a "loveless awe" (*P*, 111). Yet after, having experienced his deep sense of shame and changing his behaviour to that of religious devotee, he is shown to find that he can "no longer disbelieve in the reality of love since God Himself had loved his individual soul with divine love from all eternity" (*P*, 161–62). This indicates that, at the very least, one can read Stephen as previously having reserved judgement as to whether he was lovable, a typical perception of the self of those classified as insecure avoidants.[9] As already noted, Lee Kirkpatrick found that the ability to form a perceived relationship with God was dependent on internal working models. He further explains that if an avoidant person "applies his or her attachment machinery to ideas about God, the system is likely to output the idea that this God is distant, inaccessible, and uncaring."[10] The portrayal of Stephen, at his most pious, is of a young man who is convinced that God is loving, a synonym of caring. However, as Joyce later has him confess to his friend, Cranly, "I tried to love God [. . .]. It seems now I failed," one can certainly read Stephen as finding God inaccessible and distant in so much as he found it impossible to perceive a reciprocal relationship with him (*P*, 261).

From an attachment perspective, Stephen's expressed view that he "failed" to love God, to form an emotional bond with him, is a particularly significant if one takes into account Kirkpatrick's view of the way in which a worshiper tends to love God:

> [T]he love felt by a worshiper toward God more closely resembles a child's love for a caregiver [. . .] a relatively pure manifestation of the attachment system. It is "attachment love," if you will. Conversely, the love felt by a worshiper *from* God resembles the love a parent feels for his or her child; it is "caregiver love," unconfounded by attachment or sexuality.[11]

Stephen's attempt to love God followed by his perceived "failure" could therefore be seen to parallel the relationship he had with his mother. In temporarily finding "a belief in the reality of love," one can interpret Stephen as having found what Kirkpatrick refers to as "caregiver-love," something he would have attributed to his mother before he was left to emotionally fend for himself at Clongowes Wood. Yet his reticence or inability to form an "attachment love" with God can be read as reflecting Stephen's internal working model of others, particularly the emotional distance that had grown between himself and his mother, culminating in his professed feeling of "futile isolation" (*P*, 105). In other words, there was an intrinsic doubt that he could be be let down again and find that perhaps God's love and support were not infinite.

Support for this interpretation is evident in the portrayal of Stephen's reaction to the director of Belvedere when he raises the question of him joining the priesthood, causing his mind to return to Clongowes Wood:

> The troubling odour of the long corridors of Clongowes came back to him and he heard the discreet murmur of the burning gasflames. At once from every part of his being unrest began to irradiate. [. . .]
> Some instinct, waking at these memories, *stronger than education or piety*, quickened within him at every near approach to that life, an instinct subtle and hostile, and armed him against acquiescence. (*P*, 174, my emphasis)

Stephen's "instinct," which goes beyond his religious teachings and devotions, could be read in Jungian terms as a "psychic process, not under conscious control" an "apperception."[12] However, from an attachment perspective it can be read as relating to his internal working models, based on past experience. When bullied, sick and unjustly punished whilst at Clongowes Wood, he could not rely on his attachment figure to be available for him. He therefore realises that ultimately the only person he can depend on is himself, thereby rendering devotion to God a futile activity. Typically seen in someone with insecure avoidant traits, Stephen is portrayed as coming to the realisation that he "no longer believe[s]" (*P*, 268).[13] Unafraid of being alone, he feels able to leave his "home," "fatherland," and "church" to pursue his "mode of life or art as freely as [he] can" (*P*, 268–69).

Jung believed that for centuries religions "gathered the psychic energy of individuals and nations alike into traditions that bore witness to life's meaning and acted as underground springs nourishing different civilisations" and that without religion this energy "poured back into the psyche," its misplacement leading to neurosis.[14] It could be argued, therefore, that Stephen is, at the very least, prone to neurosis due to his rejection of religion. But one has to question what is meant by religion and whether Stephen has truly freed himself from its indoctrination. As Jung did not see religion as a particular creed but rather as being open toward the transcendent self, in order to meet the requirements of the soul through symbolic life, Stephen's wish to enable his "spirit" to "express itself in unfettered freedom" through his art, can be said to leave himself open to transcendence.

From a more conventional view of religious practice, despite Stephen's protestation in *Portrait* that he "will not serve," his friend Cranly discerns how "curious" it is that Stephen's "mind is supersaturated with the religion" in which he claims to have no belief (*P*, 260–61). If he has been unable to leave behind his religious indoctrination it is possible to argue that the Stephen presented in *Ulysses*, is a young man who has actually been unsuccessful in his attempt to "fly by" the net of religion (*P*, 220). Hence the depiction of his continued visions and dreams of his mother could be read as a result of his heightened internal judgement such that, try as he may, he feels guilty for having "sinned mortally" after refusing to pray for her and is experiencing a similar sense of shame that he felt in his adolescence. Such a reading has been made by Charles Peake, who explains in detail why he reads the power of religion in Stephen's mind as "undefeated."[15] However, it is worth exploring a comment made by Stanislaus Joyce after he left the church which can be seen to offer an alternative and more cogent reading regarding Stephen's anxiety due to his troubled conscience.

An entry in *The Complete Dublin Diary of Stanislaus Joyce* makes the point that it was *leaving* the church that actually resulted in an increased sense of right and wrong:

> The chief thing I found when I left the Church was that "ugly little beast," a conscience. [. . .] Besides, Confession and Penance, which are in a way the chastisement of sin, kill the conscience, because chastisement is expiation and kills the acuteness of one's sense of the wrong consummated, but it humiliates and emphasises one's vague sense of having done wrong. So long as any governing body has the authority to tell you what you shall consider either right or wrong, your conscience is not your own. It is uncomfortable, however, for the free conscience to be unable to blame anybody but itself and to be forced to regard every act in the past of which it disapproves as indelible.[16]

It is possible to read a similar scenario being played out in Stephen's psyche; one that both acknowledges he is no longer constrained by the nets of religion yet corroborates Stephen's "agenbite of inwit." Having flown the nets of religion, much like Icarus, he crashes down to earth (metaphorically speaking) in terms of now having to take full responsibility for his actions.

The reasoning expressed by Stanislaus as to how organised religion can nullify the conscience to a certain extent can also be seen within the narrative of *Portrait*, once one becomes aware of what is stated in the *Spiritual Exercises* regarding the Examination of Conscious and evil thoughts:

> *I presuppose that there are within me three kinds of thoughts; to wit, one my own, which springs entirely from my own liberty and will; and two others, which come from without, one form the good spirit, and the other from the evil* (2).
>
> (2) *Within me,* here, as in so many other places, S. Ignatius uses the first person singular, in order that the exercitant may apply everything to himself.[17]

Although the existence of the free will is acknowledged, it is also possible for the exercitant to attribute any thoughts and consequent actions to an evil spirit.

In *Portrait* it is the priest in the confessional of Church Street Chapel who provides Stephen with a reason for his actions:

> The devil has led you astray. Drive him back to hell when he tempts you [. . .]— the foul spirit who hates our Lord. [. . .]
> Blinded by his tears and by the light of God's mercifulness he bent his head and heard the grave words of absolution spoken and saw the priest's hand raised above him in token of forgiveness. (*P*, 157)

As with the short story "Grace" in *Dubliners,* where Mr. Kernan is persuaded by his friends to join them in "a retreat," Joyce depicts how easy it is to "wash the pot" and "'enounce the devil" (*D,* 118; 124). Yet unlike Stephen in *Portrait,* one is given the distinct impression that if Mr. Kernan is indicative of the rest of the group, there will be no true probing of the conscience or any feelings of shame: "I'll just tell him my little tale of woe. I'm not such a bad fellow" (*D*, 124). Ironically, although the contrite Stephen is portrayed as experiencing a form of "spiritual exaltation," it transpires to be only temporary and with his consequent loss of faith, from a Catholic perspective, he ends up in a far worse spiritual state than Mr. Kernan in "Grace" (*P*, 162).

With Stephen finding himself unable to believe in God and by extension the devil (as, according to the Old Testament Lucifer was an archangel created by God), his "free conscience" is in a position where, to quote Stanislaus, it is "unable to blame anybody but itself." Therefore, when the Stephen of *Ulysses* is introduced to the reader, he can be interpreted as a character who cannot, as the priest had done, blame the devil or an evil spirit for his actions and who cannot gain absolution by confessing. However, Stephen's conscience, in addition to its secular resurgence, can still be viewed as being predisposed to his religious training, in so much as he is someone who has been taught to introspect and soul search. By virtue of the admittance Joyce gives the reader to Stephen's stream of consciousness in *Ulysses*, one can interpret Stephen as being unable to desist from such activity ("Memories beset his brooding brain" [*U*, 1.265–66]). He is therefore persistently racked with remorse, which transmutes into his repeated recollections of his mother and her dying moments.

REMORSE, GUILT, AND AVOIDANT ATTACHMENT

In *Ulysses* Joyce leaves no doubt that Stephen conceptualises remorse as "I have wronged another," which I will argue has led to an element of self-punishment in his mourning. It is known that "feelings of guilt are a common problem" with those who have avoidant attachments following a loss, but whether Stephen conceptualises guilt in terms of sin is not clear-cut.[18] Much like Joyce himself who thought that most people retained some sort of belief in a supreme being, Stephen, despite no longer believing in the confessional or even evil spirits, retains an unresolvable tension between his claimed disbelief and his fear of the existence of an "Allseeing and Allknowing" being (*P*, 111).

Joyce makes this tension evident through Stephen's internal monologue and conversations. Stephen repeatedly refers to his "soul" in *Ulysses*. For example, he describes the vision of his mother in the Telemachus episode as: "Her glazing eyes, staring out of death, to shake and bend my soul" (*U*, 1.273). As is made clear by the priest at the retreat in *Portrait,* he had been taught that the soul could only come into being through God: "Remember, my dear little boys, our souls long to be with God. We come from God [. . .]. O think what pain, what anguish it must be for the poor soul to be spurned from the presence of the supremely good and loving Creator Who has called that soul into existence from nothingness and sustained it in life and loved it with an immeasurable love'" (*P*, 138).

Although the Stephen of *Ulysses* is no longer able to respond to the words of the priest, as his mother would have wished, Geert Lernout notes his reticence to blaspheme: "As long as he is sober, Stephen is strangely reluctant to own up to his rejection of the Church and instead some of the most powerful anti-clerical and anti-religious comments are made by his friends Buck Mulligan and Kevin Egan. [. . .] Buck Mulligan blasphemes almost continually, while Stephen carefully avoids using the Lord's name in vain."[19] When he is drunk, as in his conversation with Bloom in the cabman's shelter, although Stephen refers to God with a certain amount of irony he still indicates a belief that the soul comes from God. When Bloom states: "You as a good catholic [. . .] believe in the soul" Stephen replies: "They tell me on the best authority it is a simple substance and therefore incorruptible. It would be immortal, I understand, but for the possibility of its annihilation by its First Cause Who, from all I can hear, is quite capable of adding that to the number of His other practical jokes'" (*U*, 16.748–59). Although Stephen's response reads more like a journalistic report, the lack of any further emotional engagement perhaps reflecting the late hour, he does not refute Bloom's statement and acknowledges the existence of the "First Cause."

Stephen can therefore be viewed as maintaining his belief in an "Allseeing and Allknowing" being whilst having rejected the dogma of organised religion (*P*, 111). This can be said to gesture toward a reading whereby he conceptualises his guilt in terms of having sinned but does not point to a definitive interpretation. What Joyce does make abundantly clear is that Stephen genuinely feels guilty for his actions and his propensity to introspection, to brood, has exacerbated such feelings.

It has been argued that "remorse inevitably follows genuine guilt" and in Stephen's case the portrayal of his remorse can be said to exhibit elements of distortion.[20] Proeve and Tudor discuss how remorse can become what is termed "distorted" and how this can manifest itself in various ways.[21] One example is that it continues "for too long," resulting in one "brooding over oneself or one's relationships" and another is the possibility of memories of the transgression intruding "at inappropriate times and circumstances" with "all sorts of unpredictable things" acting as triggers to those memories.[22] With both of these examples it is possible to see where their work dovetails with that of attachment theorists. Before discussing chronic remorse in relation to Stephen as a character with avoidant traits, it is worth considering how remorse is shown to lead to intrusive memories.

That Joyce was all too aware of such intrusion is shown in the "Oxen of the Sun" episode of *Ulysses* where he parodies Cardinal Newman:

There are sins or (let us call them as the world calls them) evil memories which are hidden away by man in the darkest places of the heart but they abide there and wait. [. . .] Yet a chance word will call them forth suddenly and they will rise up to confront him in the most various circumstances, a vision or a dream or [. . .] at midnight when he is now filled with wine.' (*U*, 14.1344–52)

This quotation clearly foreshadows Stephen's hallucination of his mother, whilst in an inebriated state, in the "Circe" episode. The points made by Proeve and Tudor regarding intrusive memories bear resemblance to those made by Bowlby and other attachment theorists with regards to the resurfacing of repressed grief in those with avoidant traits. Bowlby noted how those with avoidant traits are likely to show "prolonged absence of conscious grieving" but that eventually they will "break down" and certain triggers, such as the anniversary of the death or reaching the same age of the deceased can precipitate this (*AL3*: 153–58).

More recently Mikulincer et al. have conducted experiments that support Bowlby's theory of the resurfacing of suppressed emotion by showing that under strain (high cognitive load) "an avoidant mind [. . .] is less able to exclude loss related information from awareness and to segregate or dissociate painful memories."[23] Furthermore, although not specifically referring to those with avoidant traits, Parkes and Prigerson also note how pangs of grief, which are particularly prevalent in the early stages of grief, can still be triggered later by certain reminders.[24] Throughout *Ulysses* one can therefore view Stephen's psyche as tormented by both his remorse and his grief and their relevant associative triggers.

To escape the psychological intrusions and hence visions of his mother would require resolution of his guilty conscience and remorse, along with a progression in the grief process, the accomplishment of each being dependent on the other. Although the first anniversary of May Dedalus's death is approaching, Stephen is portrayed as still exhibiting anger, something seen in the early phase of grief. As the vision of his mother appears whilst he stands on the gun rest of Martello tower, he hits out at the God his mother believed in "Ghoul! Chewer of corpses!" (*U*, 1.278).[25] (C. S. Lewis admits to doing a similar thing after his wife died, calling God a "cosmic sadist."[26]) Needing to move on in the grief process, but finding himself unable to, Stephen is also shown to hit out at his mother "No mother! Let me be and let me live" (*U*, 1.279).

When Stephen's guilt and remorse are depicted as coming to the fore, they are often associated with a thought or vision of staring eyes, symbolic of his mother's eyes that undoubtedly looked toward him as she asked for his prayers. For example, when walking on Sandymount Strand in the "Proteus" episode, thinking of a recent drowning and whether he could save a drowning man, his thoughts are shown to change from the victim to his mother: "A drowning man. His human eyes scream to me out of horror of his death. I . . . With him together down . . . I could not save her. Waters: bitter death: lost" (*U*, 3.328–300). Stephen's thought association is very strong here: from the man's eyes to his mother, to the waters, (which in "Telemachus" he had associated with "the green sluggish" bile his mother had vomited), to a sense of loss (*U*, 1.109). Yet, more often than not, the eyes are not just fearful, but rather they are threatening.

On the Martello Tower Stephen visualises his mother with eyes "to strike [him] down" as a result of the remembrance of his dream where "all prayed on their knees" (*U*, 1.276–77). But during his hallucination of his mother in "Circe" as she exclaims: "Beware God's hand! / (*A green crab with malignant red eyes sticks deep its grinning claws in Stephen's heart*)" (*U*, 15.4219–20). Reading from a Jungian perspective, Jean Kimball reads the crab as an "archetypal creature" from Stephen's unconscious.[27] Citing Jung's interpretation of the Crab dream in his 1917 *Psychology of the Unconscious Processes,* she notes how in German the crab "is an animal that walks backwards," as well its "association with cancer" and that Jung therefore interprets Stephen's hallucination as representing his "'overpowering and infantile craving' for love"; a "'symbol of the unconscious contents' that pull the dreamer backward."[28] As both Bowlby and Holmes note that those who are compulsively self-reliant/avoidant "have a latent yearning for love and care," from an attachment perspective Kimball's suggestion that what Stephen craves is love is not contentious (see *MB*, 165).[29] But one could also argue here that the crab is a symbolic conflation of his mother and the clergy.

As already noted by Kimball, the crab is associated with cancer. Furthermore, its eyes are described as "malignant," which means both "cancerous" and "menacing." The link with the mother who asked him to pray is obvious. However the "grinning claws" which penetrate "deep" into "Stephen's heart" can be associated with the priestly smile of the Jesuit priests who in *Portrait* not only "probed deeply" like a "knife" into his conscience, but also "smiled" when offering him the "secret knowledge and secret power"; the priesthood that would have taken his artistic life force, "end[ing] for ever, in time and eternity, his freedom" had he acquiesced to his offer of joining the priesthood in his youth (*P*, 123; 166–75). This scene can therefore be said to exemplify how, following his refusal to pray, religion and death are often inextricably linked in Stephen's thoughts. His ensuing shout of *"Non serviam!"* shows clearly his rejection of the church in which his mother held faith; the same "system" which Joyce believed made his mother "a victim" and which she would have had him follow.[30]

With his continual thought association and brooding on his mother's death almost a year after the event, Stephen's remorse can also be said to be distorted through its chronic manifestation. However, reading Stephen as someone who has a propensity to form avoidant attachments and in light of research which has shown that feelings of guilt "are a common problem with avoidant people," it is also possible for the reader of *Ulysses* to interpret Stephen's feelings of remorse as being exacerbated by his avoidant traits.[31] Colin Parkes suggests that avoidant people "blame themselves for their inability to express love and other feelings, as well as for the harm done to others by their behavior."[32] Toward the end of *Portrait* Joyce indicates that Stephen's mother and Stephen himself are both fully aware of the emotional distance between them via an entry in Stephen's diary, recalling his mother's words to him: "She prays now, she says that I may learn in my own life and away from home and friends what the heart is and what it feels" (*P*, 275). His mother appears to be expressing the hope that his physical distance from her, as well as his friends, will lead to a decrease in the emotional distance that currently affects his relationships. Her reasoning can be read as reflecting the wish that in her absence he will realise that she had loved him and supported him as best she could. But since, as I have argued, it is possible to read Stephen's removal from the family home to Clongowes as having contributed in no small way to his avoidant traits, there seems little chance of his mother's wishes being fulfilled. Indeed, when Joyce reintroduces Stephen to the reader in *Ulysses*, it is clear that he has continued to emotionally enclose himself in his self-reliant world.

Although in the "Telemachus" episode of *Ulysses* Joyce does have Stephen recall how, on having returned to Dublin to be with his ailing mother, he had at one time approached her sick bed in "awe and pity," it does not detract from his recalled inability to express his feelings, by putting to one side his claimed disbelief in Catholicism and praying for her (*U*, 1.251). His actions can be seen as resulting in a feeling that he harmed her emotionally in her final hours. Filled with remorse for the emotional distress he believes he caused his mother on her deathbed, his aunt has extrapolated the effect of his actions further to an accusation that he actually killed her. Such allegations can only serve to deepen any feeling of self-blame and consequently increase any guilt and shame. Indeed, Stephen's perception of himself in *Ulysses* seems to have changed from that in *Portrait*. In the "Telemachus" episode, following his remembrance of carrying "the boat of incense [. . .] at Clongowes," he thinks "I am another now and yet the same" (*U*, 1.311–12). Stephen is now a person who wronged his mother.[33]

In *Portrait*, Stephen makes a similar comment to Cranly when looking back to his childhood: "I was not myself as I am now, as I had to become" (*P*, 261). Here, the meaning could be seen as two-fold. Firstly, as I argued in Chapter 9, one can read this as Stephen's recognition that his experiences at Clongowes have resulted in his self-reliance and independence. Secondly, it could also denote Stephen's realisation that his rejection of the Catholic Church was, as he saw it, essential for his artistic development: "his soul had arisen from the grave of boyhood" allowing him to "create proudly out of the freedom and power of his soul" (*P*, 184). One can certainly appreciate the influence of Symons in Joyce's writing here. However, what is important in considering Stephen's remorse is the subtle difference between Stephen's thought as he stands on top of the Martello Tower and the words he spoke to Cranly. Whereas in *Portrait* he saw himself as necessarily needing to change, in *Ulysses* the different phraseology can be seen as reflecting his knowledge that as a result of exercising his own free will he emotionally harmed his dying mother and if his aunt is to be believed, he actually killed her.

Proeve and Tudor make the following argument with regards to remorse and self-perception:

> Seeing oneself as a wrongdoer is not merely a matter of recognising that one has accrued some debt or "demerit points." Rather, one's relationship to others (and not just to the one that was wronged) is altered because of this fact about one. Thus, part of the horror experienced by the remorseful murderer is that he has *become* "a murderer" through his deed.[34]

The above example of the murderer is a very apt one when considering Stephen in *Ulysses* following his aunt's accusation. Bowlby recognised that anger is often seen in the initial stages of grief and Hogan has commented that such anger may result in there being dissention among the family members, such that "they may even blame one another for the suffering and death of the loved one" (see *AL3*: 85).[35] Although initially hurtful, those who feel secure and at ease with how they have behaved may merely dismiss such accusations as a manifestation of the accuser's grief. Yet Joyce shows that Stephen, filled with remorse for his action, has ruminated on Mulligan's comments such that, in his inebriated state in the "Circe" episode he experiences an hallucination of his mother in which he defends himself against the accusation of murder: "They say I killed you, mother. [. . .] Cancer did it, not I. Destiny" (*U*, 15.4186–87).

The importance of Proeve and Tudor's argument here is in relation to one's sense of self, to how the wrongdoer realises that his relationship with others will change. Since Stephen is portrayed as distant from his family and friends and can be read as a character who has been endowed with avoidant traits, he can also be viewed as someone who will have "little confidence that he will receive kindness or comfort from relatives or others and expect instead, blame and punishment" (*AL3*: 240). The accusations made by his aunt and the instruction she had given Mulligan to "not have anything to do with" Stephen can therefore be interpreted as reinforcing both his internal model of himself and others and also his feelings of remorse and self-blame (*U*, 1.89).

Trapped by his guilt and shame, the portrayal of Stephen's Hamlet-like insistence on continuing to wear black reflects the work of Stroebe et al., who acknowledge that "[g]rief may influence mourning and mourning may equally influence feelings of grief."[36] His behaviour can be said to illustrate Bowlby's argument that if the bereaved "find some form of self-reproach" it is possible that their grief "may contain an element of self-punishment" (*MB*, 119). No longer able to expiate his sins via the confessional, Joyce appears to have reflected Stephen's need for atonement by his strict adoption of the mid-Victorian practice (which was considerably relaxed by 1904), whereby a son's deep mourning for his mother meant wearing the appropriate clothing for a year and a day.[37] Much like his attempt in *Portrait* to mitigate his shame by his strict observance of religious devotions, it appears that his adherence to rules of convention, which as an artist he finds difficult to follow for any length of time, is the worst type of punishment he can imagine for himself. However, because his resolution to wear anything but black is voluntary, it is conceivable that it will have little effect on easing his remorse.[38]

Joyce shows Mulligan as at a loss to understand his friend: "Etiquette is etiquette. He kills his mother but he can't wear grey trousers" (*U*, 1.121–22). Neither can he understand Stephen's avoidant behaviour: "Why don't you trust me more?" (*U*, 1.161). Of course, as a reader one may not give much store to Mulligan's dependability either, but from Mulligan's own perspective, he appears to believe himself to be friendly and relatively trustworthy. Exasperated by Stephen, he just sees him as "an impossible person" (*U*, 1.222). Moreover, when it comes to Stephen's behaviour toward his mother Mulligan defines him as someone with "the cursed strain in you only it's injected the wrong way," implying that his religious indoctrination has somehow become distorted such that, instead of behaving in a Christian manner, he "crossed her last wish" (*U*, 1.209–12). Unlike the reader, Mulligan cannot understand that Stephen's remorse and guilt have been exacerbated by his apostasy, tendency to introspection and his propensity to form avoidant attachments, all of which have led to his need for atonement and hence strict adherence to dress code, as well as his continued grief. As an apostate he can only blame himself for his behaviour toward his mother as she lay dying and the accusations from Mulligan only serve to further the load on his conscience. Furthermore, reading Stephen as someone with avoidant traits, his perceived need for independence and lack of reliance on anyone else means that he will not turn to anyone to help him in his grief.[39]

NOTES

1. Also see Parkes and Prigerson, *Bereavement*. Peter Randall, *The Psychology of Feeling Sorry*, pxiv, defines guilt as: "the unpleasant and aversive feeling arising from having done wrong."

2. Proeve and Tudor, *Remorse*, 32–33.

3. Randall, *The Psychology of Feeling Sorry*, 232.

4. Jeffrie G. Murphy, "Remorse, Apology and Mercy," 4, *Ohio State Journal of Criminal Law* (2007): 431.

5. William Shakespeare, *Macbeth*, The RSC Shakespeare Series, eds. Jonathan Bate and Eric Rasmussen (Hampshire: Macmillan, 2009), 88.

6. *The Spiritual Exercises of Saint Ignatius Loyola: Translated from the Spanish with a Commentary and a Translation of the Directorium in Exercitia*, trans. W. H. Longridge, 5th ed. (London: A. R. Mowbray, 1955), 47–48.

7. Cixous, *The Exile of James Joyce*, 328–29.

8. Lewis B. Smedes, *Shame and Grace: Healing the Shame We Don't Deserve* (New York: Harper Collins, 1993), 9. cited in Randall, *The Psychology of Feeling Sorry*, 88.

9. See David Howe, *Attachment Across the Lifecourse*, 44.

10. Kirkpatrick, *Attachment*, 124.

11. Kirkpatrick, *Attachment*, 79.

12. Jung "Psychological Types," 4:412.

13. Kirkpatrick, *Attachment*, 133, comments that studies have shown that those "reporting avoidant adult attachment relationships tend disproportionately to describe themselves as atheists or agnostics."

14. Anna Ulanov, "Jung and Religion: The Opposing Self," in *The Cambridge Companion to Jung*, eds. Polly Young-Eisendrath and Terence Dawson (Cambridge: Cambridge University Press, 1997 repr. 1999), 296.

15. Peake *James Joyce*, 274.

16. *The Complete Dublin Diary of Stanislaus Joyce*, 149–50.

17. *The Spiritual Exercises of Saint Ignatius Loyola*, 47.

18. Parkes, *Love and Loss*, 99.
19. Geert Lernout, "Religion," in *James Joyce in Context*, ed. John McCourt (Cambridge: Cambridge University Press, 2009), 337.
20. Randall, *The Psychology of Feeling Sorry*, 96.
21. Proeve and Tudor, *Remorse*, 46.
22. Proeve and Tudor, *Remorse*, 46–47.
23. Mikulincer and Shaver, "An Attachment Perspective on Bereavement," 105. With reference to M. Mikulciner, T Dolev and P. R. Shaver, "Attachment-Related Strategies during Thought-Suppression: Ironic Rebounds and Vulnerable Self Representation," *Journal of Personality and Social Psychology*, 87, (2004): 940–826.
24. See Parkes and Prigerson, *Bereavement*, 49.
25. Charles Peake has argued that Stephen is referring to God whereas John Rickard has argued he is referring to his mother. As Stephen's line comes after the Latin prayer that commends the dying to God and also is on a separate line to the next sentence, which is addressed to his mother, I have concurred with Peak's explanation. See Peake, *James Joyce*, 176–77; Rickard, *Joyce's Book of Memory*, 37.
26. Lewis, *A Grief Observed*, 33.
27. Jean Kimball, "Jung's "Dual Mother," in Joyce's *Ulysses:* An illustrated psychoanalytic Intertext," *Journal of Modern Journal of Modern Literature*, 17 (1991), 486
28. C. G. Jung, "The Psychology of the Unconscious Processes," trans. Dora Hecht, in *Collected papers on Analytical Psychology* ed. Constance E. Long (Moffat Yard, 1917), 324–44 cited in Kimball "Jung's 'Dual Mother' in Joyce's *Ulysses*," 486–87.
29. Also see Jeremy Holmes, *The Search for a Secure Base*, 37.
30. *Letters of James Joyce*, ed. Richard Ellmann, 2:48.
31. Parkes, *Love and Loss*, 99.
32. Parkes, *Love and Loss*, 100.
33. "In remorse one's self-perception is altered. One is now whatever else one was before, a person who has wronged another. . ." Proeve and Tudor, *Remorse*, 42.
34. Proeve and Tudor, *Remorse*, 42–43.
35. Hogan, *What Literature Teaches Us About Emotion*, 114.
36. Stroebe et al., "Bereavement Research: Contemporary Perspectives," 6.
37. Gifford with Seidman, *Ulysses Annotated*, 15.
38. Discussing those who carry out a crime such a murder Murphy states: 'Even in extreme self-imposed penance, penance of great suffering, one still retains an autonomy that one has denied to one's victims.' J. G. Murphy, *Remorse, Apology and Mercy*, 431.
39. See Holmes, "Attachment Theory," 99.

Chapter Thirteen

Leopold Bloom

Grieving in Isolation

Joyce modelled Leopold Bloom on various people, "some Dubliners, others Italian, Greek and Hungarian."[1] One of the Dubliners Joyce referenced to was Joseph Bloom, a Jew. Another was Alfred J. Hunter, an Ulster Presbyterian who "became a nominal Catholic when he married" and who also "would have been out of place in Dublin society."[2] John Rickard puts forward the argument that when Bloom dons his mourning clothes for Paddy Dignam's funeral, his black suit "ties him to Stephen symbolically: since "both characters have been unable to cease mourning their dead loved ones."[3] Their continued mourning gestures toward another way in which they are both "tied"; their lack of close friends with whom to share the burden of their loss and that they both shown to exhibit insecure attachment traits.

Jeremy Holmes makes the point that: "Although on the face of it, people with avoidant attachments seem to be the opposite of those with ambivalent attachments in reality they are not so different. [. . .] Both are dimly aware of the effects on others of their distorted perception of the world and of their ways of coping with it."[4] Although not talking in terms of attachment, Shechner actually describes well the different attachment traits of Stephen (which he also sees as belonging to Joyce) and Bloom in noticing their respective needs for self-reliance and positive regard: "In the rebelliousness of Stephen, Joyce depicted his own rebellion against dependency and restraint, while in Bloom the alien who wishes to be no more than an Irishman among Irishmen, he embodied the countertendency, his dread of isolation."[5] As discussed in some detail in Chapter 9, Stephen is aware of his distance from his family. But his avoidant traits are not the only thing affecting his grief. Paradoxically his religious schooling (in terms of his introspection) and his rejection of that schooling (resulting in his troubled conscience) have also played a role. In some ways, the representation of Bloom's association with religion and how it has affected his expression of grief is more complicated than that of Stephen Dedalus as he also has to deal with the religious opinions of the wider Dublin society, rather than just his own privately held views.

This chapter therefore discusses Bloom's isolation as a consequence of his acquaintances being unable to see past his Jewish heritage, a view of which Bloom is all too aware: "He [the Citizen] called me a jew [. . .] though really I am not" (*U*, 16.1082–85). The importance of friends and family in helping one to deal with one's grief is well documented by Bowlby and others, but labelled as a "perverted jew" and therefore "other," Bloom's only support in life seems to be his wife, Molly (*U*, 12.1635) (see *AL3*: 199).[6] Significantly, he also has to contend with the view taken by the Christian church on suicide, to which his Dublin acquaintances subscribe. This, I will argue, has led him to experience what psychologists term self-disenfranchised grief, the "inhibition of the grief process" due to "the imagined views of others."[7]

Rudolph Bloom and his untimely death are shown to feature constantly in his son's thoughts throughout the 16 June 1904 and the early hours of the following day. As noted in the Introduction to Part 4, whilst Joyce has the narrator describe Bloom's remorse regarding his "impatience" toward his father's beliefs in the "Ithaca" episode, the feelings defined are notable for their lack of intensity when compared to the agenbite of inwit suffered by Stephen in relation to his mother (*U*, 17.1894). The "Ithaca" episode owes a formal debt to Joyce's religious upbringing, with the question and answer form parodying the Jesuit catechism. In 1921 Joyce commented on his writing of "Ithaca" in a letter to Budgen: "the reader will know everything and know it in the baldest and coldest way."[8] Certainly, the rigidity of the catechistic format is cold in its impersonality. Yet Joyce does, on occasion, allow the emotion of intimate relationships to break through, as in the description of Bloom kissing Molly's rump, where the obvious delight he gains from this act is indubitably conveyed: "He kissed the plump mellow yellow smellow melons of her rump, on each plump melonous hemisphere, in their mellow yellow furrow, with obscure prolonged provocative melonsmellonous osculation" (*U*, 17.2241–43).[9] However, when it comes to Bloom's thoughts about his father in this episode, they appear stoical rather than overtly emotional.

Bloom, presented as no longer immature, and by virtue of his life's experiences more wise, now considers his father's beliefs and practices "not less rational than other beliefs and practices," but he understands the role his immaturity played in generating his irritation (*U*, 17.1904–5). By extension, and as a parent himself, one could imagine him consoling himself with the thought that his father would have understood his juvenile impatience. So, whereas Bloom is said to experience a sense that he behaved badly toward his father, he does not appear to be consumed by guilt. Of particular relevance, however, is that the rituals referred to are Jewish. For example, Bloom recalls the "prohibition of the use of fleshmeat and milk at one meal" (*U*, 17.1897).

Although his father was baptised in 1865, Leopold was not born until 1866 and as he is shown to remember his father's practices, it is possible to read his father as maintaining his Jewish faith despite his "conversion." This interpretation is further supported in the "Circe" episode when he visualises his father asking, "Are you not my dear son Leopold who left the house of his father and left the god of his fathers Abraham and Jacob?" (*U*, 15.261–62). This implies that he had expected Leopold to follow in his footsteps and although baptised, to subscribe to Jewish practices in private.

In the "Lestrygonians" episode Bloom's train of thought reveals that his father first became involved with the Protestants due to his lack of money: "They say they used to give pauper children soup to change to protestants in the time of the potato blight. Society over the way papa went to for the conversion of poor jews. Same bait" (*U*, 8.171–74). The implication is, that for a while at least, his father was a "Souper" (a term Joyce uses to describe one of the fates of those in Dublin in *Finnegans Wake*) and was baptised not only in an effort to fit in with the Christian community of Dublin, but additionally to maintain the help received from the society (*FW*, 131.4).[10] However, with the sectarian polemics regarding the Jews in Dublin at the time, I would interpret the primary reason for Rudolf Virag's conversion as being for the sake of the social standing of any future offspring, especially taking into account his later change of name to Rudolph Bloom. In 1911 Maurice Fishberg's study of the Jews made an associative link between their willingness to be baptised and their desire to remove "the disabilities from which they, as well as their ancestors, for generations ha[d] suffered" in terms of social success.[11] Neil Davison suggests that whether or not Joyce had read Fishberg, he would "have recognised the prevalence of such controversies about 'the Jews' in *fin-de-siècle* Europe."[12]

Of further and particular relevance is the fact that, in the middle months of 1904, close to when *Ulysses* is set, a "vitriolic outburst of anti-Semitism, and its more philosophical aftermath, became big news on the front pages of leading newspapers and magazines in Dublin."[13] Marvin Magalaner argues that Joyce must have been aware of that particular "topical controversy." pointing out that "[i]f he did not see references to it in the *Freeman's Journal,* to whose pages he alludes occasionally in his fiction, he could have found it in one of Dublin's most influential literary periodicals, *The All Ireland Review.*"[14] However, Joyce highlights the resilience and resolve of the Jews by depicting a willingness to convert in order to commune more easily with neighbours and be accepted in society. As Davison comments: "out of sheer psychological survival, the marginal Jew—like the alienated writer—recreates himself" and this is what Rudolf Virag, now Rudolph Bloom who has converted to Christianity, is shown to have done.[15]

MULTIPLE BAPTISMS BUT NO RELIGIOUS FAITH

It is known that Leopold was born in the calendar year following that of his father's baptism, but how many months had elapsed between the two events and therefore whether Ellen Bloom was pregnant when her husband was baptised is not revealed. However, Rudolph clearly maintained his connection with the Christian church by having Leopold baptised into the Protestant faith. Acknowledging Joyce's awareness of the social difficulties experienced by those of Jewish descent, it is worth considering how he originally portrayed Leopold Bloom's multiple baptisms in the proto-draft since there is some evidence of bullying by his school friends. The relevant part of the published "Ithaca" episode, reads as follows:

> Had Bloom and Stephen been baptised, and where and by whom, cleric or layman?
> Bloom (three times), by the reverend Mr. Gilmer Johnston M.A., alone, in the protestant church of Saint Nicholas Without, Coombe, by James O'Conner, Philip Gilligan and James Fitzpatrick, together, under a pump in the village of Swords, and by the reverend Charles Malone C. C., in the church of the Three Patrons, Rathgar. Stephen (once) by the reverend Charles Malone C. C., alone, in the church of the Three Patrons, Rathgar. (*U,* 17.540–47)

The "Ithaca" proto-draft of 1921 was somewhat different. Firstly, the question was different and only applied to Bloom: "Was he baptised?" Secondly, the account differed in "number, location and tone" as follows: "Twice. First, in church. Second, under pump at Santry by some schoolfellow in 'friendly' jest at his former religion. In both cases the water being poured at the same time as the words were spoken."[16] Crispi points out that whilst this earlier version was "probably meant to be more humorous" what is emphasised is "the bullying maltreatment that Leopold receives from his "friend" at school because of his familial and cultural heritage."[17] Although this element of prejudice was removed by Joyce from the episode before *Ulysses* was completed, Bloom's encounter with the bigoted Citizen in the "Cyclops" episode illustrates in a far more menacing and extreme way the religious prejudice that he finds himself subjected to. Despite his baptisms Bloom is seen ostensibly as a Jew and therefore as "other" (which I will discuss in detail later).

That Joyce saw Bloom as being bullied provides further, albeit perhaps less discernible evidence, that Bloom can be read as an anxious/ambivalent character, as it has been noted that those with ambivalent traits are more likely to be "bullied rather than bully" or to become "victims rather than victimisers."[18] Although on many occasions his maltreatment is very obviously linked to his perceived Jewishness, on some occasions it is not. For example, in the

"Aeolus" episode, Myles Crawford shows Bloom no respect, not allowing him to finish his sentence and walking off before the conversation is finished (Cf. *U*, 7.989–94). Even the "newsboys" take off "his flat spaugs and the walk" as they follow behind him (*U*, 7.444–48). As a character that wants to be viewed positively and wants to be part of a group, one would expect Bloom to be particularly sensitive to rejection and Joyce illustrates this clearly in "Hades." He is described as "chapfallen" following John Merton's "short" response to him and consequently drops "behind a few paces so as not to overhear" any further comments Merton may make (see *U*, 6.1016–28).

One is given the impression that Bloom, in his passivity, is a man of little presence or charisma, a character that would command little authority whatever his creed, but his perceived Jewishness removes any possibility of him being treated with respect. Colin MacCabe sees the suicide of Bloom's father as contributing to Bloom's passive feminised position; a reading clearly influenced by Freudian psychoanalysis.[19] However, from an attachment perspective this can be read as reflecting Bloom's anxious/ambivalent traits. Howe explains that those with anxious attachments have a tendency to believe "that they have little personal control over what happens" and therefore "adopt a passive stance towards all that life sends their way."[20]

Bloom endures many slights during the day but despite the overt racism he receives from the Citizen and the more passive racism he experiences with his acquaintances (which I will discuss in due course), Joyce provides many examples throughout the text of his sympathy and consideration toward his fellow Dubliners. His thoughtfulness and generosity toward the Dignam family are illustrated by his donation of "five shillings" given "without a second word" to a fund for the family (*U*, 10.974–77). Similarly, Joyce describes Bloom's tongue as "clack[ing] in compassion" as he learns of Mrs. Purefoy's long labour (see *U*, 8.285–90) and later in the day he is shown taking time to visit the lying in hospital to enquire after her (see *U*, 14.111–13). Extending no less to animals, his thoughtfulness is made plain in "Lestrygonians" where he notices some seagulls ("poor birds") and promptly buys some cakes to feed them with (*U*, 8.51–76). Bloom is therefore presented as a character who will take time to consider what it would be like in another's situation, whether human or animal and to behave correspondingly: "If we were all suddenly someone else" (*U*, 6.836).

Bloom's generosity and considerate way of life can be said to reflect that advocated by the Christian church into which he has been baptised, but he is shown to have no particular religious belief and very little understanding of the Catholic funeral mass. Indeed, it is clear that Joyce uses his character to challenge the church, degrading its power and criticising the clergy. Frances Restuccia has noted that even in Bloom's feeding of the birds, Joyce secularises the Eucharist in order to diminish its theological meaning: "Prior to purchasing 'two Banbury cakes for a penny,' he reads the words 'Blood of the Lamb' on Dowie's throwaway and thinks of 'Crossbuns' [hotcross buns] [...]; his first gesture after buying the cakes is to break 'the brittle paste'" (*U*, 8.11; 8.36; 8.74–75).[21] Similarly, the ironic distancing employed by Joyce, as he admits the reader to Bloom's thoughts at the communion in All Hallows and later at Dignam's funeral, has the effect of dissipating the impact of religious authority and ceremony:

> Shut your eyes and open your mouth. What? *Corpus:* body. Corpse. Good idea the Latin. Stupefies them first [. . .] Rum idea: eating bits of corpse. (*U*, 5.349–52)
> Muscular Christian. Woe betide anyone that looks crooked at him: priest. [...] Makes them feel more important to be prayed over in Latin. (*U*, 6.596–661)
> [...]
> Said he was going to paradise or is in paradise. Says that over everybody. Tiresome kind of job. But he has to say something. (*U*, 6.629–30)

These quotes demonstrate that Bloom's cynicism does not stop with the Christian rituals, it also extends to those who administer them, to the priests.

A more blatant example is provided when Joyce uses Bloom to further explore the notion, already raised in *Dubliners* and *Portrait*, of the shallowness of repentance experienced through confession, although with more derogatory humour than in his earlier work:

> Confession. Everyone wants to. Then I will tell you all. Penance. Punish me, please. Great weapon in their hands. More than doctor or solicitor. Woman dying to. And I schschschschschcsch. And did you chachachachacha? And why did you? [...] Whispering gallery walls have ears. Husband learn to his surprise. God's little joke. Then out she comes. Repentance skindeep. (*U*, 5.425–30)

Not only is Bloom portrayed as viewing the contrition shown at the confessional as "skindeep," as Pericles Lewis points out, there is an explicit connection here between the act of confession and the "sexual fantasies of women and priests."[22] This is reinforced later in the "Penelope" episode when Molly recalls her own experience of the confessional and questions asked by the priest regarding where she had been touched: "on the leg, high up was it" (*U*, 18.107–16). The narrative could have been influenced by a story Nora told Joyce about a priest who sat her on his lap, put his hand up her skirt and then told her to go to confession.[23] However, in *Ulysses*, whilst Joyce depicts the priest as gaining further information from Molly, possibly for his own titillation, he stops short of portraying any sexual abuse.

Joyce does not, however, show any restraint when using Bloom to express a certain condemnation in respect of what he perceives as the greed of the clergy. After passing one of the Dedalus children in the street and reflecting on the number of children in the family, Bloom's thought association is shown to lead him to contemplate the behaviour of the priests and soon after that of the nuns:

> Birth every year almost. That's in their theology or the priest won't give the poor woman the confession, the absolution. Increase and multiply. Did you ever hear such an idea? Eat you out of house and home. No families themselves to feed. Living on the fat of the land. Their butteries and larders. [. . .] All for number one. (*U*, 8.31–39)
> [. . .]
> Devil of a job it was collecting accounts of those convents. [. . .] I suppose they really were short of money. Fried everything in the best butter all the same. No lard for them. (*U*, 8.143–51)

Bloom's accusations of avarice can be seen to reflect the comments made by Edward Boyd Barrett regarding their seductive and coercive methods, previously discussed in Chapter 11. By placing Bloom on the outside of the Christian community, Joyce is able to use him to critique the church through a supposedly objective lens, which he could not do with the character of Stephen who has been subjected to their indoctrination. It also makes plain why Bloom has not turned to the church in his grief. Collectively, the narrator's comments regarding Bloom's "impatience" with regards to his father's beliefs in "Ithaca," the portrayal of Bloom's thoughts during the religious rituals, his rejection of the possibility of an afterlife in "Hades" ("once you are dead you are dead"), confirm his position as one who lacks any form of religious belief (*U*, 6.677). As an agnostic he would not be able to form an attachment with any God of any creed. Indeed, Lernout interprets Bloom as viewing "religion, and more specifically Catholicism, as little more than an extremely successful scam."[24]

Despite his criticism of the church, Joyce does have Bloom consider the role of religion in a more positive light when in All Hallows, which again brings out his anxious/ambivalent attachment traits. Here he has Bloom acknowledge that religious practice can lead to companionship: "First communicants. Hokypoky penny a lump. Then feel all like one family party, same in the theatre, all in the swim. They do. I'm sure of that. Not so lonely" (*U*, 5.361–63). As someone sensitive to rejection it is in keeping with his character traits that he would acknowledge the sense of belonging within the religious community as being advantageous. Although being a member of a group one may lose a certain amount of autonomy, it is known that anxious/ambivalent individuals can see such loss as an acceptable price to pay for perceived security.[25] However, for Bloom, as for Stephen, (and indeed Joyce) there is a snag: "Thing is if you really believe in it" (*U*, 5.364–65).

Bloom's apparent lack of any religious conviction is particularly relevant when considering the representation of how he has dealt with his bereavements. Colin Murray Parkes references a study of "121 people bereaved by accident, suicide, homicide or natural death" which "found that belief in an afterlife was associated with more recovery, greater well-being and less avoidance of grief than was lack of belief."[26] In depicting Bloom as rejecting religion Joyce has denied him this particular aspect of psychological support, as well as the social support of the church community, both of which may have had the prospect of helping him in coming to terms with his grief.[27]

Although in All Hallows Joyce has Bloom acknowledge the social aspect of the religious community, such thoughts do not extend to Dignam's funeral service, and there is no consideration of the comfort that may be obtained from a particular belief system. His interior monologue, which tends to consider more practical and money saving ideas for funerals does, however, reveal an irreverent sense of humour. Following Kernan's quoting of the bible ("*I am the resurrection and the life*") and his expressed belief that the script "touches a man's inmost heart," Bloom, whilst verbally agreeing is actually thinking: "Your heart perhaps but what price the fellow in the six feet by two with his toes to the daisies? [. . .] That last day idea. [. . .] Come forth, Lazarus! And he came fifth and lost the job" (*U*, 6.670–79).

Luca Crispi, in reviewing the drafts of *Ulysses* points out that they reveal "a more spiritual side to Bloom that is mostly elided from *Ulysses*" and therefore "not available to reader." He specifically refers to the question posed in "Ithaca" in regards to any remorse Bloom may have felt in relation to his father's beliefs and practices and where the response in the proto-draft reads: "No, he suspected that there were one or two secrets on the otherside which would be told him triumphantly in the years time to come."[28] Crispi's wording regarding the availability of such information to the reader implies that this is a side to Bloom's character that, although not revealed in the published text of *Ulysses* is nevertheless there. However, as this was removed from the text, it is questionable whether to read Bloom in this way. Firstly, it would detract from the ironic impact Joyce conveyed via Bloom's thoughts on religion and secondly it would contradict Bloom's expressed view of "once you are dead you are dead" (*U*, 6.677). Bloom is portrayed as a man who is grappling with questions of science rather than those of faith, which his conversation with Stephen in the cabman's shelter exemplifies (see *U*, 16.748–84). Here, with "a smile of unbelief" he argues that parts of the Holy Writ were "forgeries" that had been "put in by monks" (*U*, 16.778–82). However, his lack of faith not only denies him the possibility of a deity to provide psychological comfort, it also makes him an anomaly within an overtly religious community.

THE PERCEPTION OF BLOOM AS JEWISH: AN IMPOSED IDENTITY

Bloom's secular way of life means that his acquaintances, in order to define him, look to his lineage and therefore label him a Jew. The consequence of what is effectively an imposed identity is that he is seen as "other," making him an exile in Dublin even though he is Dubliner. Although Joyce had no close Jewish friends in Dublin, Ira Nadel reports that he "recognised the universal condition of the Jew which meant exclusion and mistrust which his friendships and experiences in Trieste corroborated and enlarged"[29] One of the facts he discovered was that "the converted or atheist Jew often remained a Jew in [. . .] the eyes of others."[30] The following quote from Lewis Hyman's *The Jews of Ireland* explains the difficulties of the Irish Jew:

> The mere concept of the Irish Jew raised a laugh in the Ireland of Joyce's day. Edward Raphael Lipset (1869–1921), A Dublin Jew, Journalist, novelist, and playwright, wrote impressions of the Jews in Ireland in 1906, under the pen-name of Halitvack: "There is an invisible but impassable barrier between Jew and Christian—a barrier which the one part will not, and the other cannot break through. You cannot get one native to remember that a Jew may be an Irishma."[31]

Whilst simultaneously parodying the title of a book by M. J. MacManus, *So This Is Dublin,* Joyce also raises the matter of exclusion in the *Wake:* 'So This Is Dyoublong?' (*FW*, 13.4). It is clearly an issue that occupied Joyce and in *Ulysses* it is the "impassable barrier" to which Hyman and Lipset refer, that seems in no small way to have denied Bloom social support in his grief.

One of the ways in which Bloom's marginality and lack of social position is depicted is through the way the various characters address each other. "While many of the men in the numerous pubs are on first name basis with each other, nobody calls Bloom by his first name."[32] He is verbally held at a distance. In direct contrast to the bigotry and violence of the Citizen, which Bloom will later face, there are many passive and understated, although no less poignant, examples of how Bloom experiences acts of prejudice due to his perceived Jewishness. One such example is his journey in the funeral carriage to Paddy Dignam's funeral.

Since medieval times Jews have been associated with money lending and commerce and Bloom's astute money management, in so much as he does not spend it all on drink, is a detail Joyce provides about his character that can be seen to mark him out from his companions in the coach. When a comment is made about a beggar Cunningham makes a backhanded remark whilst looking at Bloom: "We have all been there [. . .]. Well, nearly all of us"

(*U*, 6.259–61).³³ Later in the novel Joyce makes it plain that Cunningham's remark was unfounded and that Bloom had "been there," through the conversation that takes place in the "Sirens" episode between Ben Dollard and Father Cowley when it is commented that Bloom "was on the rocks" (*U*, 11.485) and also through Bloom's own interior monologue: "Ten bob I got for Molly's combings when we were on the rocks in Holles Street" (*U*, 13.840–41).

Following Cunningham's comment and possibly in response to his sense of disparity with the others in the carriage, Bloom, who is generally quiet and left to his thoughts during the journey to the cemetery, is shown to "speak with sudden eagerness" (*U*, 6.262). Joyce creates the impression that Bloom is trying to promote some form of inclusivity by showing his awareness of the story of Reuben J Dodd and his son. However, for a supposedly amusing anecdote Bloom's phraseology appears formal rather than colloquial ("That's an awfully good one" [*U*, 6.264]) and sometimes journalistic ("There was a girl in the case" [*U*, 6.269]), which only serves to further emphasise his difference from his companions. Consequently, Simon Dedalus keeps interrupting and misunderstands what Bloom is trying to say, causing Cunningham to take over the telling of the story, "rudely" thwarting Bloom's speech (6.277). David Wright's comment that, in contrast to Stephen, "Bloom accepts the importance of engagement with other people, despite failure and trauma," picks up on the portrayal of the different attachment traits of the two characters. It seems that Bloom's need for positive regard and fear of rejection means that, despite being "rudely" interrupted, he cannot help himself when it comes to attempting to continue with the story as he endeavours to fit in with the group, but yet again he is thwarted by Cunningham (see *U*, 6.285–90).³⁴ The fact that others are willing to interrupt and talk over him denotes both his status as an outsider and a also form of rejection through their denial to allow him a voice. He is, apparently, not worth listening to.

The coach scene illustrates that Bloom, who wants to be accepted in society, has many acquaintances but no real friends with whom he can form a meaningful relationship. In addition to being perceived as a Jew, his freemasonry can also be seen as exacerbating the mistrust and suspicion with which he is evidently viewed. Davison explains that on being named the Holy See three years before Joyce's birth, "Leo XIII began a crusade that called for all Catholics to join the fight against Socialist, Freemasons, Jews, and a host of other enemies of the Church. The Pope himself had a particular fear of Freemasonry as a destructive element amongst Catholic populations."³⁵ In the "Cyclops" episode Joyce uses Bloom's dispute with the Citizen—who refers to him as a "bloody freemason" amongst other things—to exemplify overtly the hated and contempt that the Jews were often met with (*U*, 12.300).

With Davison's report of evidence that Joyce had read Otto Weininger's *Sex and Character,* it is possible that he had the following quote in mind when creating the Citizen:

> When we hate we delude ourselves into believing that we are being threatened by somebody else, and we pretend that we are purity itself under attack, instead of admitting to ourselves that we must weed out the evil in ourselves, since it lurks in our own hearts and nowhere else. We construct the evil in order to have the satisfaction of throwing an inkwell at him. The only reason why the belief in the devil is immoral is that it is an unacceptable method for making our struggle easier, and that it shifts the blame.[36]

The final two sentences quoted here can be seen to relate just as easily to the confessional scene in *Portrait,* discussed in Chapter 12, as they do to the "Cyclops" episode in *Ulysses* where the Citizen throws a biscuit tin at Bloom rather than a metaphorical inkwell. Described by Davison as representing "the convolutions both bigotry and violent republicanism make to sustain their hatreds" the Citizen "can see nothing but a nation-wide egoism" and labels Bloom a stranger and swindler (Cf. *U*, 12.1150–51).[37]

It is worth taking a moment to consider the social psychology of a devotee of a particular belief system and why a different belief will be seen as idolatrous. Kirkpatrick notes how "the human psychological architecture [. . .] is in many ways a collection of dedicated social-cognitive processing systems" and goes on to explain that:

> The Operation of each of these social-cognitive systems, along with the attachment system, is evident in diverse ways across religions. Gods and other supernatural beings might be treated psychologically as attachment figures, but also (or instead) as [. . .] coalitional partners ("God is on our side"), [or] social-exchange partners (who offer particular provisions in exchange for proper behaviour, sacrifices etc.).[38]

Viewing God as a coalitional or social-exchange partner means that any other form of practice or behaviour can only be seen as profane and therefore Bloom is perceived by the Citizen and the wider Dublin community as a threat.

Reading from a Freudian perspective, Paul Schwaber argues that, leading up to the physical abuse from the Citizen, Bloom, in the knowledge that Molly is at that moment with Boylan, "is defending against anguish by diverting through repression, his passion and anger and [. . .] unconsciously looking for trouble."[39] However, reading Bloom as someone with anxious/ambivalent traits it is difficult to agree with Schwaber. His need for positive regard and as already noted, the fact that he is also more likely to be bullied rather than be a bully—which Bloom clearly feels to be the case when one considers his waking dream in "Circe" ("When in doubt persecute Bloom")—raises the possibility of an alternative reading (*U*, 15.975–76). It seems that Bloom, who it has already been established does not have the best conversational skills, is actually trying to engage with and fit in with his acquaintances. Whilst his slip regarding "the wife's admirers" shows that his mind is clearly preoccupied with Molly, this is all the more reason that at that moment in time Bloom would want to feel the comfort of companionship, albeit with those with whom his is not particularly close (*U*, 12.767). Rather than aggression he wants acceptance, which although he doesn't receive it in actuality, symbolically he does as parodically he is accepted into heaven, having stood up to the evils of prejudice, when leaving Barney Kiernan's.

The Citizen's behaviour is notable for its extremism and it is difficult to find any behaviour at the other end of the spectrum within the novel; to find the portrayal of any munificence, in word or deed, toward Bloom. Even when Cunningham, Power and Nolan are discussing his donation to the Dignam family, Cunningham is depicted as unable to resist a sarcastic and implicitly anti-Semitic comment regarding Bloom's generosity: "strange but true" (*U*, 10.978). This causes Nolan to respond with a quote from *The Merchant of Venice*: "I'll say there is much kindness in the Jew"; a line in the play aimed at the Jewish money lender, Shylock, whose malevolence can be seen to emanate, at least partly, from the way he is treated by his gentile acquaintances (*U*, 10.980).[40] Although Bloom is clearly not to be read as a villain, the slights he receives from Cunningham and the physical violence from the Citizen show that he is scarcely any more welcome than such an unsavoury character would be. This therefore reinforces that, at best, he is viewed with dubiousness and suspicion. Roy Gottfried points out that perhaps one of the few genuine acts of good will that occur during the day is in the "Sirens" episode when Richie Goulding offers to eat with him in the Ormond Bar.[41]

Thus, whilst Bloom, in his grief for both his father and his son, can be seen to have excluded himself from any support associated with religion, the prejudicial contempt shown toward him by his Dublin acquaintances demonstrates a further and *imposed* denial of any social support, in so much as they have chosen to marginalise him by labelling him a Jew. In his inflicted status of "other" he has no one in whom to confide. Research that lends support to Attachment Theory has found that bereaved persons who believed they had high levels of social support coped better that those who believed their social support to be low, with reports of less stress and fewer physical symptoms.[42]

Discussing Bloom's solitary status in general terms, rather than in relation to the grief process, Declan Kiberd takes a positive view of Bloom, suggesting that he "rather likes to live at an angle to the community." He argues that Bloom's "inner life offers rich compensations for the poverty of social intercourse in a city whose denizens are often more fluent than articulate and where every conversation seems to be repeated many times over."[43] However, he takes a different view when he considers why Bloom is actually attending Dignam's funeral when he "scarcely" knew him and suggests that "as an outsider' Bloom may be "seeking acceptance in a major Irish ritual from which he cannot decently be excluded."[44] Reading Bloom as an anxious/ambivalent individual, it is entirely plausible to interpret his attendance as part of his struggle to gain acceptance. His conversational efforts in the carriage, although failing dismally, appear to support this. Similarly his waking dream in nighttown, in which he takes on the persona of Alderman of Dublin, "the world's greatest reformer" and "Leopold the first" can also be interpreted as a particularly vivid illustration of his need for acceptance and security (see *U*, 15.1365–475).

It has been noted that anxious/ambivalent individuals can harbour "fantasies of power" and in his dream-like state in "Circe" Bloom appears to allow such desires to come to the fore in order to mentally reverse the treatment he had received throughout the day.[45] This is particularly evident in his vision of the Citizen's response to him: "(*chocked with emotion, brushes aside a tear in his emerald muffler*) May the good God bless him!'" (*U*, 15.1617–18). Reflecting the precariousness of his self-esteem, even in his dream-like state Bloom is unable to maintain a positive vision of treatment by others and of himself.[46] From being called "His Most Catholic Majesty" the tone changes and he is called "an anythingarian seeking to overthrow our holy faith," a "bad man," an "abominable person" and so on. (*U*, 15.1630–718). The "anxious internal working model all too readily supports strong negative thoughts about the self."[47]

One can interpret Bloom as being caught in a self-perpetuating cycle, at least in his relationship with the wider community. Isolated due to his perceived Jewishness, receiving rebuffs and prejudicial treatment, feeling negative yet trying to fit in—both conversationally and through his actions—receiving further rebuffs and so on. With Bloom's difficulty in being accepted within the community, despite his continued efforts, plus the additional burden of how society viewed suicide at that time, (expressed robustly by Mr. Power in the "Hades" episode: "the worst of all [. . .] The greatest disgrace to have in the family"), one can conclude that the likelihood of Bloom feeling able to discuss the loss of his father, from the time of his death up to 16th June 1904, would be remote (*U*, 6.335–38).

SUICIDE, STIGMA, AND SELF-INITIATED DISENFRANCHISED GRIEF

Travelling in the funeral carriage, Bloom's reluctance to mention the anniversary of his father's death is clearly illustrated through his simple expression of a need to "go down to the county Clare on some private business" as an explanation as to why he is not joining Molly on tour (*U*, 6.216–17). One can assume he does not wish to mention the anniversary for fear he may be asked the cause of death. This gestures toward Bloom having succumbed to what is now termed self-initiated disenfranchised grief in relation to his father's death.

Jeffrey Kauffmann explains that: "In self-initiated disenfranchisement the source of the inhibition of the grief process is the imagined views of others" and with the stigma that surrounded suicide at that time, it is little wonder that Bloom is portrayed as avoiding the subject of his father's death.[48] Kenneth J. Doka, in "How we die: Stigmatized Death and Disenfranchised Grief" refers to the work of Goffman, who introduced the concept of stigma:

> Stigma refers to some relational attribute that mars one's social identity. In other words, a stigma is an attribute of an individual that would alter others' assessment of that individual. The critical aspect of a stigma is that it has the possibility to overwhelm other social roles. The stigma once it becomes known, becomes the mark of identity, the focal point of interaction.
> [. . .]
> Goffman further notes that stigmas can be discrediting and discernable. A *discrediting stigma* is one that is evident or widely known. A *discreditable stigma* is one that is not widely known but that could be discrediting if found out by others, such as a criminal record.[49]

Throughout *Ulysses*, as the examples discussed above show, Bloom can be seen as experiencing discrediting stigmatisation by virtue of his Jewish ancestry whilst living in a mainly Christian society. However, since the taking of one's own life was "regarded as a form of murder" and "an offence against God," his father's suicide also leaves him harbouring a discreditable stigma, which if known could further thwart his ambition of being accepted by his fellow Dubliners.[50]

In the funeral carriage, Bloom becomes aware that Cunningham is acquainted with how his father died through his avoidance of eye contact following Mr. Power's comments on suicide: "He looked away from me. He knows" (*U*, 6.358). The depiction of Bloom's realisation reveals that he did not personally impart this information, again implying that he has deliberately remained silent on the subject of his father's demise. Cunningham's effort to change the tone of the conversation by advocating "a charitable view of it" as a form of "Temporary insanity," can be viewed as relating to his own awkwardness in Bloom's presence, rather than any particular feeling of sympathy (*U*, 6.339–40). Since Cunningham has already made a backhanded comment to Bloom regarding money, "rudely" thwarted his speech and later goes on to make what could be construed as an anti-Semitic comment regarding Bloom's donation to the Dignam fund, it is somewhat ironic that Joyce has Bloom think of him as "Sympathetic" and a person who "always" has "a good word to say" (*U*, 6.345–46). Mr. Cunningham's duplicity actually appears to equal that of Father Conmee and provides another example of the hypocrisy that can be exhibited by those who present a pious persona.

Although shown as seeking acceptance, the simple use of the word "they" nevertheless creates a certain sense of distance, separating Bloom from his fellow Dubliners, when he considers their views on suicide: "They have no mercy on that here or infanticide" (*U*, 6.345–46). His thoughts pertain to the harsh and unjustifiable cultural practices and strict legal penalties that were historically imposed following a suicide, including "forfeiture of all property and goods, denial of Christian burial" and "desecration of the corpse."[51] His musings juxtapose the impersonal treatment of the cadavers of suicide victims by the church and the consequent social segregation with the very personal anguish Bloom feels: "Refuse Christian burial. They used to drive a stake of wood through his heart in the grave. As if it wasn't broken already" (*U*, 6.346–48). Admitting the reader to Bloom's thoughts, the final sentence here delivers its emotional intensity through its simplicity. Whatever one's view of suicide, the ensuing sense of pathos and the sadness invoked ensures the reader's sympathy remains with Bloom.

The concept of a broken heart gestures toward a belief that his father committed suicide due to his grief following the loss of his wife. From an attachment perspective, this assumption on Bloom's part is not unrealistic, as literature has documented how the impulse to search and reunite with a lost spouse can lead to suicide.[52] It is possible that Joyce had a letter from his father in mind when writing this. The biography of John Stanislaus Joyce relates how, when writing to his son for money, he refers to the "'miserable existence I have put over since *August 13th 1903*,' the day he lost May" and final sentence before signing off sounds very much like a suicide note: "Goodbye, Jim, and may God protect you, is the prayer of your still fond and loving, though broken-hearted / *Father*."[53]

In narrating Dignam's burial, Joyce shows how the private thoughts of Bloom during this public ritual turn to his father. As the coffin "dive[s] out of sight," "Far away a donkey bray[s]," causing Bloom's thoughts to move to Irish superstition and sayings and then on to his father's death: "Rain. No such ass. Never see a dead one, they say. Shame of death. They hide. Also poor papa went away" (*U*,6.833–38).⁵⁴ The final short three sentences of this quote are revealing in terms of Bloom's self-initiated disenfranchisement of his grief. "Shame of death. They hide" can be seen as relating to the burial of the dead and how they are hidden away. Zygmunt Bauman writes how:

> Funerals differ in their ritual, but they are always acts of exclusion [. . .] They expel the dead from the company of the normal, innocuous, these to be associated with. But they do more than that. Through applying to the dead the same technique of separation as they do to the carriers of infections diseases or contagious malpractices, they cast the dead in the category of threats that lose their potency if kept at a distance.⁵⁵

Placing the dead in cemeteries, often behind walls that are particularly tall, the dead are hidden away from the living. Bloom's thoughts clearly associate the burial ritual (the hiding of the dead) with his father going away to a solitary hotel room to end his life in what the church and society considered a sinful and shameful manner. Moreover, Bloom, in his kept silence, has also attempted to hide away the mode of his father's death. Although all of the penalties relating to suicide had been repealed by 1870, it is known that Victorian families of suicide victims nevertheless "shrank from the stigma such a death attached to them" and "tired as hard as ever to conceal suicides whenever they could."⁵⁶ Sadly, the fear of stigmatisation has not abated and even in today's society there are those who will hide the circumstances of a suicide in order to protect the family from perceived stigma.⁵⁷ Bloom's employment of such tactics, as he attempts to be accepted more fully by his acquaintances, can therefore be seen as prototypical.

    The pain that Bloom feels regarding his father's lonely death is reflected in the refrain "poor papa," which is repeated several times throughout *Ulysses*. That his death may not have been peaceful is depicted in Bloom's remembrance of him being found "at the foot of the bed" which could indicate excessive movement in his final moments [*U*, 6.363]. However, his refrain could also reflect some remorse. Since Bloom has already been portrayed as suffering from causation guilt regarding his son's death, his linking of infanticide and suicide in his thoughts could imply a feeling of responsibility on Bloom's part, in so much as he did not realise his father was harbouring suicidal thoughts following the loss of his wife; a feeling that is often experienced by those whose loved ones have taken their own lives.⁵⁸ This reading is further supported through Bloom's thought association also linking Rudy's death with his father's through the refrain "Rattle his bones. Over the stones. Only a pauper. Nobody owns" (*U*. 6.332–33). The first time he thinks of the refrain is just after he has thought "If it's healthy it's from the mother. If not from the man" (*U*, 6.329). The second time is after he realises Martin

Cunningham knows his father took his own life ("He knows. Rattle his bones" [*U*, 6.358]). S. L. Goldberg reads the full refrain as being "explored in the different contexts of experience brought together by Bloom," among them "the general social hostility to suicide, the heartbreak and loneliness that cause it, the private hell from which it springs."[59]

The "general hostility" to which Goldberg refers, leads the reader to acknowledge Bloom's own "private hell" that his father's mode of death has inflicted. The psychological effects of suicide on those who survive the victim have been described as "sentenc[ing] the survivors to deal with many negative feelings, and, more, to be become obsessed with thoughts regarding their own actual or possible role in having precipitated the suicidal act or having failed to abort it."[60] I would not describe Joyce's portrayal of Bloom as being "*obsessed*" with his father's death—that domain belongs to Stephen in regards to his mother. Nevertheless, he is still clearly carrying the load of his father's suicide and still grieving for him. Studies have shown that suicide survivors take longer for the symptoms of mourning to abate and on this day of mourning for Paddy Dignam, "poor papa" is continually on his mind: from his childhood memories, to his detailed recollection of the inquest into his death, to the contents of the suicide note he has felt unable to throw away.[61]

As someone who is already perceived as different, the risk of disclosure is shown to prove too much for Bloom to consider. The difficulty he faces is described well by Doka who states that "stigmatised deaths place survivors in a double blind. If they risk disclosure, they may be perceived different by others and fail to receive the support they seek. Yet if they do not risk disclosure, they deny themselves the possibility of support, and they conceal an important attribute of identity."[62] Even if Bloom did manage to gain some form of acceptance, to trust someone as an attachment figure takes time. Bowlby notes that: "In order to provide the continuity of potential support that is the essence of a secure base, the relationships between the individuals concerned must persist over a period of time, measured in terms of years" (*MB*, 1277). Thus, surrounded by acquaintances and still seeking acceptance, the only attachment figure available to Bloom is Molly. However, with their lack of communication regarding their feelings over Rudy's death, one is left wondering how much emotional support Bloom would have received from her when dealing with his grief for his father.

Although Molly is shown to think of her father-in-law in sympathetic terms ("poor old man I suppose he felt lost") at no time does she express sympathy for her husband and the added difficulty he may experience in dealing with a socially unacceptable form of death (*U*, 18.1062). Bloom, on the other hand, is not only left with the burden of being further stigmatised by his Dublin acquaintances but also worries that he too may commit suicide (see *U*, 17.1765–68). Jordon quotes several studies that show that "losing a loved one to suicide may elevate the mourner's own risk for suicidal behaviour and completion" and with the benefit of such information, the reader can view Bloom's fear as not unreasonable.[63] At the beginning of "Lestrygonians," by the quayside, Joyce has Bloom momentarily think: "If I threw myself down?" (*U*, 8.52). Having no other attachment figure but Molly and aware of her forthcoming meeting with Boylan, he has a fear he may even lose her and perhaps at the moment one can read him as feeling as lost and alone as his father did.

In the Ormond bar in the "Sirens" episode, "loneliness is the dominant mood."[64] Bloom is aware of his reliance on Molly and his experience in the funeral carriage has heightened his awareness of the apparent gulf that exists between himself and his Dublin acquaintances (soon to be further enhance by the behaviour of the Citizen). On a day when thoughts of his bereavements, both of his father and his son, are prominent in his mind, he has no one with whom to share them and one can surmise that this has always been the case.

NOTES

1. Louis Hyman, *The Jews of Ireland: From Earliest Times to the Year 1910* (Shannon: Irish University Press, 1972), 169.

2. Costello, *James Joyce*, 228–31. For a more detailed description of the Hunter and Bloom family, see Louis Hyman, *The Jews of Ireland*, 169–76.

3. Rickard, *Joyce's Book of Memory*, 41.

4. Holmes, *The Search for a Secure Base*, 99.

5. Shechner, *Joyce in Nighttown*, 47.

6. Parkes, *Bereavement*, 155; Sheila Payne et al., *Loss and Bereavement*, 40–66; Kirkpatrick, *Attachment*, 157.

7. Jeffrey Kauffman, "The Psychology of Disenfranchised Grief: Liberation, Shame, and Self-Disenfranchisement," cited in *Disenfranchised Grief: New Directions, Challenges and Strategies for Practice*, ed. Kenneth J. Doka (Illinois: Research Press, 2002), 71.

8. *The Letters of James Joyce*, ed. by Stuart Gilbert, 159–60.

9. *The Letters of James Joyce*, ed. by Stuart Gilbert, 159–60.

10. "Souper" was a term usually used for Catholics who converted to Protestantism in return for soup during the time of the famine, but although Bloom's father was Jewish, as Joyce states: "same bait."

11. Maurice Fishberg, *The Jews: A Study of Race and Environment* (London: Walter Scott, 1911), 451.

12. Davison, *James Joyce*, 138.

13. Marvin Magalaner, "The Anti-Semitic Limerick Incidents and Joyce's "Bloomsday," *PMLA* 68 (1953): 1219.

14. Mgalaner, 'The Anti-Semetic Limerick," 1219.

15. Davison, *James Joyce*, 182.

16. Crispi, *Joyce's Creative Process*, 85.
17. Crispi, *Joyce's Creative Process*, 85.
18. Howe, *Attachment Across the Lifecourse*, 133.
19. See MacCabe, *James Joyce*, 123.
20. Howe, *Attachment Across the Lifecourse*, 139.
21. Frances L. Restuccia, *Joyce and the Law of the Father* (New Haven: Yale University Press, 1989), 76.
22. See Pericles Lewis, *Religious Experience and the Modernist Novel* (Cambridge: Cambridge University Press, 2010), 11–12.
23. See *Selected Letters of James Joyce*, ed. Ellmann, 45–46.
24. Lernout, *Help My Unbelief*, 169.
25. See Holmes, *The Search for a Secure Base*, 3.
26. Parkes, *Bereavement*, 79. With reference to Smith et al "Belief in an Afterlife as a Buffer in Suicide and other Bereavements," *Omega*, 24, no. 3 (1992): 217.
27. For example, see Nottingham, *Religion and Society*, 30; Parkes, *Bereavement*, 171.
28. Crispi, *Joyce's Creative Process*, 77–78.
29. Ira B. Nadel, *Joyce and the Jews: Culture and Texts* (Basingstoke: Macmillan, 1989), 198.
30. Davison, *James Joyce*, 122.
31. Hymann, *The Jews of Ireland*, 176 citing the *Jewish Chronicle*, December 21, 1906.
32. Peter I. Barta, *Bely, Joyce and Döblin: Peripatetics in the City Novel*, The Florida James Joyce Series (Gainsville: University Press of Florida, 1996), 56.
33. See Fishberg, *The Jews*, 393–94.
34. David G. Wright, *Characters of Joyce* (Dublin: Gill & Macmillan, 1983), 80.
35. Davison, *James Joyce*, 54.
36. Weininger, *Sex and Character*, 220.
37. Davison, *James Joyce*, 220; Ellmann, *The Consciousness of Joyce*, 63.
38. Kirkpatrick, *Attachment*, 338–40.
39. Schwaber, *The Cast of Characters*, 103.
40. The lines spoken by Antonia are: "Content, in faith. I'll seal to such a bond, / And say there is much kindness in the Jew" (I.iii.149–50). William Shakespeare, *The Merchant of Venice*, ed. J. L. Halio (Oxford: Carendon Press, 1993), 126.
41. See Gottfried, *The Art of Joyce's Syntax*, 61.
42. See Payne et al., *Loss and Bereavement*, 66.
43. Kiberd, *Ulysses and Us*, 89.
44. Kiberd, *Ulysses and Us,* 102.
45. See case study of Oliver in Holmes, *The Search for a Secure Base*, 38–39.
46. Holmes states "In both variants of insecure attachment, self-esteem is precarious." *The Search for a Secure Base*, 10.
47. Howe, *Attachment Across the Lifecourse*, 149.
48. Jeffrey Kauffman, 'The Psychology of Disenfranchised Grief: Liberation, Shame, and Self-Disenfranchisement," cited in *Disenfranchised Grief: New Directions*, 71.

49. Kenneth J. Doka, "How we die: Stigmatized Death and Disenfranchised Grief," in *Disenfranchised Grief: New Directions, Challenges and Strategies for Practice*, ed. Kenneth J. Doka (Research Press, 2002), 324. With. Reference to E. Goffman, *Stigma: Notes on the Management of Spoiled Identity* (Englewood Cliffs, NH: Prentice Hall, 1963).

50. Pat Jalland, *Death in the Victorian Family* (Oxford: Oxford University Press, 1996), 69–70.

51. Jalland, *Death in the Victorian Family*, 70; Michael McDonald and Terence Murphy, *Sleepless Souls: Suicide in Early Modern England* (Oxford: Clarendon, 1990), 42.

52. See Phillip R. Shaver and R. Chris Fraley, "Attachment, Loss and Grief: Bowlby's Views and Current Controversies," in *Handbook of Attachment: Theory, Research and Clinical Applications*, ed. Jude Cassidy, and Philip R. Shaver, 2nd ed., (New York: The Guildford Press, 2008), 50.

53. John Wyse Jackson, and Peter Costello, *John Stanislaus Joyce: The Voluminous Life and Genius of James Joyce's Father* (London: Fourth Estate, 1998), 294.

54. Gifford and Seidman, point to "the Irish superstition that a donkey braying at mid-day forecasts rain and the also the 'Irish saying, "Three things no person ever saw: a highlander's kneebuckle, a dead ass, a tinker's funeral."'" *Ulysses Annotated*, 121–22.

55. Zygmunt Bauman, "Survival as social conduct," in *Theory, Culture and Society*, 9 (1992): 1–36, cited in Jennifer Webb and Lorraine Webb, "Dead or Alive," in *Images of the Corpse: From the Renaissance to Cyberspace*, ed. by Elizabeth Klaver (Wisconsin: University of Wisconsin Press, 2004), 210–11.

56. McDonald and Murphy, *Sleepless Souls*, 351; See Jalland, *Death in the Victorian Family*, 70–76 for specific examples of the responses to suicide in the late nineteenth century.

57. See Dorothy Ratnarajah, and Margot J. Scholfield, "Survivors' Narratives of the Impact of Parental Suicide," in *Suicide and Life-Threatening Behaviour*, 38 (October 2008): 618–30.

58. John R. Jordan, "Is Suicide Bereavement Different? A Reassessment of the Literature," in *Suicide and Life-Threatening Behaviour*, 31 (Spring 2001): 92. With reference to M. Cleiren and R. Dieskstra, "After the loss: Bereavement after Suicide and Other Types of Death," in *The Impact of Suicide*, edited by B. Mishara (New York: Springer, 1995), 7–39.

59. Goldberg, *The Classical Temper*, 276.

60. *Survivors of Suicide*, ed. A. C. Caine (Springfield, IL: Thomas, 1972) cited in J. William Worden, Grief Counseling and Grief therapy: A Handbook for the Mental Health Practitioner, 4th ed. (New York: Springer, 2009), 179–80.

61. See Jordan, "Is Suicide Bereavement Different?" 98.

62. Doka, "How We Die," 326.

63. John R Jordan, "Is Suicide Bereavement Different?" 95.

64. Kain, *Fabulous Voyager*, 77.

Summary and Conclusion

Reading a work of literature requires use of one's cognitive abilities of creative imagination to understand the characters and in doing so it is possible to attribute to them a theory of mind. Indeed, Lizzy Welby has argued that *Ulysses* can be viewed as "a study in Theory of Mind and Meta Representation *par excellence*."[1] Theory of mind acknowledges a humanistic approach to literary characters and I have argued that Joyce encourages the reader to take such an approach to his work. However, as Culpeper has espoused, one's "impression of a character" is formed using both cognitive factors and textual factors.[2] Joyce provides a myriad of information regarding his characters within the text; a text which encompasses thematic schemes, symbolism, realism, and an array of narrative methods and styles. Piecing together the information and using knowledge of Attachment Theory allows for interpretations of his protagonists to emerge that differ from those offered by other theories.

The work of Alexander F. Shand can be said to be important in validating the use of Attachment Theory in literary criticism as it demonstrates the existence of a relationship between creative writing and theories of grief put forward by those working in the field of psychological enquiry and in particular Attachment Theory. It highlights the longstanding dialogue between the ideas about grief as they are represented in literature and the clinical settings in which Attachment Theory found its institutional home. Interpreting Joyce's texts through Bowlby's lens, there appears to be a link between Joyce's representation of character, their portrayed behaviour and thoughts at times of emotional anxiety, particularly grief, and the respective parenting that each of the characters were portrayed as having experienced. The evident self-reflexive elements of Joyce's work have resulted in some of his own behavioural traits being reflected in the character of Stephen Dedalus. However, with his keen observation of others, it is inevitable that Joyce would have witnessed certain attachment traits and the varied responses to loss. Of course, the theoretical terminology would not have been available to him, but as discussed in Chapter 2, attachment behaviours associated with grief can be viewed as universal, immutable across cultures and throughout history.

Using Attachment Theory as a frame of reference has facilitated the discussion of some aspects of Joyce's work that have previously not been focused on in any particular detail. If one takes as an example the character of Master Dignam, he is often mentioned briefly, but from the extensive review of critical literature I have undertaken, I have not been able to find an analysis of any length regarding Joyce's representation of him. Perhaps this is because his experiences do not seem to fit the Freudian paradigms that were dominant in psychologically inflected literary criticism. Taking into account the child's domestic situation and relationship with his parents, which Bowlby saw as fundamental to understanding a child's attachment behaviour, in addition to the information provided by virtue of Master Dignam's internal monologue, enables a detailed analysis of his initial grief response. Evidence emerges of his anxious/ambivalent traits and how they were playing a role in his negotiation of the early stages of the grief process.

On territory familiar to Freudians, such as memory, Attachment Theory can again be seen to facilitate the emergence of new insights. Removing the element of libidinal drives allows for interpretations which take into account the support network of the bereaved, both prior to the loss (from infancy onwards) and after the loss, the possibility of continuing bonds with the deceased and the fact that the bereaved may move back and forth between the different stages of the grief process. It is possible to show that reading Stephen Dedalus as an avoidant individual provides an explanation for his self-reliance and distancing from his friends, family and also God, thus affording an alternative interpretation to those provided by Freudian critics, who read him as subject to an Oedipal complex. Acknowledging his avoidant traits also provides coherence to his grief response in all its complexity. That is: his tendency to stifle his grief reaction, which comes to the fore in *Ulysses* as the anniversary of his mother's death draws near; his propensity to feelings of guilt and also to expect blame from others, exacerbating his remorse, which in turn was fueled by his tendency to introspection; and the element of self-punishment in his insistence on wearing black. Although critics have inevitably commented on Stephen's guilt and remorse and hence his vision/ hallucination of his mother, using knowledge of Attachment Theory enables a piecing together of how the hurts of childhood influence Stephen's view of himself and hence how he believes others see him. This in turn enables interpretation of the behaviours he adopted as a consequence, his particular response to the loss of his mother, and his inability to move on in the grief process.

Although Bloom's grief reaction to the death of his father has not been totally ignored by critics, emphasis is usually placed on how Bloom has been affected by the death of his son, Rudy. The latter seems more amenable to a Freudian reading, whereas an attachment approach helps elucidate the rich significance of Bloom's relationship with his father (which does not fit the Oedipal model). Piecing together the information regarding Leopold Bloom as expressed by other members of the community, from the thoughts of his wife Molly and his own thoughts about himself, his life and those he loves and has loved, provides a picture of someone who has developed anxious/ambivalent traits and as such a need for positive regard. Realising Leopold Bloom's need for social acceptance enables the reader to reason why he has attended the funeral of Paddy Dignam and why, despite the slights received, he continually tries to fit in with his acquaintances. This in turn explicates his perceived necessity for self-disenfranchised grief in relation to his father. Already trying to overcome the perception that he is Jewish due to his lineage, even though he has been baptised twice but actually follows no religious practices, it can be seen that the added stigma of a suicide within his family would only serve to distance him further from those he is trying to connect with.

Researchers have admitted that although it is possible to categorise certain types of attachment behaviour, no one person will fit "totally into any one group."[3] That being said, it is clear that critics often described the main insecure attachment traits of both Stephen and Bloom, even if they were not identified as such. It can therefore be argued that, regardless of the theoretical stance critics are reading from, such behavioural traits are evidently discernable in Joyce's writing.

Although this book has focused on his representation of grief and associated anxieties, the humour Joyce instilled within the pages of *Ulysses* have still been evident, mainly through the thoughts of Bloom and quite often in relation to religion. Through Joyce's use of narrative techniques such as internal monologue and the stream of consciousness, it is possible to access the private, psychological world of his protagonists as they negotiate their way through the events of the day. For Bloom, humorous thoughts often present as a form of psychological defence; a way of keeping his mood relatively buoyant. For example, in the funeral coach, Bloom has thought of his dead son, his father's suicide note, listened to the talk regarding Blazes Boylan, with whom is wife will shortly have a liaison, and suffered the passive-aggressive responses of his acquaintances. Then, as the conversation turns to the deceased, he thinks of Dignam's excessive drinking and in a moment of wry humour, how he spent "a lot of money" colouring his nose (*U*, 6.308–9). However, his mood is shortly to be brought down again as a carriage with a child's coffin turns his thoughts once again to Rudy and then to his father. This is one example of many in Hades where the juxtaposition of comedic thoughts with quite emotional thoughts of loss and life make the latter all the more poignant. Similarly, whilst in All Hallows, before attending Paddy Dignam's funeral, his thoughts regarding the communion and the confessional show a certain amount of irreverent of humour. Yet between those thoughts he acknowledges that being in the Church "family" means that one is "not so lonely" (*U,* 5.163). The fact that the "Lotus Eaters" episode focuses on his secret correspondence with Martha, which in itself is a sad reflection of his current relations with Molly, and that he had also been thinking of his father's suicide alone in the hotel room, this very short sentence conjures up various forms of loneliness that can be experienced.

Vargish and Mook have described the "epistemological location of Modernism" as neither the objective world nor the subjective perceiver but their interaction."[4] There is a certain correspondence between this view of modernism and the basic tenets of Attachment Theory, which acknowledges how behaviour is related to how one sees oneself, as well as those with whom we interact, and how we believe we are perceived by them. Such perceptions can be subject to erroneous representation due to faulty internal working models, caused by the lack of a secure base, which in turn affects our confidence in the world and how we react to life experiences such as loss. In *Ulysses* the objective world is "THE HEART OF THE HIBERNIAN METROPOLIS" (*U,* 7.1) with its bustling activity, but the community is represented "as a collection of individual selves," where each can be imaged as having their own prototypical memories that affect their interaction with the world.[5]

In Virginia Woolf's Essay, "Modern Fiction," where she praises the work of Joyce, she advocates basing one's writing on feeling with "as little mixture of the alien and external as possible."[6] As MacKay points out, by pairing "alien and external" there is an implication that "what is "external" is necessarily "alien.""[7] Joyce's work certainly shows the external world as alienating. From an attachment perspective, Stephen's avoidant traits, his lack of trust and hence fostered self-reliance, means that he feels alienated from those with whom he communes, even his family, as is made plain in *Portrait*. For Bloom the opposite applies. His anxious/ambivalent traits make him want to be noticed, to be "an Irishman among Irishmen," yet his perceived Jewishness relegates him to the edges of his social sphere, despite his efforts, making him an alien in his own country and perpetuating the loneliness and anxiety he feels throughout the day.[8]

Attachment Theory can therefore be seen to provide a vocabulary and a theoretical framework for describing and understanding Joyce's texts, whilst also encouraging readers to attend to parts of the Joycean oeuvre that have been neglected by Freudian critics. As it is a theory based on cognitive, emotional, and behavioural elements, rather than internal fantasy as in

Freudian theory, a lot of empirical research has been carried out following on from Bowlby's work. This has been particularly useful in understanding, for example, religious activity and sexual behaviour, as I have discussed, but also choices of career, since "individuals select environments consistent with their beliefs about self and other."[9] It therefore helps to explain Stephen's willingness to leave Ireland without fear of being alone in order to become an authentic artist. Joyce's modernism, or "new realism" as he referred to it, his narrative techniques and representation of cognitive processes, along with the sociological, domestic, and psychological information within his work, make it particularly open to critical analysis using such methodology.[10]

Apart from the analysis of the poems offered by Jeremy Holmes in his book regarding the work and life of John Bowlby, Attachment Theory does not appear to have been used as a framework for detailed literary critical analysis before (see *JB*, 96–102). I believe that, by taking a humanistic approach to the characters, Attachment Theory can provide a useful frame of reference for the reader in understanding the relationship of the characters with their world. The concept of internal working models provides a new perspective from which to view their behaviours; one which does not involve internal fantasy but rather the affective interaction of one person with another. It opens up another avenue in the debate regarding cognition and literature, in turn pushing the boundaries of literary criticism as advocated by critics such a Jonathan Culler.[11]

NOTES

1. Lizzy Welby, "Configuring Cognitive Architecture: Mind-Reading and Meta-Representation in *Ulysses*," in *Cognitive Joyce*, 206.

2. Jonathan Culpeper, *Language and Characterisation*, 28.

3. See Kim Bartholomew and Leonard M. Horowitz, "Attachment Styles Among Young Adults: A Test of a Four Category Model," in *Journal of Personality and Social Psychology*, 61 (1991) 226–44.

4. Vargish and Mook, *Inside Modernism*, 90. This argument can be seen as following on from Rolo May's description of the act of creation as resulting from the encounter of the between the "subjective pole" and the "objective pole" of the creator with "a continual dialectical process" occurring between "the world and self and self and world." May, *The Courage to Create*, 50.

5. Marina MacKay, "The Modernist 'Novel,'" in *The Cambridge History of Modernism*, ed. Vincent Sherry (Cambridge: Cambridge University Press, 2016), 321.

6. Virgina Woolf, "Modern Fiction," in *Essays of the Self: Selected Essays of Virginia Woolf*, ed. Joanna Kavenna (Devon: Notting Hill Editions, 2014), 19.

7. MacKay, "The Modernist 'Novel,'" 312.

8. Shechner, *Joyce in Nighttown*. 47.

9. Fenney and Noller, *Adult Attachment*, 106.
10. Power, *Conversations*, 64.
11. Jonathan Culler, "In Defence of Overinterpretation," 109–23.

Bibliography

Abbot, H. Porter. "How Do We Read What Isn't There to Be Read? Shadow Stories and Permanent Gaps." In *The Oxford Handbook of Cognitive Literary Studies*, edited by Lisa Zunshine, 104–19. New York: Oxford University Press, 2015.

Ainsworth, Mary D. Salter. "Attachment: Retrospect and Prospect." In *The Place of Attachment in Human Behaviour*, edited by Colin Murray Parkes and Joan Stevenson-Hinde, 3–30. London: Tavistock, 1982.

Anderson, Chester G. "'Introduction' to Part III." In *The Seventh of Joyce*, edited by Bernard Benstock. Bloomington: Indiana University Press, 1982.

Archer, John. *The Nature of Grief: The Evolution and Psychology of Reactions to Loss.* London: Routledge, 1999.

Archer, John. "Theories of Grief: Past, Present and Future Perspectives." In *Handbook of Bereavement and Research Practice: Advances in Theory and Intervention*, edited by Margaret S. Strobe, Robert O. Hansson, Henk Schut, and Wolfgang Stroebe, 45–65. Washington: American Psychological Association, 2008.

Arnold, Joan Hagan and Penelope Buschman Gemma. *A Child Dies: A Portrait of Family Grief*. Maryland: Aspen, 1983.

Barta, Peter I. *Bely, Joyce and Döblin: Peripatetics in the City Novel*. The Florida James Joyce Series. Gainsville: University Press of Florida, 1996.

Barrett, Edward Boyd. *The Jesuit Enigma*. London: Cape, 1928.

Bartholomew, Kim and Leonard M. Horowitz. "Attachment Styles Among Young Adults: A Test of a Four Category Model." *Journal of Personality and Social Psychology*, 61 (1991): 226–44.

Bauman, Zygmunt. *Mortality, Immortality and Other Life Strategies*. Cambridge: Polity Press, 1992.

Bauman, Zygmunt. "Survival as Social Conduct." *Theory, Culture and Society*, 9 (1992): 1–36.

Beja, Morris. *James Joyce: A Literary Life.* Literary Life Series. Basingstoke: Macmillan, 1992.

Bell, Robert H. *Jocoserious Joyce: The Fate of Folly in Ulysses*. New York: Cornell University Press, 1991.
Belluc Sylvian and Valérie Bénéjam. "Introduction." In *Cognitive Joyce*, edited by Sylvian Belluc and Valérie Bénéjam, 1–29. Studies in Literature and Performance Series. Basingstoke: Palgrave Macmillan, 2018.
Bennett, Andrew. *Suicide Century: Literature and Suicide from James Joyce to David Foster Wallace*. Cambridge: Cambridge University Press, 2017.
Benstock, Bernard. *Narrative Con/Texts in Ulysses*. Urbana: University of Illinois Press, 1991.
Benstock, Bernard. *Narrative Con/Texts in Dubliners*. Hampshire: Macmillan, 1994.
Birmingham, Kevin. *The Most Dangerous Book: The Battle for James Joyce's Ulysses*. London: Head of Zeus, 2014.
Bloom, Harold. *Yeats*. Oxford: Oxford University Press, 1970.
Bonheim, Helmut. *Joyce's Benefictions*. Perspectives in Criticism Series. Berkley: University of California Press, 1964.
Bowker, Gorden. *James Joyce: A Biography*. London: Weidenfeld & Nicolson, 2011.
Bowlby, John. "The Role of Childhood Experience in Cognitive Disturbance." In *Cognition and Psychotherapy*, edited by Michael J. Mahoney and Arthur Freeman, 181–200. New York: Plenum Publishing, 1985.
Bowlby, U. Personal Communication, 1991. In Jeremy Holmes, *John Bowlby and Attachment Theory*, edited by Laurence Spurling. The Makers of Modern Psychotherapy Series London: Routledge, 1993; reprint, East Sussex: Bruner-Routledge, 2004.
Bradley, Bruce S. J. *James Joyce's Schooldays*. Dublin: Gill and Macmillan, 1982.
Brandabur, Edward. *A Scrupulous Meanness: A Study of Joyce's Early Work*. Urbana: University of Illinois Press, 1971.
Brivic Sheldon. "James Joyce: From Stephen to Bloom." In *Psychoanalysis & Literary Process*, edited by Frederick Crews, 118–62. Cambridge: Winthrop, 1970.
Brown, Dennis. *The Modernist Self in Twentieth-Century English Literature*. Hampshire: Palgrave, 1989.
Brown, Richard. *James Joyce and Sexuality*. Cambridge: Cambridge University Press, 1985.
Brown Simon. *Alice in Wonderland (1903)*. Accessed July 2018. http://www.screenonline.org.uk/film/id/974410.
Budgen, Frank. *James Joyce and the Making of Ulysses*. 2nd edition. London: Grayson & Grayson, 1937.
Bulson, Eric. *The Cambridge Introduction to James Joyce*. Cambridge: Cambridge University Press, 2006.
Burton Robert. *The Anatomy of Melancholy*, edited by Thomas C. Faulkner, Nicolas K. Kiessling and Rhonda L. Blair. 6 vols. Oxford: Henry Cripps, 1621, edited copy. Oxford: Clarendon Press, 1989.
Bush, Ron. "'Intensity by Association': T. S. Eliot's Passionate Allusions." *Modernism/Modernity*, 20, no. 4 (2014): 709–27.

Cecconi, Elisabetta. *"Who Chose This Face for Me?" Joyce's Creation of Secondary Characters in Ulysses*. European University Studies Series XIV, Anglo Saxon Language in Literature. Bern: Peter Lang, 2007.

Charles-Edwards, David. *Counselling Issues for Managers No. 1: Death and Bereavement and Work*. London: CEPEC, 1992.

Cixous, Hélène. *The Exile of James Joyce*. Translated by Sally A. J. Purcell. New York: David Lewis, 1972.

Connolly, Thomas, E. *James Joyce's Books, Portraits, Manuscripts, Notebooks, Typescripts, Page Proofs Together with Critical Essays About Some of His Work*. 5th edition. New York: Mellen, 1997.

Cosgrove, Brian. *James Joyce's Negations: Irony, Indeterminacy and Nihilism in Ulysses and Other Writings*. Dublin: University College Dublin Press, 2007.

Costello, Peter. *James Joyce: The Years of Growth 1882 1915*. West Cork: Roberts Rinehart, 1992.

Crispi, Luca. *Joyce's Creative Process and the Construction of Character in Ulysses: Becoming the Blooms*. Oxford: Oxford University Press, 2015.

Culler, Jonathan. *Structuralist Poetics: Structuralism, Linguists and the Study of Literature*. London: Routledge & Kegan Paul, 1975.

Culler, Jonathan. "In Defence of Overinterpretation." In *Interpretation and Overinterpretation*, edited by Stefan Collini, 109–23. Cambridge: Cambridge University Press, 1992, digital, 2004.

Culpeper, Jonathan. *Language and Characterisation: People in Plays and Other Texts*. Edinburgh: Pearson Education, 2001.

Cupckik, Gerald C., Keath Oatley, and Peter Vorderer. "Emotional Effects of Reading Excerpts from Short Stories by James Joyce." *Poetics* 25 (1998): 363–77.

Dallos, Rudi and Arlene Vetere. *Systemic Therapy and Attachment Narratives: Applications in a Range of Clinical Settings*. London: Routledge, 2009.

Damon, S. Forster. "The Odyssey in Dublin." In *James Joyce: Two Decades of Criticism*, edited by Seon Givens, 203–42. New York: Vanguard Press, 1963.

Darwin Charles. *The Expression of the Emotions in Man and Animals*. 3rd edition. Great Britain: John Murray, 1872; London: Harper Collins, 1889; reprint, 1998.

Davison, Neil R. *James Joyce, Ulysses, and the Construction of Jewish Identity: Culture, Biography, and "The Jew" in Modernist Europe*. Cambridge: Cambridge University Press, 1996.

Dettmar, Kevin J. H. *The Illicit Joyce of Postmodernism: Reading Against the Grain*. Madison: University of Wisconsin Press, 1996.

Dixon, Thomas. "From Passions to Emotions." In *Emotions: A Social Science Reader*, edited by Monica Greco and Paul Setnner, 22–83. Routledge Student Reader Series. London: Routledge, 2008.

Doka, Kenneth J. "Disenfranchised Grief." In *Disenfranchised Grief: Recognizing Hidden Sorrow*, edited by Kenneth J. Doka, 3–11. New York: Lexington Books, 1989.

Doka, Kenneth J, ed. *Disenfranchised Grief: New Directions Challenges and Strategies for Practice*. Illinois: Research Press, 2002.

Doka, Kenneth J. "How We Die: Stigmatized Death and Disenfranchised Grief." In *Disenfranchised Grief: New Directions Challenges and Strategies for Practice*, edited by Kenneth J. Doka, 323–36. Illinois: Research Press, 2002.

Doka, Kenneth J. "Disenfranchised Grief in Historical and Cultural Perspective." In *Handbook of Bereavement and Research Practice: Advances in Theory and Intervention*, edited by Margaret S. Strobe, Robert O. Hansson, Henk Schut, and Wolfgang Stroebe, 223–40. Washington: American Psychological Association, 2008.

Doka, Kenneth J. and Terry L. Martin. *Grieving Beyond Gender: Understanding the Ways Men and Women Mourn.* Series in Death, Dying and Bereavement, revised edition. New York: Routledge, 2010.

Downing, Gregory M. "Diverting Philology: Language and Its Effects in Popularised Philology and Joyce's Work." In *James Joyce: The Study of Languages*, edited by Dirk Van Hulle, 121–66. New Comparative Poetics Series No. 6. Bruxelles: PIE-Peter Lange, 2002.

Dunbar, Robin. *Grooming, Gossip and the Evolution of Language.* Cambridge, MA: Harvard University Press, 1996.

Ellmann, Richard. *James Joyce.* London: Oxford University Press, 1959; reprint, 1966.

Ellmann, Richard, ed. *Letters of James Joyce.* 3 vols. London: Faber and Faber, 1966.

Ellmann, Richard, ed. *Selected Letters of James Joyce.* London: Faber and Faber, 1975.

Ellmann, Richard. *The Consciousness of Joyce.* London: Faber and Faber, 1977.

Ellmann, Richard. *James Joyce.* New and revised edition with corrections. Oxford: Oxford University Press, 1983.

Evans, Dylan. *An Introductory Dictionary of Lacanian Psychoanalysis.* Sussex, Routledge: 1998.

Fallis, Richard. *The Irish Renaissance: An Introduction to Anglo-Irish Literature.* Dublin: Gill and Macmillan, 1978.

Feeney, Judith and Patricia Noller. *Adult Attachment.* Sage Series of Close Relationships. London: Sage, 1996.

Felski, Rita. "Introduction." *New Literary History*, 42, no. 2 (2011): v–ix.

Feshbach, Sidney. "Fallen on His Feet in Buenos Ayres (D 39): Frank in 'Eveline.'" *James Joyce Quarterly*, 20, no. 2 (1983): 223–26.

Field, Nigel P. "Unresolved Grief and Continuing Bonds: An Attachment Perspective." *Death Studies*, 30 (2006): 739–56.

Field, Nigel P. "Whether to Relinquish or Maintain a Bond with the Deceased." In *Handbook of Bereavement and Research Practice: Advances in Theory and Intervention*, edited by Margaret S. Strobe, Robert O. Hansson, Henk Schut, and Wolfgang Stroebe, 113–32. Washington: American Psychological Association, 2008.

Fishberg, Maurice. *The Jews: A Study of Race and Environment.* London: Walter Scott, 1911.

Foster, John Wilson. *Fictions of the Irish Literary Revival: A Changeling Art.* New York: Syracuse University Press, 1987.

Foster, R. F. *Modern Ireland 1600–1972*. Allen Lane, 1988; London: Penguin, 1989.
Freedman, M. "Notes on Grief in Literature." In *Loss and Grief: Psychological Management and Medical Practice*, edited by B. Schoenberg A. C., Carr, D. Peretz, and A. H. Kutscher, 339–46. New York: Columbia University Press, 1970.
French, Marilyn. *The Book as World: James Joyce's Ulysses*. New York: Paragon House, 1993.
Freud, Sigmund. *The Future of an Illusion*. Translated by W. D. Robson-Scott. The International Psycho-Analytical Library. Edited by Ernest Jones, no. 15. London: Hogarth Press, 1928; reprint 1953.
Freud, Sigmund. *Collected Papers*. Volume 4 translation supervised by Joan Riviere. London: Hogarth, 1925; 10th reprint, 1957.
Freud, Sigmund. *Inhibitions, Symptoms and Anxiety*. Translated by Alix Strachey, edited and revised by James Strachey. London: Hogarth, 1936; revised edition, 1961.
Freud, Sigmund. "The Question of a *Weltanschauung*." In *The Freud Reader*, edited by Peter Gay, 783–96. New York: Norton, 1989; reprint, 1995.
Friedman, Alan Warren. *Fictional Death and the Modernist Enterprise*. Cambridge: Cambridge University Press, 1995.
Fulton Robert. "Anticipatory Mourning: A Critique of the Concept." *Morality*, 8 (2003): 342–51.
Garrett, Peter K. "Introduction." In *Twentieth Century Interpretations of Dubliners: A Collection of Critical Essays*, edited by Peter K. Garrett, 1–17. New Jersey: Prentice-Hall, 1968.
Gibson, Andrew. "Macropolitics and Micropolitics in 'Wandering Rocks.'" In *Joyce's "Wandering Rocks,"* edited by Andrew Gibson and Steven Morrison, 27–56. European Joyce Studies. Amsterdam: Rodopin, 2002.
Gibson, Andrew. *The Strong Spirit: History, Politics and Aesthetics in the Writings of James Joyce*, 1898–1915. Oxford: Oxford University Press, 2013.
Gifford, Don. *Joyce Annotated: "Notes for Dubliners" and "A Portrait of the Artist as a Young Man."* 2nd edition. Berkley: University of California Press, 1982.
Gifford, Don with Robert J. Seidman. *Ulysses Annotated: Notes for James Joyce's Ulysses*. Revised and expanded edition. California: University of California Press, 1989.
Gilbert, Stuart, ed. *The Letters of James Joyce*. London: Faber and Faber, 1957.
Gillespie, Michael Patrick. *Inverted Volumes Improperly Arranged: James Joyce and His Trieste Library*. Studies in Modern Literature Series No. 10. Michegan: UMI Research Press, 1983.
Goldberg, S. L. *The Classical Temper: A Study of James Joyce's Ulysses*. London: Chatto and Windus, 1961.
Goldie, Peter. "Narrative and Perspective: Values and Appropriate Emotions." In *Philosophy and the Emotions*, edited by Anthony Hatzimoysis, 201–20. Cambridge: Cambridge University Press, 2003.
Gombrich, E. H. *Art and Illusion*. London: Paidon Press, 1972.
Goodwin, Sarah Webster and Elisabeth Bronfen. *Death and Representation*. Baltimore: Johns Hopkins University Press, 1993.

Gottfried, Roy K. *The Art of Joyce's Syntax in Ulysses.* London: Macmillan, 1980.
Haag, Stefan. "Listen and Be Touched: Aural Space in 'Wandering Rocks.'" In *Joyce's "Wandering Rocks,"* edited by Andrew Gibson and Steven Morrison, 107–20. European Joyce Studies 12. Amsterdam: Rodopi, 2002.
Hägglund, Martin. *Dying for Time: Proust, Woolf, Nabokov.* Massachusetts: Harvard University Press, 2012.
Harkness, Marguerite. *A Portrait of the Artist as a Young Man: Voices of the Text.* Twaynes Masterwork Studies No. 38. Boston: Twayne, 1990.
Hart, Clive. "Wandering Rocks." In *James Joyce's Ulysses: Critical Essays*, edited by Clive Hart and David Hayman, 181–216. Berkeley: University of California Press, 1977.
Harvey, John. H. *Perspectives on Loss and Trauma: Assaults on the Self.* California: Sage, 2002.
Hays, Judith C. and Cristina C. Hendrix. "The Role of Religion in Bereavement." In *Handbook of Bereavement and Research Practice: Advances in Theory and Intervention*, edited by Margaret S. Strobe, Robert O. Hansson, Henk Schut, and Wolfgang Stroebe 327–48. Washington: American Psychological Association, 2008.
Healey, George H., ed. *The Complete Dublin Diary of Stanislaus Joyce.* London: Cornell University Press, 1971.
Henke, Suzette, A. *James Joyce and the Politics of Desire.* Routledge: London, 1990.
Henke, Suzette. "Stephen Dedalus & Women: A Portrait of the Artist as a Young Misogynist." In *Women in Joyce*, edited by Suzette Henke and Elaine Unkeless, 82–107. Urbana: University of Illinois Press, 1982.
Herring, Philip F. *Joyce's Ulysses Notesheets in the British Museum.* Charlotttesville: University Press of Virginia, 1972.
Hoffman, Frederick, J. *Freudianism and the Literary Mind.* 2nd edition. Louisiana: Louisiana State University Press, 1957.
Hoffmeister, Adolph. "Portrait of Joyce." In *Portraits of the Artist in Exile: Recollections of James Joyce by Europeans*, edited by Willard Potts, 127–36. Seattle: University of Washington Press, 1979.
Hogan, Patrick Colm. *What Literature Teaches Us About Emotion.* Studies in Emotion and Social Interaction, Second Series. Cambridge: Cambridge University Press, 2011.
Holmes, Jeremy. "Attachment Theory: A Secure Base for Policy?" In *The Politics of Attachment: Towards a Secure Society*, edited by Sebastian Kraemer and Jane Roberts, 27–42. London: Free Association Books, 1996.
Holmes, Jeremy. *The Search for A Secure Base: Attachment Theory and Psychotherapy.* East Sussex: Brunner-Routledge, 2001; reprint, 2002.
Holmes, Jeremy. "Superego: An Attachment Perspective." *International Journal of Psychoanalysis*, 92 (2011): 1221–40.
Homer. *The Odyssey.* Translated by Robert Fitzgerald. New York: Doubleday, 1962.
Howe, David. *Attachment Across the Lifecourse: A Brief Introduction.* Basingstoke: Palgrave Macmillan, 2011.

Humphrey, Robert. *Stream of Consciousness in the Modern Novel*. California: University of California Press, 1954.

Hyman, Louis. *The Jews of Ireland: From Earliest Times to the Year 1910*. Shannon: Irish University Press, 1972.

Ingersoll, Earl G. *Engendered Trope in Joyce's Dubliners*. Carbondale: Southern Illinois University Press, 1996.

Inglis, Tom. "Religion, Identity, State and Society." In *The Cambridge Companion to Modern Irish Culture*, edited by Joe Cleary and Clare Connolly, 59–77. Cambridge: Cambridge University Press, 2005.

Jackson, John Wyse, and Peter Costello. *John Stanislaus Joyce: The Voluminous Life and Genius of James Joyce's Father*. London: Fourth Estate, 1998.

Jalland, Pat. *Death in the Victorian Family*. Oxford: Oxford University Press, 1996.

James, David. "Modernist Narratives: Revisions and Rereadings." In *The Oxford Handbook of Modernisms*, edited by Peter Brooker, Andrzej Gasiorek, Deborah Longworth, and Andrew Thacker, 85–107. Oxford: Oxford University Press, 2010.

Jameson, Fredric. *The Political Unconscious: Narrative as a Socially Symbolic Act*. Ithaca: Cornell University Press, 1981.

Jones, Robert S. P. "Language, Form and Emotion in James Joyce's Portrait of an Artist as a Young Man: A Literary Analysis." *Advances in Language and Literary Studies*, no. 8 (2017), 158–63.

Jordan, John R. "Is Suicide Bereavement Different? A Reassessment of the Literature." In *Suicide and Life-Threatening Behaviour*, 31 (2001): 91–102.

Joyce, James. *Pomes Penyeach: And Other Verses*. London: Faber and Faber, 1966.

Joyce, James. *The Critical Writings*, edited by Ellsworth Mason and Richard Ellmann. New York: Cornell University Press, 1989.

Joyce, Stanislaus. *My Brother's Keeper: James Joyce's Early Years*. London Faber and Faber, 1958; reprint, Cambridge: Da Capo, 2003.

Joyce, Stanislaus. "Extracts from James Joyce: A Memoir." In *James Joyce: Critical Assessments of Major Writers*, edited by Colin Milton, 4 vols., 1: 126–27. Abingdon: Routledge 2012.

Jung, C. G. "Psychological Types." In *The Collected Works of C. J. Jung*, translated by R. F. C. Hull, edited by Herbert Read and others, 463–67. 2nd edition, volume 4. London: Routledge & Kegan Paul, 1969.

Jung, C. G. "The Psychology of the Unconscious Processes." In *Collected Papers on Analytical Psychology*, translated by Dora Hecht, edited by Constance E. Long, 324–44. Moffat Yard, 1917.

Jung, C. G. "Psychotherapists or the Clergy." In *The Collected Works of C. J. Jung*, translated by R. F. C. Hull, edited by Herbert Read and others, 327–47. 2nd edition, volume 11. London: Routledge & Kegan Paul, 1969.

Jung, Carl Gustav. *Psychology and Religion*. New Haven: Yale University Press, 1938; reprint, 1968.

Juri, Luis J. and Mario Marrone, "Attachment and Bereavement." In *Attachment Theory and the Psychoanalytic Process*, edited by Mauricio Cortina and Mario Marrone, 242–67. London: Whurr Publishers, 2003.

Kain, Richard M. *Fabulous Voyager: James Joyce's Ulysses*. Chicago: University of Chicago Press, 1947.
Kain, Richard, ed. An Interview with Carola Giedion-Welcker and Maria Jolas." *James Joyce Quarterly*, 11 (Winter 1974): 120
Keen, Suzanne. *Empathy and The Novel*. Oxford: Oxford University Press, 2007.
Keen, Suzanne. "Readers' Temperaments and Fictional Character." *New Literary History*, 42, no. 2 (2011): 295–314.
Kenner, Hugh. *Ulysses*. London: Allen and Unwin, 1980.
Kenny, Diana T. *From Id to Intersubjectivity: Talking about the Talking Cure with Master Clinicians*. London: Karnac, 2014.
Kershner, R. Brandon. *Joyce, Bakhtin and Popular Literature: Chronicles of Disorder*. Chapel Hill: The University of North Carolina Press, 1989.
Kershner, R. Brandon. *The Culture of Ulysses*. Hampshire: Palgrave Macmillan, 2010.
Kiberd, Declan. *Ulysses and Us: The Art of Everyday Living*. London: Faber and Faber, 2009.
Kimball, Jean. *Odyssey of the Psyche: Jungian Patterns in Joyce's Ulysses*. Carbondale: Southern Illinois University Press, 1997.
Kimball, Jean "Jung's 'Dual Mother' in Joyce's *Ulysses:* An illustrated Psychoanalytic Intertext." *Journal of Modern Literature*, 17 (1991): 478–90.
Kirkpatrick, Lee A. *Attachment, Evolution and the Psychology of Religion*. New York: Guildford Press, 2005.
Kirkpatrick, Lee. A. and Phillip R. Shaver. "Attachment Theory and Religion: Childhood Attachments, Religious Beliefs, and Conversion." *Journal for the Scientific Study of Religion*, 29 (1990): 314–34.
Lamarque, Peter and Stein Haugom Olson. *Truth, Fiction and Literature: A Philosophical Perspective*. Oxford: Clarendon Press, 1994.
Lamos, Colleen. *Deviant Modernism: Sexual and Textual Errancy in T.S. Eliot, James Joyce, and Marcel Proust*. Cambridge: Cambridge University Press, 1998.
Lange, Carl Georg and William James. *The Emotions*. New York: Hafner, 1922; reprint, 1967.
Lawrence, Karen. "Paternity as Legal Fiction in *Ulysses*." In *James Joyce: The Augmented Ninth*, edited by Bernard Benstock, 223–43. New York: Syracuse University Press, 1988.
Leonard, Garry M. *Reading Dubliners Again: A Lacanian Perspective*. Syracuse: Syracuse University Press, 1993.
Lernout, Geert. "Religion." In *James Joyce in Context*, edited by John McCourt, 332–34. Cambridge: Cambridge University Press, 2009.
Lernout, Geert. *Help My Unbelief: James Joyce and Religion*. London: Continuum, 2010.
Leverage Paula, Howard Mancing, Richard Schickert, and Jennifer Marston Williams. "Introduction." In *Theory of Mind and Literature*, edited by Paula Leverage, Howard Mancing, Richard Schickert, and Jennifer Marston, 1–11. Williams, IN: Purdue University Press, 2011.

Levinson, Jerrold. "Emotion in Response to Art." In *Emotion and the Arts*, edited by Mette Hjort, and Sue Laver, 20–49. Oxford: Oxford University Press, 1977.

Lewis, C. S. *A Grief Observed*. London: Faber and Faber, 1961; reprint, 1978.

Lewis, Pericles. *Religious Experience and the Modernist Novel*. Cambridge: Cambridge University Press, 2010.

Littlewood, Jane. *Aspects of Grief: Bereavement in Adult Life*. London: Routledge, 1992; reprint, 1993.

Longridge, W. H. trans. *The Spiritual Exercises of Saint Ignatius Loyola: Translated from the Spanish with a Commentary and a Translation of the Directorium in Exerciti*. 5th edition. London: A. R. Mowbray, 1955.

Lowe-Evans, Mary. *Catholic Nostalgia in Joyce and Company*. The Florida James Joyce Series. Gainesville: University Press of Florida, 2008.

MacCabe, Colin. *James Joyce and the Revolution of the Word*. London: MacMillan, 1979; reprint, 1981.

MacKay, Marina. "The Modernist 'Novel.'" In *The Cambridge History of Modernism*, edited by Vincent Sherry, 307–25. Cambridge: Cambridge University Press, 2016.

McCourt, John. *The Years of Bloom: James Joyce in Trieste 1904–1920*. Wisconsin: The University of Wisconsin Press, 2000.

McDonald, Michael and Terence Murphy. *Sleepless Souls: Suicide in Early Modern England*. Oxford: Clarendon, 1990

Maddox, Brenda. *Nora: A Biography of Nora Joyce*. Hamish Hamilton, 1988; reprint, London: Minerva, 1989.

Maddox, James H. Jr. *Joyce's Ulysses and the Assault Upon Character*. Sussex: Harvester Press, 1978.

Magalaner, Marvin. "The Anti-Semitic Limerick Incidents and Joyce's 'Bloomsday.'" *PMLA*, 68 (1953): 1219–23

Mahaffey, Vicki. "Darkening Freedom: Yeats, Joyce and Beckett." In *The Cambridge History of Modernism*, edited by Vincent Sherry, 446–662. Cambridge: Cambridge University Press, 2016.

Main, Mary. "Metacognitive Knowledge, Metacognitive Monitoring, and Singular (Coherent) vs. Multiple (Incoherent) Model of Attachment: Findings and Directions for Future Research." In *Attachment Across the Lifecyle*, edited by Colin Murray Parkes, Joan Stevenson-Hinde, and Peter Marris, 127–59. London: Routledge, 1991.

Marrone Mario and Maricio Cortina. "Introduction: Reclaiming Bowlby's Contribution to Psychoanalysis." In *Attachment Theory and the Psychoanalytic Process*, edited by Mauricio Cortina and Mario Marrone, 1–24. London: Whurr Publishers, 2003.

Marthaler, Bernard, L. and others, eds. *New Catholic Encyclopedia*. 2nd edition. Volume 13. 15 volumes. Detroit: Gale in Association with The Catholic University of America, 2003.

Mattoon, Mary Ann. *Jungian Psychology in Perspective*. New York: The Free Press, 1981.

May, Rollo. *The Courage to Create*. London: Collins, 1976.

Melton, J. Gordon. "Rosicrusian Religion." In *Encyclopaedia Britannica Online*. Accessed 30 July 2018. www.Brtannica.com/topic/Rosicrusians

Mercanton Jacques. "The Hours of Joyce." In *Portraits of the Artist in Exile: Recollections of James Joyce by Europeans*, edited by Willard Potts, 206–52. Seattle: University of Washington Press, 1979.

Mikulincer, Mario and Phillip R. Shaver. *Attachment in Adulthood: Structure, Dynamics and Change*. New York: Guilford Press, 2007; reprint, 2010.

Mikulincer, Mario and Phillip R. Shaver. "An Attachment Perspective on Bereavement." In *Handbook of Bereavement and Research Practice: Advances in Theory and Intervention*, edited by Margaret S. Stroebe et al., 87–112. Washington, DC: American Psychological Association, 2008.

de Montaigne, Michel. "On Experience." In *The Complete Essays of Michel do Montaigne*, translated by M. A. Screech, 1207–69. London: Allen Lane, The Penguin Press, 1991.

Murphy, Jeffrie G. "Remorse, Apology and Mercy." *Ohio State Journal of Criminal Law*, 4 (2007): 423–53.

Myers, Frederic W. H. *Human Personality and Its Survival of Bodily Death*, edited. by Richard Hodgson and Alice Johnson. 2 vols. London: Longmans Green, 1903; reprint, 1915.

Nadel, Ira B. *Joyce and the Jews: Culture and Texts*. Basingstoke: Macmillan, 1989.

Norris, Margot. *Suspicious Readings of Joyce's Dubliners*. Pennsylvania: University of Pennsylvania Press, 2003.

Norris, Margot. *Virgin and Veteran Readings of Ulysses*. New York: Palgrave Macmillan, 2011.

Norris Margot. "Character, Plot and Myth." In *The Cambridge Companion to Ulysses*, edited by Sean Latham, 69–80. New York: Cambridge University Press, 2014.

Nottingham, Elizabeth K. *Religion and Society*. Doubleday Short Studies in Sociology Series. New York: Random House, 1954.

Oatley Keith and Mitra Gholamain. "Emotions and Identification: Connections Between Readers and Fiction." In *Emotion and the Arts*, edited by Mette Hjort and Sue Laver, 263–81. Oxford: Oxford University Press, 1997.

Oatley, Keith. *Best Laid Schemes: The Psychology of Emotions*. Cambridge: Cambridge University Press, 1992; reprint, 1999.

O'Brien, Darcy. *The Conscience of James Joyce*. Princeton: Princeton University Press, 1968.

O'Brien, Edna. *James Joyce*. Lives Series. London: Weidenfield & Nicholson, 1999.

Ó hÓgáin, Dáithí. *The Lore of Ireland: An Encyclopaedia of Myth, Legend and Romance*. Woodbridge: Boydell, 2006.

Paosada, Germán and Jill M. Trumbell, "Universality and Cultural Specificity in Child-Mother Attachment Relationships: In Search for Answers." In *Attachment Across Clinical and Cultural Perspectives A Relational Psychoanalytic Approach*, edited by Sonia Gojman-de-Millan, Christian Herreman, and L. Alan Sroufe, 30–52. Psychoanalytic Inquiry Book Series. London: Routledge, 2017.

Parker, Stephen. "*Jung's Essay on Ulysses.*" Accessed 05 January 2012. http://jung-currents.com/jungs-essay-on-ulysses.

Parkes, Colin Murray. *Bereavement: Studies of Grief in Adult Life*. 3rd edition. London: Penguin, 1988.

Parkes, Colin Murray and Holly G. Prigerson. *Bereavement: Studies of Grief in Adult Life*. 4th edition. London: Routledge, 2010.
Parkes, Colin Murray. *Love and Loss: The Roots of Grief and its Complications*. London: Routledge, 2006.
Parrinder, Patrick. "A Portrait of the Artist." In *James Joyce's A Portrait of the Artist as a Young Man: A Casebook*, edited by Mark A. Wollaeger, 85–128. Oxford: Oxford University Press, 2003.
Payne, Sheila, Sandra Horn, and Marilyn Relf. *Loss and Bereavement*. Health Psychology Series Buckingham: Open University Press, 1999.
Peake, C. H. *James Joyce: The Citizen and the Artist*. London: Arnold, 1977.
Pierce, David. *Reading Joyce*. Harlow: Pearson Longman, 2008.
Pound, Ezra. "'Dubliners' and Mr. James Joyce." In *James Joyce: The Critical Heritage*, edited by Robert H. Deming. 2 vols. London: Routledge, 1970.
Power, Arthur. *Conversations with James Joyce*. London: Millington, 1974; reprint with corrections, Dublin: Lilliput Press, 1999.
Proeve, Michael and Steven Tudor. *Remorse: Psychological and Jurisprudential Perspectives*. Surrey: Ashgate, 2010.
Raleigh, John Henry. *The Chronicle of Leopold and Molly Bloom: Ulysses as Narrative*. Berkley: University of California Press, 1977.
Randall, Peter. *The Psychology of Feeling Sorry: The Weight of the Soul*. London: Routledge, 2013.
Ratnarajah, Dorothy and Margot J. Scholfield. "'Survivors' Narratives of the Impact of Parental Suicide." *Suicide and Life-Threatening Behaviour*, 38 (October 2008): 618–30.
Reed, Bruce. *The Dynamics of Religion: Process and Movement in Christian Churches*. London: Drayton, Longman and Todd, 1978.
Restuccia, Frances L. *Joyce and the Law of the Father*. New Haven: Yale University Press, 1989.
Rickard, John S. *Joyce's Book of Memory: The Mnemotechnic of Ulysses*. Durham: Duke University Press, 1999.
Riquelme, John Paul. *Teller and Tale in Joyce's Fiction: Oscillating Perspectives*. Maryland: Johns Hopkins University Press, 1983.
Riquelme, John Paul. "Desire, Freedom, and Confessional Culture in *A Portrait of the Artist as A Young Man*." In *A Companion to James Joyce*, edited by Richard Brown, 34–53. Oxford: Blackwell Publishing, 2008.
Robinson, Jennifer. *Deeper Than Reason: Emotion and Its Role in Literature, Music and Art*. Oxford: Oxford University Press, 2005.
Rosenblatt, Paul, C. *Bitter Bitter Tears: Nineteenth Century Diarists and Twentieth Century Grief Theories*. Minneapolis: University of Minnesota Press, 1983.
Rossman, Charles. "The Reader's Role in *A Portrait of the Artist as a Young Man*." In *James Joyce: Critical Assessments of Major Writers*, edited by Colin Milton, 259–73. 4 Vols. Abingdon: Routledge, 2012.
Schneider, Ulrich. "Titles in Dubliners." In *Rejoycing: New Readings of Dubliners*, edited by Rosa Bosinelli, M. Bollettieri, and Harold F. Mosher Jr., 195–205. Lexington: University Press of Kentucky, 1998.

Scholes, Robert and Richard M. Kain, eds. *The Workshop of Daedalus: James Joyce and the Raw Materials for a Portrait of the Artist as a Young Man.* Illinois: Northwestern University Press, 1965.

Schutte, William M. *Joyce and Shakespeare: A Study in the Meaning of Ulysses.* Yale University Press, 1957; Connecticut: Archon Books, 1971.

Schwaber, Paul. *The Cast of Characters: A Reading of Ulysses.* New Haven: Yale University Press, 1999.

Shand, Alexander F. *The Foundations of Character: Being a Study of the Tendencies of the Emotions and Sentiments,* 2nd edition. London: MacMillan, 1920.

Sharoni, Josephine. "The Failure of the Parental Metaphor: A Lacanian Reading of James Joyce's 'Eveline.'" *Journal of Modern Literature*, 39, no. 4 (2016), 33–48.

Shakespeare, William. *The Merchant of Venice*, edited by J. L. Halio. Oxford: Carendon Press, 1993.

Shakespeare, William. *Macbeth*, edited by Jonathan Bate and Eric Rasmussen. The RSC Shakespeare Series. Hampshire: Macmillan, 2009.

Shakespeare, William, *The Merchant of Venice*, edited by J. L. Halio. Oxford: Clarendon Press, 1993.

Shaver, Phillip R. and R. Chris Fraley. "Attachment, Loss and Grief: Bowlby's Views and Current Controversies." In *Handbook of Attachment: Theory, Research and Clinical Applications*, edited by Jude Cassidy and Philip R. Shaver, 48–77. 2nd edition. New York: The Guildford Press, 2008.

Shechner, Mark. *Joyce in Nighttown: A Psychoanalytic Inquiry into Ulysses.* Berkley: University of California Press, 1974.

Smedes, Lewis B. *Shame and Grace: Healing the Shame We Don't Deserve.* New York: Harper Collins, 1993.

Smidt, Kristian. *James Joyce and the Cultic Use of Fiction.* Revised edition. Oslo: Oslo University Press, 1959.

Smith, Murray. "On the Twofoldness of Character." *New Literary History*, 42, no. 2 (2011): 277–94.

Smith, P. C., L. M. Range and A. Ulmer. "Belief in an Afterlife as a Buffer in Suicide and Other Bereavement." *Omega*, 24, no.3 (1992).

Soupault, Philippe. "James Joyce." In *Portraits of the Artist in Exile: Recollections of James Joyce by Europeans*, edited Willard Potts, 108–18. Seattle: University of Washington Press, 1979.

Spoo, Robert. *James Joyce and the Language of History: Dedalus's Nightmare.* Oxford: Oxford University Press, 1994.

Sroufe, L. Alan. "Attachment Theory: A Humanistic Approach for Research and Practice Across Cultures." In *Attachment Across Clinical and Cultural Perspectives: A Relational Psychoanalytic Approach*, edited by Sonia Gojman-de-Millan, Christian Herreman, and L. Alan Sroufe, 1–29. Psychoanalytic Inquiry Book Series. London: Routledge 2017.

Steinberg, Erwin R. *The Stream of Consciousness and Beyond.* Pittsburgh: University of Pittsburgh Press, 1973.

Strange, Julie Marie. *Grief and Poverty in Britain, 1870–1914.* Cambridge: Cambridge University Press, 2005.

Stroebe et al. "Bereavement Research: Contemporary Perspectives." In *Handbook of Bereavement and Research Practice: Advances in Theory and Intervention*, edited by Margaret S. Strobe, Robert O. Hansson, Henk Schut, and Wolfgang Stroebe 3–24. Washington: American Psychological Association, 2008.

Strong, L. A. G. *The Sacred River: An Approach to James Joyce*. London: Methuen, 1949.

Sultan, Stanley, *The Argument of Ulysses*. Columbus: Ohio State University Press, 1964.

Symons, Arthur. *The Symbolist Movement in Literature*. 2nd edition, revised. London: Constable, 1911.

Tacey, David. *How to Read Jung*. London: Granta, 2006.

The Society of St. Pius X. Accessed 1 November 2013. http://www.sspx.co.uk/mass/requiem/index.htm

Thomas, Brook. *James Joyce's Ulysses: A Book of Many Happy Returns*. Louisiana State University Press, Baton Rouge, 1982.

Thurston, Luke. "Scotographica: Joyce and Psychoanalysis." In *A Companion to James Joyce*, edited by Richard Brown, 407–26. Oxford: Blackwell Publishing Ltd., 2008.

Tigges, Wim. "Dervaun Seraun!: Resignation or Escape?" *James Joyce Quarterly*, 32 (1994), 102–4.

Tindall, William York. *A Reader's Guide to James Joyce*. New York: Farrar, Straus & Giroux, 1959; reprint, 1978.

Torchiana, Donald T. *Backgrounds for Joyce's Dubliners*. Boston, Allen and Unwin, 1986.

Trotter, David, *Cinema and Modernism*. Massachusetts: Blackwell, 2007.

Tymoczko, Maria. *The Irish Ulysses*. Berkley: University of California Press, 2004.

Ulanov, Anna "Jung and Religion: The Opposing Self." In *The Cambridge Companion to Jung*, edited by Polly Young-Eisendrath and Terence Dawson, 296–313. Cambridge: Cambridge University Press, 1997; reprint, 1999.

Vargish, Thomas and Delo E. Mook. *Inside Modernism: Relativity Theory, Cubism, Narrative*. New Haven: Yale University Press, 1999.

Wade, Allan, ed. *The Letters of W. B. Yeats*. London: Hart-Davis, 1954.

Wagner, Richard. *Judaism in Music and Other Essays*. Translated by W. Ashton Ellis. Lincoln: University of Nebraska Press, 1995.

Wall, Richard. *Anglo-Irish Dialect Glossary for Joyce's Works*. Gerrards Cross: Smythe, 1986.

Walzl, Forence L. "Joyce's 'The Sisters': A Development." *James Joyce Quarterly*, 50 (2013): 73–117.

Warner, John, M. *Joyce's Grandfathers: Myth and History in Defoe, Smollett, Sterne, and Joyce*. Georgia: The University of Georgia Press, 1993.

Webb, Jennifer and Lorraine Webb. "Dead or Alive." In *Images of the Corpse: From the Renaissance to Cyberspace*, edited by Elizabeth Klaver, 206–27. Wisconsin: University of Wisconsin Press, 2004.

Weininger, Otto. *Sex and Character: An Investigation of Fundamental Principles*. Translated by Ladislaus Löb, edited by Daniel Steuer with Laura Marcus. Vienna, 1903; Bloomington: Indiana University Press, 2005.

Weizmann, Chaim and Richard Gottheil. *What Is Zionism? Two Chapters from "Zionism and the Jewish Future."* London: Zionist Organisation, 1918.

Welby, Lizzy. "Configuring Cognitive Architecture: Mind-Rading and Meta-Representation in *Ulysses*." In *Cognitive Joyce*, edited by Sylvian Belluc and Valérie Bénéjam, 193–207. Studies in Literature and Performance Series. Basingstoke: Palgrave Macmillan, 2018.

Wilson, David Sloan. *Darwin's Cathedral: Evolution, Religion and the Nature of Society*. Chicago: University of Chicago Press, 2002.

Winstanley. Julie, *Key Concepts in Psychology*. Palgrave Key Concepts Series. Basingstoke: Palgrave Macmillan, 2006.

Wollaeger, Mark A., ed. *James Joyce's A Portrait of the Artist as a Yung Man: A Casebook*. Oxford: Oxford University Press, 2003.

Woolf, Virginia. "Modern Fiction." In *Essays of the Self: Selected Essays of Virginia Woolf*, edited by Joanna Kavenna, 17–22. Devon: Notting Hill Editions, 2014.

Worden, J. William. *Grief Counseling and Grief Therapy: A Handbook for the Mental Health Practitioner*. 4th edition. New York: Springer, 2009.

Wright, David G. *Characters of Joyce*. Dublin: Gill & Macmillan, 1983.

Zunshine, Lisa. *Getting Inside Your Head: What Cognitive Science Can Tell Us About Popular Culture*. Baltimore: Johns Hopkins University Press, 2012.

Index

afterlife, 117, 157, 163, 165, 192
alcohol abuse, 64–65, 70, 72
Attachment Theory, 4, 6, 15, 19–20, 22, 24, 29, 44, 95, 147, 163, 177, 207–9;
 adolescence, 13;
 Adult Attachment Interview (AAI), 14;
 anxious/ambivalent attachment, 12–13, 63–65, 87–88, 95, 123, 125, 133–34, 141, 185, 188–89, 197;
 avoidant attachment, 12–13, 23, 71, 95, 102, 111, 157, 172, 175–79, 181, 185;
 disorganised attachment, 12;
 evolutionary and ethological science, 19–20, 35, 158;
 grief, ix–x, 1–2, 4, 13–16, 20–22, 35, 46, 49–50, 53, 59, 62–64, 69, 71–72, 78, 82, 95, 116–18, 126, 140, 164–65, 169, 177–78, 180–81, 186, 199, 202, 205–6;
 internal working models, 12–14, 20–21, 96, 172, 208, 209;
 rejection, 125–26;
 religion and, 5, 16, 56, 114, 148–51, 172, 191–92, 195, 209;
 secure attachment, 13, 45, 56, 102, 123;
 self-knowledge and, 93–94, 140, 185;
 sexual abuse and, 46;
 sexual behaviour and, 35–36, 52, 138, 209.
 See also Attachment Theory and literary interpretation; Bowlby, John; Shand, Alexander
Attachment Theory and literary interpretation, ix–x, 1, 3–4, 20, 23–25, 28–30, 33–37, 41, 45–46, 48, 52, 56, 65–67, 71, 74–75, 78, 82, 87–89, 101, 108, 110–18, 123, 130, 132–34, 138, 141, 172–73, 179, 181–82, 189, 195–97, 202, 206, 208

Bowlby, John, 1–4, 7n5, 11–16, 17n15, 19, 21, 33, 35–36, 45, 46, 49, 52, 53, 58n27, 62, 63–64, 65, 83, 77, 95, 102, 116–17, 118, 125–26, 127, 151, 164, 177, 201

Crispi, Luca, 5, 28–29, 188, 192

Darwin, Charles, 15, 21
Dubliners, ix, 2, 5, 24, 35, 78;
 "The Dead," 41, 63, 78, 81–89, 125;
 "Eveline," 41, 69–79, 89, 117;
 "Grace," 175;

"The Sisters," 2, 41, 43, 45–56, 59, 63, 67

Eliot, T. S., 129
emotion:
    literature and, 1, 22, 24, 42–43;
    narrative form and, 93–94;
    use of terminology, 41–42

Freud, Sigmund, ix, 2–3, 11–13, 20, 24, 27–28, 33, 36, 64, 104–5, 150, 161, 163–64, 209;
    Freudian interpretation of Joyce's work, 36, 50–51, 86–87, 108, 111–13, 124–25, 133, 189, 195, 206–8;
    "Mourning and Melancholia," 14–16, 36
Finnegans Wake, 35, 107, 187

grief, ix, 1, 4, 93, 98, 115, 119, 169, 181, 201;
    anticipatory, 52–54;
    causation guilt, 127–28, 200;
    disenfranchised, 81–83, 85, 89, 148, 186, 198, 207;
    dreams, 49–51, 102, 117–18;
    emotional response to, 4, 41, 78, 93, 136–37;
    grieving rules, 82–83;
    guilt, 117–18, 139, 142, 147, 169, 174–78, 180, 182, 206;
    idealisation, 81, 83–84;
    religion and, 3, 147;
    sexual relations and, 132, 136–38, 140;
    social support and, 98, 182, 185, 192–93, 196, 201–2;
    stages of, 14–16, 21–22, 50, 71–72, 82, 127.
    See also Attachment Theory; sudden death; suicide

historicism, 20
Homer, 20, 22

Joyce, James, ix–x, 2, 23;
    autobiographical references, 34, 93, 101;
    biographical information, 2, 4, 6, 23, 30, 42, 70, 72, 94, 96–97, 102, 110, 116, 118, 129, 136, 152–53, 161, 163, 165;
    letters, 5, 118, 153, 157, 161–64, 186;
    narrative techniques, 1, 3–4, 6, 20, 23–25, 30, 33, 35–36, 41, 43, 47, 55, 59–61, 66–67, 70, 74–76, 83, 101, 115, 117, 124, 129, 189, 199, 202, 207, 209.
    See also Dubliners; *Finnegans Wake*; *Portrait of the Artist*; religion; *Stephen Hero*; *Ulysses*
Joyce, John, 70, 96–97, 199
Joyce, Nora (nee Barnacle), 2, 73, 129, 136, 153, 157, 161–62, 165, 190
Joyce, Stanislaus, 2, 101, 160–62, 174, 175.
    See also religion
Jung, C. F., 3, 36, 150, 157, 161, 163–64, 178;
    Jungian interpretations of Joyce's work, 37, 115, 173

Klein, Melanie, 3, 11–12

Lacan, Jacques, 3, 20;
    Lacanian interpretation of Joyce's work, 37, 48, 54, 77–78, 138
Lang, Carl, 21
Lewis, C. S., 4
literary characters, theory, 27;
    dehumanising approach, 27;
    humanising approach, 3, 27–29, 35, 41, 94, 205, 209.
    See also reader response
literature and the mind, 1–2, 35, 94, 205

modernism, 3, 6, 129, 208–9

Oatley, Keith:

emotion, communicative
   function, 77;
emotion, derivation of,
   42–43, 49, 114;
emotion of loss, 4
"overinterpretation" of texts,
   29–30, 34, 209

Portrait of the Artist, ix, 2, 4–5, 24,
   36, 45, 93–94, 101–15, 118–19,
   152–53, 162, 166, 170, 173, 179–
   81, 195, 209;
   avoidant traits of Stephen, 34, 105,
      110–14, 179, 208;
   Clongowes Wood College, 4, 33–34,
      48, 60, 94–96, 102–10, 112–14,
      119, 140, 170, 172–73, 179–80;
   familial relationships, 101, 109,
      111–14, 119–20, 179, 208.
   See also religion
Pound, Ezra, 24

Raleigh, John Henry, 5, 124
reader response, 42, 83;
   Culpeper, Jonathan, 3, 27,
      35, 116, 202;
   Felski, Rita, 28;
   Keen, Suzanne, 27–29, 35;
   Smith, Murray, 27–28, 34, 70
reading, process of, 34–35, 83
religion, 5–6, 83, 147, 148–49, 163,
   186, 191, 207;
   Bloom's lack of, 189–93, 207;
   Catholicism, 54, 71, 117, 151, 157–
      59, 161–63, 189, 191, 194;
   conscience and, 169–70, 174–75;
   Dedalus, Stephen and, 6, 114–15,
      120, 147–48, 151–52, 165–66,
      169–76, 179–82, 185, 192;
   introspection, 147, 170, 175–76, 185;
   Jesuit priests/order, 51, 107–10,
      158–60, 179, 191, 199;
   Jews/Judaism, 6, 20, 26, 96, 128–29,
      147, 151–52, 186–89, 193–94,
      196–98, 207–8;

Joyce, James and, 41–42, 93,
   117, 147, 153, 157–63, 165,
   176, 186, 192;
Joyce, Stanislaus and, 157, 160, 174;
Protestantism, 151, 187;
social relations, 147–48, 158–59,
   186, 191–93, 196–97.
See also Attachment Theory; grief;
   religious rituals
religious rituals, 148;
   baptism, 151, 187–88;
   confession, 50, 66, 190;
   eucharist, 50, 189–91;
   funerals/burials, 189–90, 192, 199;
   Jewish, 186–87
remorse, 6, 101, 118–19, 147–48, 169–
   70, 175, 177–82, 186, 200, 206

sexual relationships, 141;
   adultery, 131, 132, 134, 140–41;
   coerciveness, 136;
   exhibitionism, 138–39;
   imagined, 87;
   jealousy, 87, 135;
   moral guilt, 139;
   voyeurism, 137–40.
   See also grief
shame, 171, 175, 180, 181, 200
Shand, Alexander, F., ix–x, 3, 14–16,
   21–23, 33, 76–77, 93, 98, 205
Shakespeare, William:
   Freud reference to, 15;
   Joyce references to, 170, 196;
   Shand reference to, 22
Stephen Hero, 4, 62, 111, 114,
   153, 158, 162
stigma, 198, 200, 201, 207;
   discreditable, 198;
   discrediting, 198
sudden death, 60
suicide, 20, 14, 169, 186, 189, 197–
   202, 207–8.
   See also stigma
survival wish, 130–31

Ulysses, ix, 2–4, 20, 23–24, 27, 30, 36, 41, 61–62, 98, 118, 207;
"Aeolus," 189;
"Circe," 30, 101, 109–10, 117–19, 124–26, 128–30, 132, 139, 178, 181, 187, 196–97;
"Cyclops," 188, 194–96;
"Eumaeus," 131–32, 176, 186, 192;
"Hades," 59, 63–67, 89, 127–31, 139, 189–92, 193–94, 197–201, 207–8;
"Ithaca," 30–31, 96, 124, 126–28, 133, 139–40, 148, 151, 186, 188, 191–92, 201;
"Lestrygonians," 129, 132, 137, 187, 189–91, 202;
"Lotus Eaters," 51, 131, 190–92, 208;
"Nestor," 118–19, 176;
"Oxen of the Sun," 30–31, 117, 128–29, 177, 189;
"Penelope," 96–98, 125, 128, 132–42, 190, 201;
"Proteus," 115–16, 178;
"Scylla and Charybdis," 22, 101, 130–31;
"Sirens," 128, 135, 194, 196, 202;
"Telemachus," 4, 23, 72, 101–2, 106, 115–17, 119, 158, 170, 176, 178–82;
"Wandering Rocks," 59–68, 159–60, 189, 196.
See also *Ulysses*, main characters of
Ulysses, main characters of:
Bloom, Ellen (nee Higgins, mother of Leopold), 96–97, 124, 188;
Bloom, Leopold, 2, 5–6, 23, 27–28, 30–31, 36, 62–64, 66, 93, 96–98, 116, 123–42, 147–48, 150–52, 176, 185–202, 207–8;
Bloom, Milly, 97, 132, 140;
Bloom, Molly, 5, 23, 28, 93, 96–98, 123–28, 131–42, 186, 190, 195–96, 198, 201–2, 207–8;
Bloom, Rudolph (father of Leopold), 96, 124, 147, 186–89, 191, 197–201, 207–8;
Bloom, Rudy, 2, 97, 127–33, 136–37, 139–40, 142, 200–201, 207;
Boylan, Hugh Blazes, 28, 131–32, 134, 138, 140–41, 195, 202, 207;
the Citizen, 152, 186, 188–89, 193–97, 202;
Cunningham, Martin, 63–64, 160, 193–94, 196, 198–99, 201;
Dedalus, Dilly, 78, 113;
Dedalus, Mary ("May") (mother of Stephen), 72, 101, 117–19, 147, 162, 165, 178–80;
Dedalus, Simon (father of Stephen), 63, 127, 129–30, 194;
Dedalus, Stephen, 4, 6, 22–23, 30–31, 36, 66, 69, 72, 93, 98, 101, 106, 109, 115–20, 124, 128–33, 147–48, 150–53, 158, 161, 165–66, 169–70, 173–82, 185–86, 191–92, 194, 201, 205–6;
Dignam, Master, 29, 41, 43, 59–68, 70, 87, 160, 206;
Dignam, Mrs, 65;
Dignam, Paddy, 64–65, 97, 201, 207;
Mulligan, Malachi ("Buck"), 128, 170, 176, 181–82.
See also *Portrait of the Artist*

Weininger, Otto, 152, 195

About the Author

Linda Horsnell gained her PhD at the University of East Anglia, where she is currently a visiting researcher. She is also a study support assistant at the University of Suffolk. She has previously published papers in the peer review journals *Brief Encounters* and *Exclamation* and a book review in *Notes and Queries*.

www.ingramcontent.com/pod-product-compliance
Lightning Source LLC
Chambersburg PA
CBHW020742020526
44115CB00030B/847